Houghton
Mifflin
Harcourt

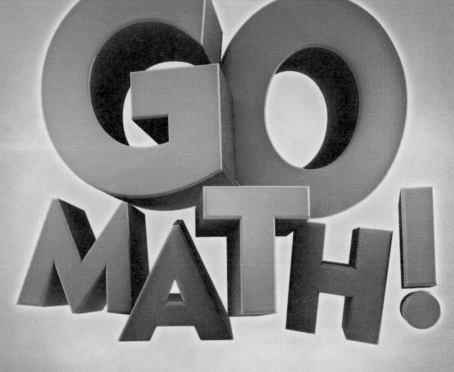

Volume 2

Made in the United States
Text printed on
recycled paper

Houghton Mifflin Harcourt

ISBN 978-0-544-43274-1

15 0928 22 21 20 19

4500760105   D E F G

Dear Students and Families,

Welcome to **Go Math!**, Grade 2! In this exciting mathematics program, there are hands-on activities to do and real-world problems to solve. Best of all, you will write your ideas and answers right in your book. In **Go Math!**, writing and drawing on the pages helps you think deeply about what you are learning, and you will really understand math!

By the way, all of the pages in your **Go Math!** book are made using recycled paper. We wanted you to know that you can Go Green with **Go Math!**

Sincerely,

The Authors

Made in the United States
Text printed on recycled paper

GO MATH!

Authors

Juli K. Dixon, Ph.D.
Professor, Mathematics Education
University of Central Florida
Orlando, Florida

Edward B. Burger, Ph.D.
President, Southwestern University
Georgetown, Texas

Steven J. Leinwand
Principal Research Analyst
American Institutes for
    Research (AIR)
Washington, D.C.

Contributor

Rena Petrello
Professor, Mathematics
Moorpark College
Moorpark, CA

Matthew R. Larson, Ph.D.
K-12 Curriculum Specialist for
    Mathematics
Lincoln Public Schools
Lincoln, Nebraska

Martha E. Sandoval-Martinez
Math Instructor
El Camino College
Torrance, California

English Language Learners Consultant

Elizabeth Jiménez
CEO, GEMAS Consulting
Professional Expert on English
    Learner Education
Bilingual Education and
    Dual Language
Pomona, California

VOLUME 1
Number Sense and Place Value

 Common Core **Critical Area** Extending understanding of base-ten notation

Vocabulary Reader **Whales** 1

1 Number Concepts 9

Domains Operations and Algebraic Thinking
Number and Operations in Base Ten

COMMON CORE STATE STANDARDS 2.OA.C.3, 2.NBT.A.2, 2.NBT.A.3

Critical Area

GO DIGITAL
Go online! Your math lessons are interactive. Use iTools, Animated Math Models, the Multimedia eGlossary, and more.

Chapter 1 Overview
In this chapter, you will explore and discover answers to the following **Essential Questions**:
- How do you use place value to find the values of numbers and describe numbers in different ways?
- How do you know the value of a digit?
- What are some different ways to show a number?
- How do you count by 1s, 5s, 10s, and 100s?

Personal Math Trainer
Online Assessment and Intervention

Numbers to 1,000   71

Domain Number and Operations in Base Ten

COMMON CORE STATE STANDARDS   2.NBT.A.1, 2.NBT.A.1a, 2.NBT.A.1b, 2.NBT.A.3, 2.NBT.A.4, 2.NBT.B.8

Addition and Subtraction

 Critical Area Building fluency with addition and subtraction

Critical Area

GO DIGITAL

Go online! Your math lessons are interactive. Use *iTools*, Animated Math Models, the Multimedia *e*Glossary, and more.

Chapter 3 Overview

In this chapter, you will explore and discover answers to the following **Essential Questions**:

• How can you use patterns and strategies to find sums and differences for basic facts?

• What are some strategies for remembering addition and subtraction facts?

• How are addition and subtraction related?

Personal Math Trainer
Online Assessment and Intervention

Chapter 4 Overview

In this chapter, you will explore and discover answers to the following **Essential Questions:**

- How do you use place value to add 2-digit numbers, and what are some different ways to add 2-digit numbers?
- How do you make an addend a ten to help solve an addition problem?
- How do you record the steps when adding 2-digit numbers?
- What are some ways to add 3 numbers or 4 numbers?

Practice and Homework

Lesson Check and Spiral Review in every lesson

4 2-Digit Addition 233

Domains Operations and Algebraic Thinking

Number and Operations in Base Ten

COMMON CORE STATE STANDARDS 2.OA.A.1, 2.NBT.B.5, 2.NBT.B.6, 2.NBT.B.9

GO DIGITAL

Go online! Your math lessons are interactive. Use *iTools*, Animated Math Models, the Multimedia *eGlossary*, and more.

Chapter 7 Overview

Essential Questions:

- How do you use the values of coins and bills to find the total value of a group of money, and how do you read times shown on analog and digital clocks?

- What are the names and values of the different coins?

- How can you tell the time on a clock by looking at the clock hands?

Chapter 8 Overview

Essential Questions:

- What are some of the methods and tools that can be used to estimate and measure length?

- What tools can be used to measure length and how do you use them?

- What units can be used to measure length and how do they compare with each other?

- How can you estimate the length of an object?

x

VOLUME 2
Measurement and Data

 Critical Area Using standard units of measure

© Houghton Mifflin Harcourt Publishing Company

Chapter 9 Overview

In this chapter, you will explore and discover answers to the following **Essential Questions**:

- What are some of the methods and tools that can be used to estimate and measure length in metric units?
- What tools can be used to measure length in metric units and how do you use them?
- What metric units can be used to measure length and how do they compare with each other?
- If you know the length of one object, how can you estimate the length of another object?

Practice and Homework

Lesson Check and Spiral Review in every lesson

Chapter 10 Overview

In this chapter, you will explore and discover answers to the following **Essential Questions**:

- How do tally charts, picture graphs, and bar graphs help you solve problems?
- How are tally marks used to record data for a survey?
- How is a picture graph made?
- How do you know what the bars in a bar graph stand for?

GO DIGITAL

Go online! Your math lessons are interactive. Use *iTools*, Animated Math Models, the Multimedia *e*Glossary, and more.

Chapter 11 Overview

In this chapter, you will explore and discover answers to the following **Essential Questions**:

• What are some two-dimensional shapes and three-dimensional shapes, and how can you show equal parts of shapes?

• How can you describe some two-dimensional and three-dimensional shapes?

• How can you describe equal parts of shapes?

Personal Math Trainer
Online Assessment and Intervention

Geometry and Fractions

 Critical Area Describing and analyzing shapes

Making a Kite

by Kathryn Krieger and Christine Ruiz

Common Core   **CRITICAL AREA** Using standard units of measure

Ellie and Mike get the materials to make a kite. Then they make the body of the kite.

Materials

paper kite pattern
tape
straw
10 small paper clips
scissors
hole punch
string
3 sheets of paper
streamer paper

1 Fold the pattern in half.

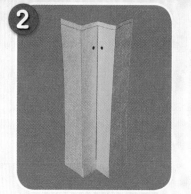

2 Fold along both dashed lines.

3 Tape on each end.

What are the parts of a kite?

Mike does not want the front of the kite to bend too much. He uses a straw to make the kite stronger.

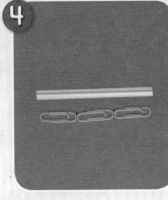

4 Measure 3 paper clips long. Cut.

5 Tape the straw on the line.

Why is a straw used as part of the kite?

The kite must have a string for Ellie or Mike to hold. If the kite does not have a string, it will blow away. Ellie will tie the string onto the kite.

6
Punch one hole.

7
Measure 3 paper-lengths of string. Cut.

8
Put the string through the hole and tie it.

Why is a string needed on a kite?

A tail will help the kite fly straight. Mike measures streamer paper and will tape it to the kite. Then the kite will be finished!

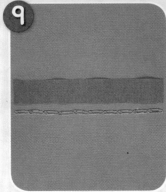

9 Measure 10 paper-clip-lengths of streamer paper. Cut.

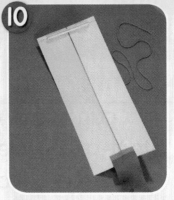

10 Tape the streamer to the kite as a tail.

Why is a tail needed on a kite?

You can make a kite too.
Start at the beginning of
this story. Follow the steps.

How do all of the parts help the kite fly?

Write About the Story

Draw and write a story about making a kite. Explain how to measure the parts of the kite in your story.

Vocabulary Review

measure

length

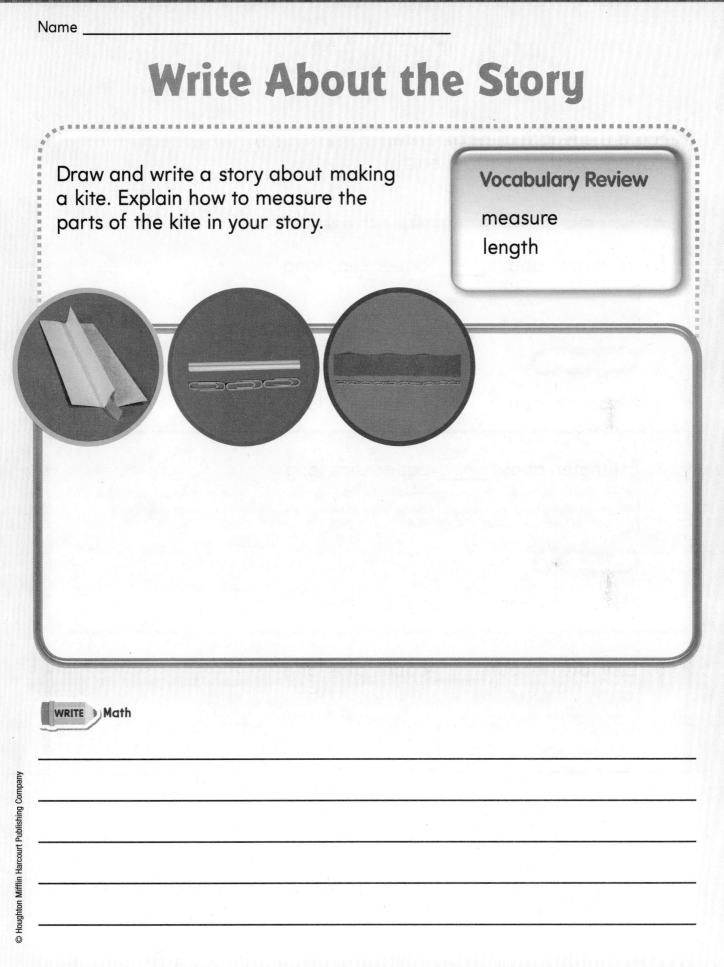

WRITE Math

_____

_____

_____

_____

_____

What is the length?

Estimate the length of each straw.
Then measure the length of each
straw using small paper clips.

I. Estimate: about _____ paper clips long

Measure: about _____ paper clips long

2. Estimate: about _____ paper clips long

Measure: about _____ paper clips long

3. Estimate: about _____ paper clips long

Measure: about _____ paper clips long

MATH BOARD — Look around the classroom. Find other objects to measure. Measure the length of each object using small paper clips.

462

Money and Time

Curious about Math

A sundial shows the time using the position of the sun. It has numbers around it, like a clock face. What numbers are on a clock face?

Name _____

Order Numbers to 100 on a Number Line

Write the number that is just before, between, or just after. (1.NBT.A.1)

1.
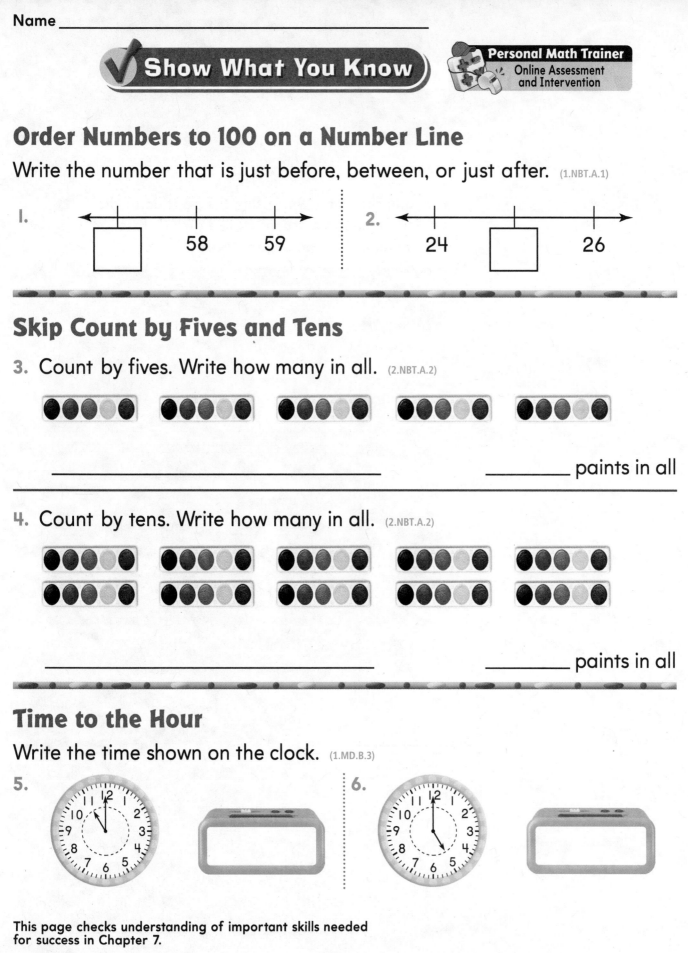
☐ 58 59

2.
24 ☐ 26

Skip Count by Fives and Tens

3. Count by fives. Write how many in all. (2.NBT.A.2)

●●●●● ●●●●● ●●●●● ●●●●● ●●●●●

_____ _____ paints in all

4. Count by tens. Write how many in all. (2.NBT.A.2)

●●●●● ●●●●● ●●●●● ●●●●● ●●●●●
●●●●● ●●●●● ●●●●● ●●●●● ●●●●●

_____ _____ paints in all

Time to the Hour

Write the time shown on the clock. (1.MD.B.3)

5.

6.

This page checks understanding of important skills needed for success in Chapter 7.

Name _____

Vocabulary Builder

Review Words

count

pattern

count on

Visualize It

Fill in the graphic organizer.
Show ways to **count on**.

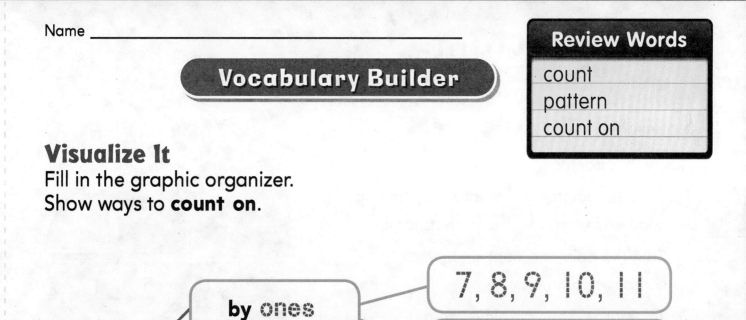

Understand Vocabulary

Write the missing numbers in each counting **pattern**.

1. **Count** by ones.   40, ____, ____, ____, 44, ____, 46, ____

2. **Count** by fives.   10, 15, ____, ____, ____, 35, ____, ____

3. **Count** by tens.   20, ____, ____, 50, ____, ____, 80, ____

Game

5 and 10 Count

Materials • 1 ▪ • 1 ▪ • ◉

Play with a partner.

1. Spin the pointer on ◉ for your starting number. Put your cube on that number.

2. Spin the pointer. Count on by that number two times.

3. Take turns. The first player to get to 100 wins. Play again.

10	5
5	10

1	2	3	4	**5**	6	7	8	9	**10**
11	12	13	14	**15**	16	17	18	19	**20**
21	22	23	24	**25**	26	27	28	29	**30**
31	32	33	34	**35**	36	37	38	39	**40**
41	42	43	44	**45**	46	47	48	49	**50**
51	52	53	54	**55**	56	57	58	59	**60**
61	62	63	64	**65**	66	67	68	69	**70**
71	72	73	74	**75**	76	77	78	79	**80**
81	82	83	84	**85**	86	87	88	89	**90**
91	92	93	94	**95**	96	97	98	99	**100**

Chapter 7 Vocabulary

a.m.

a.m.

2

cent sign

símbolo de centavo

5

decimal point

punto decimal

13

dime

moneda de 10¢

16

dollar

dólar

17

dollar sign

símbolo de dólar

18

hour

hora

30

midnight

medianoche

40

53¢

↑

cent sign

Times after midnight and before noon are written with **a.m.**

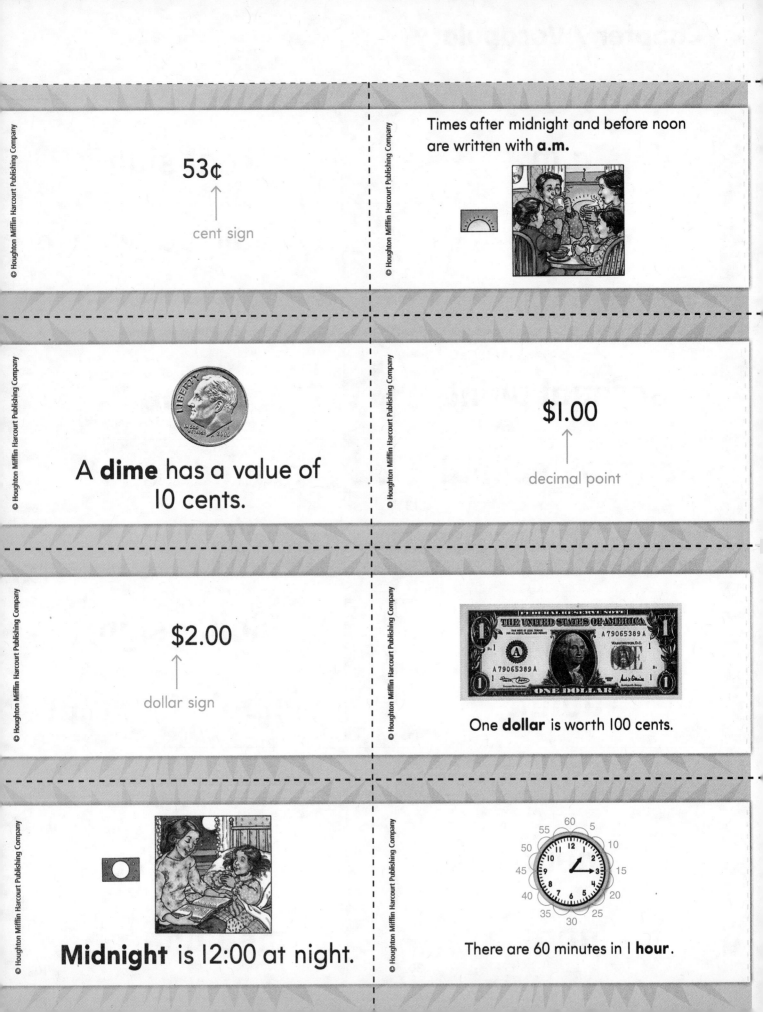

A **dime** has a value of 10 cents.

$1.00

↑

decimal point

$2.00

↑

dollar sign

One **dollar** is worth 100 cents.

Midnight is 12:00 at night.

There are 60 minutes in 1 **hour**.

minute minuto 41	**nickel** moneda de 5¢ 42
noon mediodía 43	**penny** moneda de 1¢ 46
p.m. p.m. 50	**quarter** moneda de 25¢ 52
quarter past y cuarto 54	

A **nickel** has a value of
5 cents.

5 minutes
5 minutes
5 minutes
5 minutes
5 minutes
5 minutes

There are 30 **minutes** in a half hour.

A **penny** has a value of
1 cent.

Noon is 12:00 in the daytime.

A **quarter** has a value of
25 cents.

Times after noon and
before midnight are written
with **p.m.**

8:15

15 minutes after 8
quarter past 8

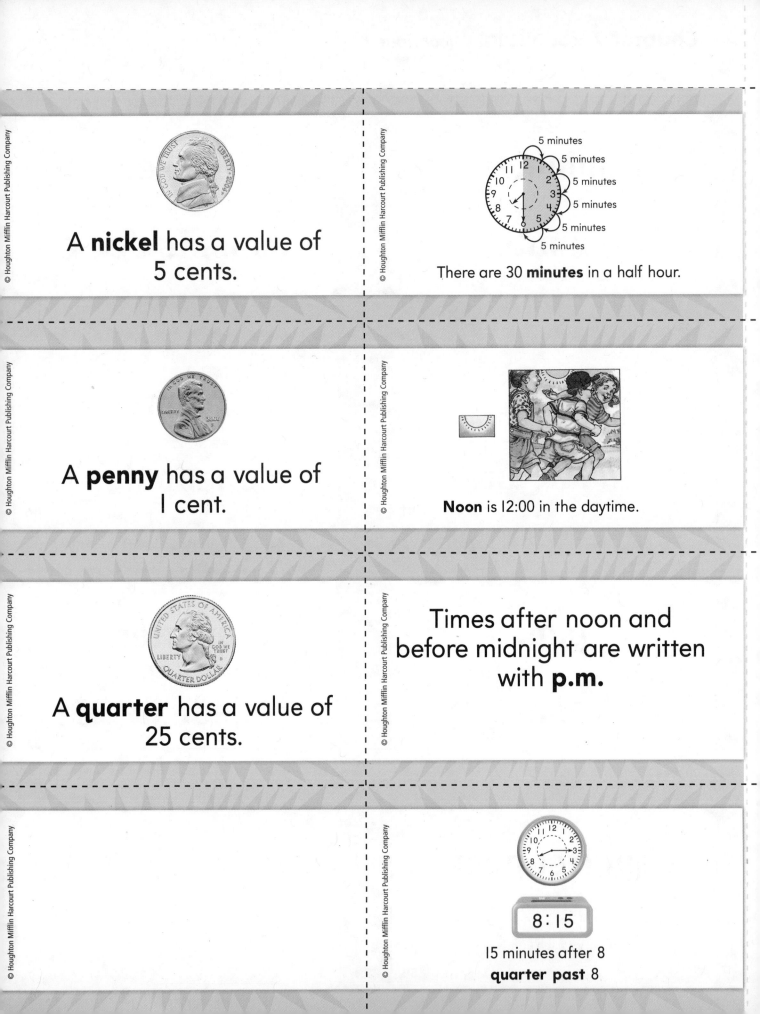

Going to Los Angeles

For 2 to 4 players

Materials

• 1 ▪ • 1 ▪ • 1 ▪ • 1 ▪ • 1 ▪ • Clue Cards

How to Play

1. Take turns to play.

2. To take a turn, toss the ▪. Move that many spaces.

3. If you land on this space:

   Blue Space Use a math word to name the picture or symbol you see. If you name it correctly, move ahead 1.

   Red Space The player to your right takes a Clue Card from the pile and reads you the question. If you answer correctly, move ahead 1.
   Return the Clue Card to the bottom of the pile.

   Green Space Follow the directions in the space.

4. The first player to reach FINISH wins.

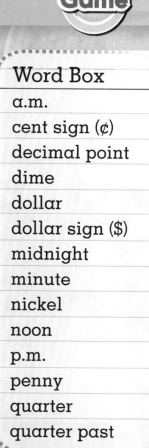

Word Box

a.m.

cent sign (¢)

decimal point

dime

dollar

dollar sign ($)

midnight

minute

nickel

noon

p.m.

penny

quarter

quarter past

DIRECTIONS 2 to 4 players. Take turns to play. To take a turn, toss the numbered cube. Move that many spaces. Follow the directions for the space you land on. First player to reach FINISH wins.

MATERIALS I connecting cube per player • I number cube • I set of clue cards

START

See art at the Getty Center. Move ahead 1.

CLUE CARD

Listen to music on Olvera Street. Take another turn.

CLUE CARD

CLUE CARD

Ride the Ferris Wheel at Santa Monica Pier. Go Back 1.

FINISH

Get lost on the freeway. Lose 1 turn.

CLUE CARD

$

Get stuck at La Brea tarpits. Lose 1 turn.

CLUE CARD

CLUE CARD

Spot a movie star in Hollywood. Trade places with another player.

The Write Way

Reflect

Choose one idea. Write about it in the space below.

• Write and draw to explain the following amount as if you were talking to a young child. Use another sheet of paper for your drawing.

$1.36

• What time is it now? Use at least **three** of these words in your answer.

    a.m.   midnight   minute   noon   p.m.   quarter past

• Write at least **three** things you know about money.

Name _____

Dimes, Nickels, and Pennies

Essential Question How do you find the total value of a group of dimes, nickels, and pennies?

Common Core
Measurement and Data— 2.MD.C.8
MATHEMATICAL PRACTICES
MP1, MP4, MP7

Listen and Draw Real World · Hands On

Sort the coins. Then draw the coins.

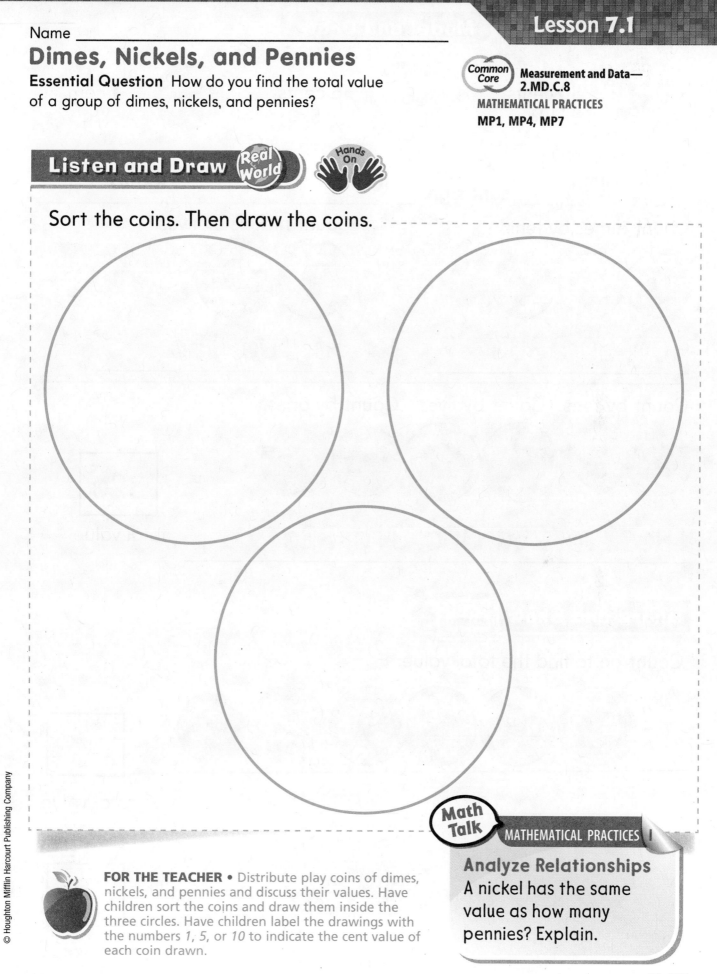

FOR THE TEACHER • Distribute play coins of dimes, nickels, and pennies and discuss their values. Have children sort the coins and draw them inside the three circles. Have children label the drawings with the numbers *1, 5,* or *10* to indicate the cent value of each coin drawn.

Math Talk MATHEMATICAL PRACTICES

Analyze Relationships A nickel has the same value as how many pennies? Explain.

Chapter 7

four hundred sixty-seven **467**

Model and Draw

10 cents
10¢

dime

¢ is the
cent sign.

5 cents
5¢

nickel

1 cent
1¢

penny

Count dimes by tens.

10¢, 20¢, 30¢

Count nickels by fives.

5¢, 10¢, 15¢

Count by tens. Count by fives. Count by ones.

10¢, 20¢, 25¢, 30¢, 31¢, 32¢

32¢

total value

Share and Show   MATH BOARD

Count on to find the total value.

1.

total value

2.

total value

Name _____

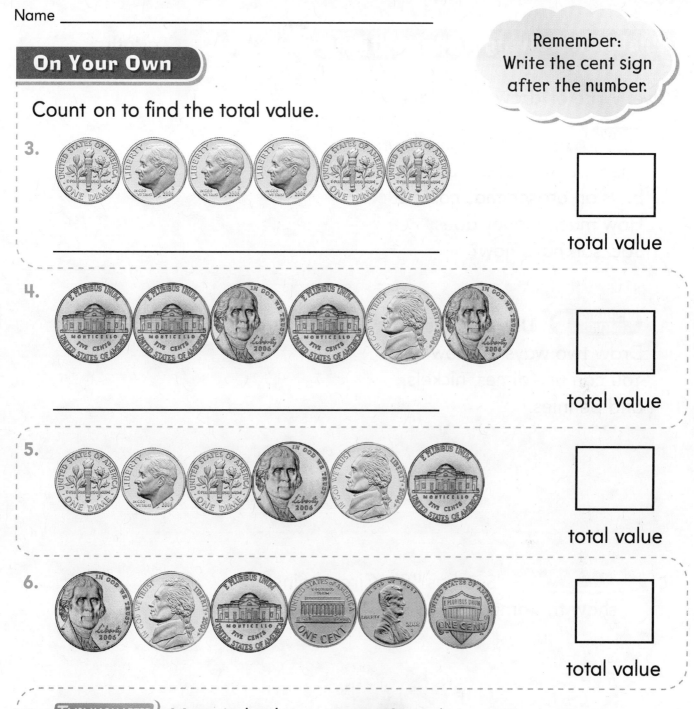

On Your Own

Count on to find the total value.

3.

total value

4.

total value

5.

total value

6.

total value

7. **THINK SMARTER** Maggie had 5 nickels. She gave 2 nickels to her sister. What is the total value of the nickels that Maggie has now?

_____

Problem Solving • Applications    WRITE Math

Solve. Write or draw to explain.

8. **MATHEMATICAL PRACTICE ①** **Analyze** Jackson has 4 pennies and 3 dimes. He buys an eraser that costs 20¢. How much money does Jackson have now?

_____

9. **MATHEMATICAL PRACTICE ④** **Use Models** Draw two ways to show 25¢. You can use dimes, nickels, and pennies.

10. **THINK SMARTER** Sue has 40¢. Circle coins to show this amount.

 TAKE HOME ACTIVITY • Draw pictures of five coins, using dimes, nickels, and pennies. Ask your child to find the total value.

Dimes, Nickels, and Pennies

Common Core **COMMON CORE STANDARD—2.MD.C.8**
Work with time and money.

Count on to find the total value.

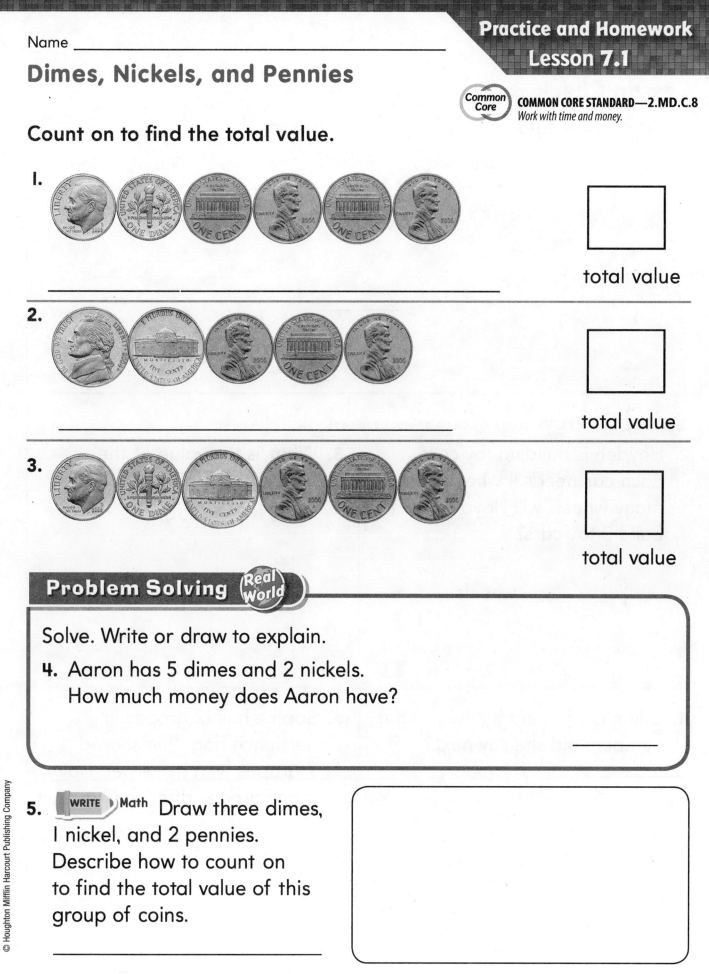

1. _____   total value

2. _____   total value

3.   total value

Problem Solving *Real World*

Solve. Write or draw to explain.

4. Aaron has 5 dimes and 2 nickels.
   How much money does Aaron have?

   _____

5. **WRITE** Math Draw three dimes,
   1 nickel, and 2 pennies.
   Describe how to count on
   to find the total value of this
   group of coins.

   _____

Lesson Check (2.MD.C.8)

1. What is the total value of this group of coins?

_____

---

2. Hayden is building toy cars. Each car needs 4 wheels. How many wheels will Hayden use to build 3 toy cars?

_____ wheels

3. What is the value of the underlined digit?

4̲29

_____

---

4. Lillian is counting by fives. What numbers did she say next?

40, ____, ____, ____, ____

5. Sophie has 12 grapes in her lunch bag. She shared 7 grapes with her sister. How many grapes does she have?

$12 - 7 =$ _____

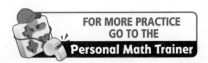

FOR MORE PRACTICE
GO TO THE
Personal Math Trainer

Quarters

Essential Question How do you find the total value of a group of coins?

Common Core — Measurement and Data — 2.MD.C.8
MATHEMATICAL PRACTICES
MP6, MP7, MP8

Listen and Draw Real World

Hands On

Sort the coins. Then draw the coins.

FOR THE TEACHER • Distribute play coins of quarters, dimes, and nickels and discuss their values. Have children sort the coins and draw them inside the three boxes. Have them label the drawings with 5¢, 10¢, or 25¢.

Math Talk

MATHEMATICAL PRACTICES 6

Describe how the value of a quarter is greater than the value of a dime.

A **quarter** has a value of 25 cents.

25¢

Count by twenty-fives.   Count by tens.   Count by ones.

25¢, 50¢, 60¢, 70¢, 71¢, 72¢

72¢

total value

Share and Show   MATH BOARD

Count on to find the total value.

Remember:
¢ is the cent sign.

1.

_____

total value

✓2.

_____

total value

✓3.

_____

total value

Name _____

On Your Own

Count on to find the total value.

4.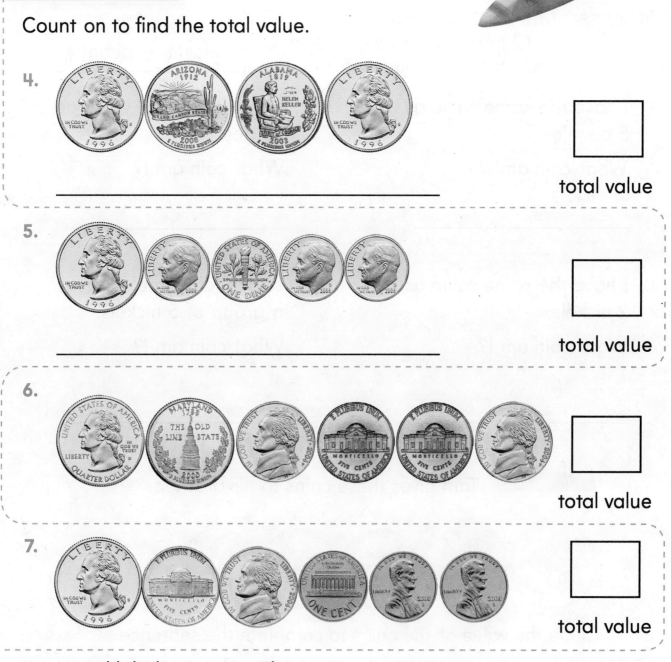

_____

□ total value

5.

□ total value

6.

□ total value

7.

□ total value

Draw and label a coin to solve.

8. **THINK SMARTER** Ed's coin has the same value as a group of 5 pennies and 4 nickels. What is his coin?

Problem Solving • Applications

WRITE Math

MATHEMATICAL PRACTICE 6 Make Connections

Read the clue. Choose the name of a coin from the box to answer the question.

nickel	dime
quarter	penny

9. I have the same value as 5 pennies.

   What coin am I?

   _____

10. I have the same value as 25 pennies.

    What coin am I?

    _____

11. I have the same value as 2 nickels.

    What coin am I?

    _____

12. I have the same value as a group of 5 nickels.

    What coin am I?

    _____

13. **THINK SMARTER** Tom gives these coins to his brother.

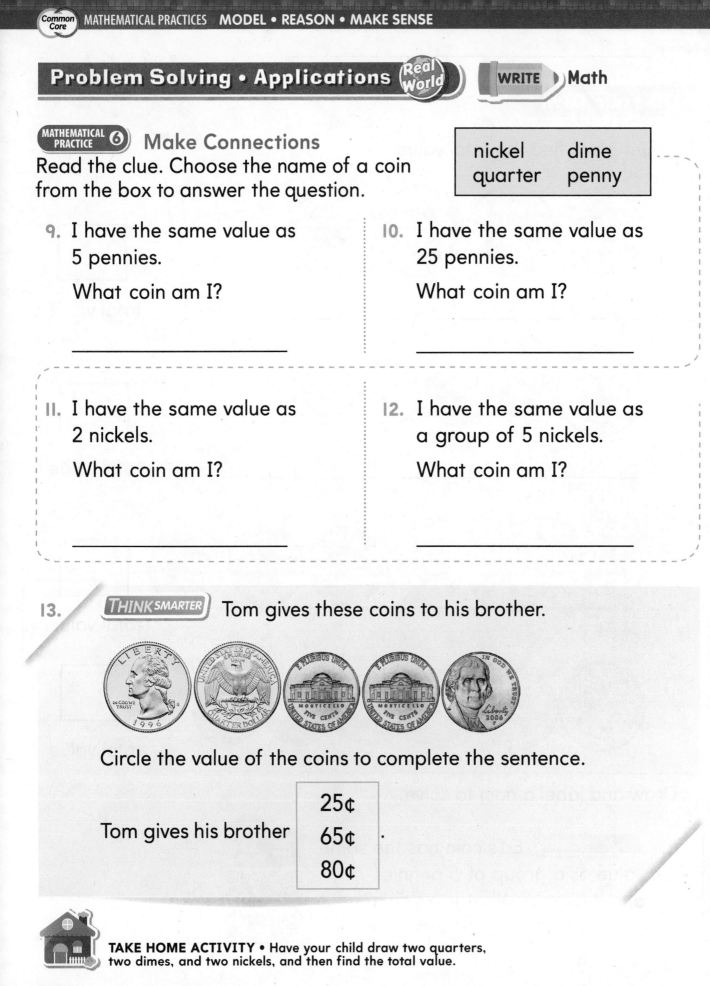

Circle the value of the coins to complete the sentence.

Tom gives his brother | 25¢ |
                       | 65¢ |
                       | 80¢ |

TAKE HOME ACTIVITY • Have your child draw two quarters, two dimes, and two nickels, and then find the total value.

Quarters

 COMMON CORE STANDARD—2.MD.C.8
Work with time and money.

Count on to find the total value.

1.

_____

☐ total value

2.

_____

☐ total value

 Problem Solving Real World

Read the clue. Choose the name of a coin
from the box to answer the question.

nickel	dime
quarter	penny

3. I have the same value as a group of
2 dimes and 1 nickel. What coin am I?

_____

4. **WRITE** Math Draw coins to show
39¢. Describe how to count
to find the total value of this
group of coins.

_____

_____

Lesson Check (2.MD.C.8)

1. What is the total value of this group of coins?

————

Spiral Review (2.OA.A.1, 2.OA.C.3, 2.NBT.A.3, 2.NBT.A.4)

2. Circle the odd number.

 8   14   17   22

3. Kai scored 4 points and Gail scored 7 points. How many points did they score altogether?

$4 + 7 =$ ———— points

4. There were 382 chairs in the music hall. Write a number greater than 382.

————

5. Write the number 61 using words.

————

FOR MORE PRACTICE
GO TO THE
Personal Math Trainer

Name _____

Count Collections

Essential Question How do you order coins to help find the total value of a group of coins?

Common Core **Measurement and Data—2.MD.C.8**
MATHEMATICAL PRACTICES
MP4, MP6, MP8

Listen and Draw *Real World*   *Hands On*

Line up the coins from greatest value to least value. Then draw the coins in that order.

greatest   least

greatest   least

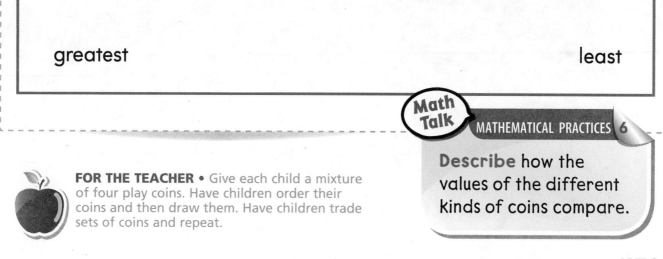

Math Talk MATHEMATICAL PRACTICES 6

Describe how the values of the different kinds of coins compare.

🍎 **FOR THE TEACHER •** Give each child a mixture of four play coins. Have children order their coins and then draw them. Have children trade sets of coins and repeat.

Model and Draw

Order the coins from greatest value to least value.
Then find the total value.

$$\overset{\text{(}}{25¢}\quad \overset{\text{(}}{25¢}\quad \overset{\text{(}}{10¢}\quad \overset{\text{(}}{1¢}\quad \overset{\text{(}}{1¢}$$

> Count the cents.
> 25, 50, 60, 61, 62

_____
total value

Share and Show MATH BOARD

Draw and label the coins from greatest
to least value. Find the total value.

> Remember: Write
> the cent sign.

1.

_____

✓ 2.

_____

✓ 3.

_____

Name _____

On Your Own

Draw and label the coins from greatest to least value. Find the total value.

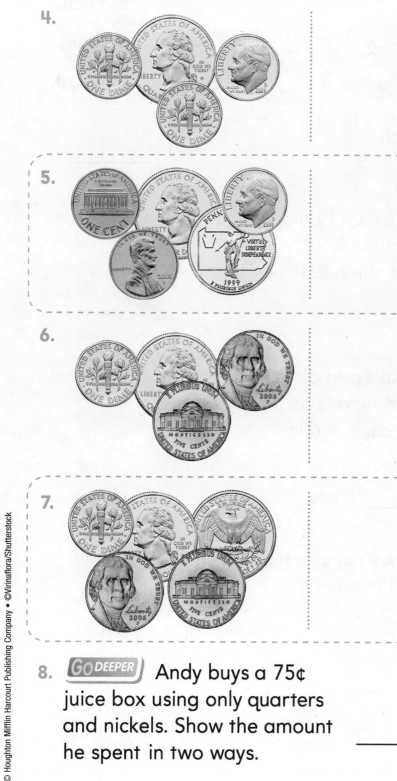

4. _____

5. _____

6. _____

7. _____

8. **GO DEEPER** Andy buys a 75¢ juice box using only quarters and nickels. Show the amount he spent in two ways.

_____ quarter _____ nickels

_____ quarters _____ nickels

Problem Solving • Applications Real World   WRITE Math

Solve. Write or draw to explain.

9. **THINK SMARTER** Paulo had these coins.

He spent 1 quarter. How much
money does he have now?   _____

10. Rachel has 2 quarters, 3 dimes, and 1 nickel.
She wants to buy a book that costs 90¢.
How much more money does she need?

_____

11. **GO DEEPER** Blake has only nickels and dimes.
He has double the number of nickels as
dimes. The total value of his coins is 60¢.
What coins does Blake have?

_____ nickels   _____ dimes

12. **THINK SMARTER** Malik has these coins in his pocket.
What is the total value of the coins?

_____

  TAKE HOME ACTIVITY • Have your child draw and label
coins with a total value of 32¢.

Name _____

Count Collections

COMMON CORE STANDARD—2.MD.C.8
Work with time and money.

Draw and label the coins from greatest to least value. Find the total value.

1.

_____

2.

_____

Problem Solving Real World

Solve. Write or draw to explain.

3. Rebecca has these coins. She spends 1 quarter. How much money does she have left?

_____

4. **WRITE Math** Draw 2 dimes, 1 nickel, and 2 quarters. Describe how to order and then count to find the total value of the coins.

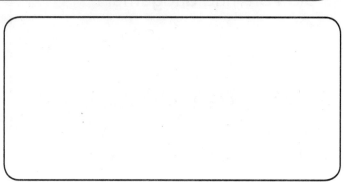

_____

Lesson Check (2.MD.C.8)

1. What is the total value of this group of coins?

_____

Spiral Review (2.OA.B.2, 2.NBT.A.1, 2.NBT.A.3, 2.NBT.B.8)

2. What number is 100 more than 562?

_____

3. Describe 58 as a sum of tens and ones.

_____

---

4. Pete helps his grandmother gather pecans. He finds 6 pecans on his left and 3 on his right. How many pecans did Pete find altogether?

$6 + 3 =$ ____ pecans

5. What number do the blocks show?

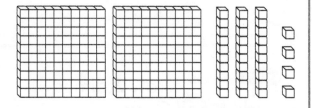

_____

FOR MORE PRACTICE
GO TO THE
Personal Math Trainer

Name _____

Show Amounts in Two Ways

Essential Question How do you choose coins to show a money amount in different ways?

Common Core **Measurement and Data—2.MD.C.8**
MATHEMATICAL PRACTICES
MP1, MP4, MP8

Listen and Draw Real World   Hands On

Show the amount with coins. Draw the coins.
Write the amount.

FOR THE TEACHER • Distribute play coins. Tell children to use coins to show 27 cents. Then have them draw the coins and write the amount. Repeat the activity for 51 cents.

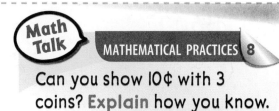

Math Talk
MATHEMATICAL PRACTICES 8
Can you show 10¢ with 3 coins? **Explain** how you know.

Chapter 7

Model and Draw

Here are two ways to show 30¢.

Look at Matthew's way. If you trade 2 dimes and I nickel for I quarter, the coins will show Alicia's way.

Count the cents. Start with the dimes.

Count the cents. Start with the quarter.

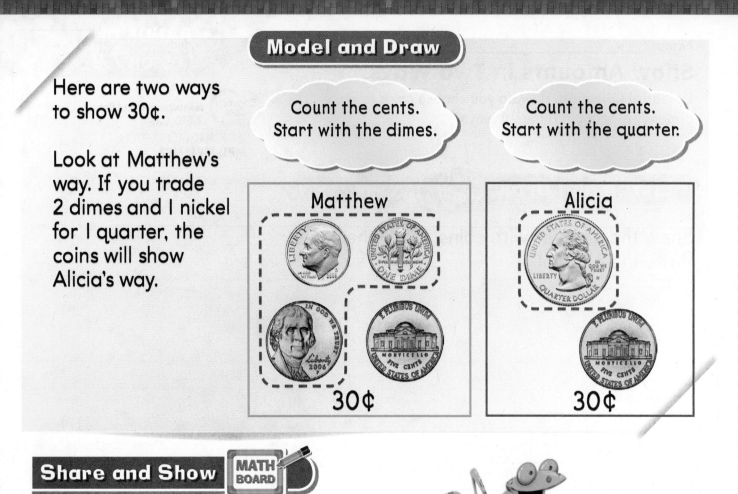

Matthew

30¢

Alicia

30¢

Share and Show MATH BOARD

Use coins. Show the amount in two ways. Draw and label the coins.

☑ 1.

61¢

☑ 2.

36¢

On Your Own

Use coins. Show the amount in two ways.
Draw and label the coins.

3.

55¢

4.

90¢

5.

75¢

6. **THINK SMARTER** Teresa has 42¢.
She has no dimes. Draw to show
what coins she might have.

Problem Solving · Applications Real World   WRITE Math

MATHEMATICAL PRACTICE ④ Model with Mathematics

Use coins to solve.

7. Lee buys a pen for 50¢. Draw coins to show two different ways to pay 50¢.

8. **MATHEMATICAL PRACTICE ①** Make Sense of Problems

Delia used 4 coins to buy a book for 40¢. Draw coins to show two ways to pay 40¢ with 4 coins.

9. **THINK SMARTER** Fill in the bubble next to all the groups of coins with a total value of 30¢.

   ○ 6 dimes

   ○ 1 quarter and 1 nickel

   ○ 2 nickels and 2 dimes

   ○ 3 nickels and 5 pennies

TAKE HOME ACTIVITY · With your child, take turns drawing different collections of coins to show 57¢.

Name _____

Show Amounts in Two Ways

Common Core **COMMON CORE STANDARD—2.MD.C.8**
Work with time and money.

Use coins. Show the amounts in two ways.
Draw and label the coins.

1.

39¢

2.

70¢

Problem Solving Real World

3. Madeline uses fewer than 5 coins
to pay 60¢. Draw coins to show
one way she could pay 60¢.

4. WRITE Math Draw coins in two
ways to show 57¢. Describe
how to chose the coins for
each way.

_____

_____

Lesson Check (2.MD.C.8)

1. Circle the group of coins that has the same total value.

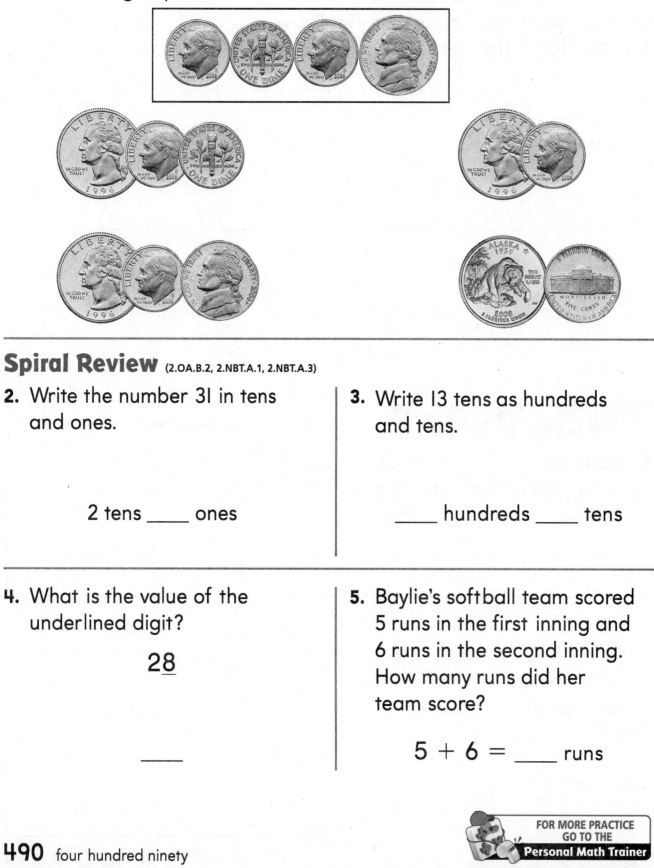

Spiral Review (2.OA.B.2, 2.NBT.A.1, 2.NBT.A.3)

2. Write the number 31 in tens and ones.

2 tens ____ ones

3. Write 13 tens as hundreds and tens.

____ hundreds ____ tens

4. What is the value of the underlined digit?

2<u>8</u>

____

5. Baylie's softball team scored 5 runs in the first inning and 6 runs in the second inning. How many runs did her team score?

$5 + 6 =$ ____ runs

FOR MORE PRACTICE
GO TO THE
Personal Math Trainer

Name _____

One Dollar

Essential Question How can you show the value of one dollar with coins?

Common Core **Measurement and Data— 2.MD.C.8**

MATHEMATICAL PRACTICES
MP4, MP6, MP7

Listen and Draw (Real World)

Draw the coins. Write the total value.

_____

_____

FOR THE TEACHER • In the first box, have children draw eight nickels and then count to find the total value. In the second box, have children draw eight dimes and then count to find the total value.

Math Talk — MATHEMATICAL PRACTICES 6

How many pennies have the same value as 80¢? Explain.

© Houghton Mifflin Harcourt Publishing Company

One **dollar** has the same value as 100 cents.

$$\$1.00 = 100¢$$

dollar sign ⟶ ⟵ decimal point

The decimal point separates the dollars from the cents.

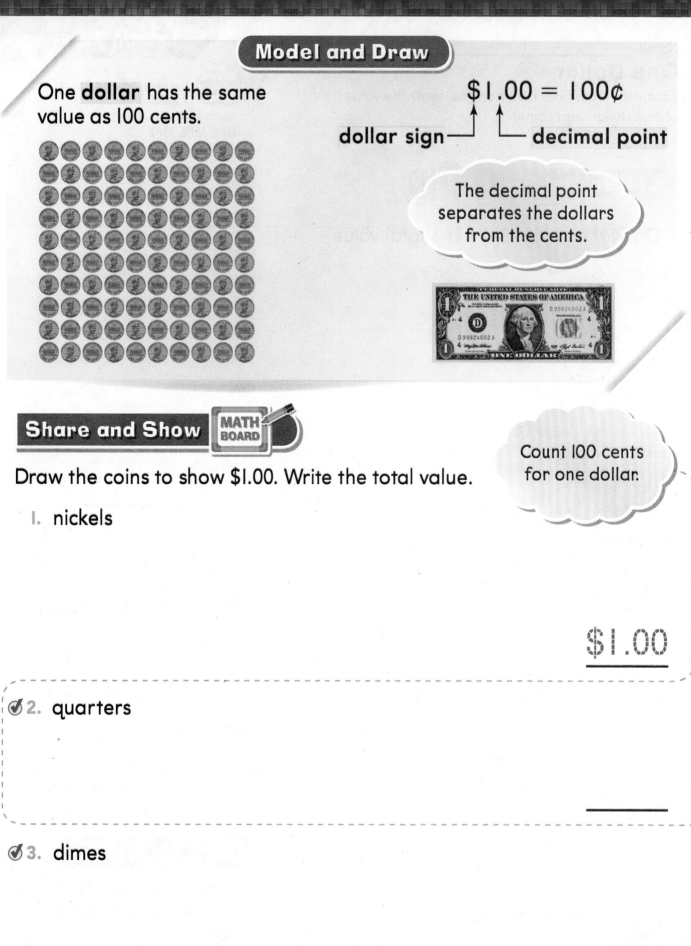

Share and Show MATH BOARD

Draw the coins to show $1.00. Write the total value.

Count 100 cents for one dollar.

1. nickels

$1.00

☑ 2. quarters

☑ 3. dimes

Name _____

Circle coins to make $1.00.
Cross out the coins you do not use.

4.

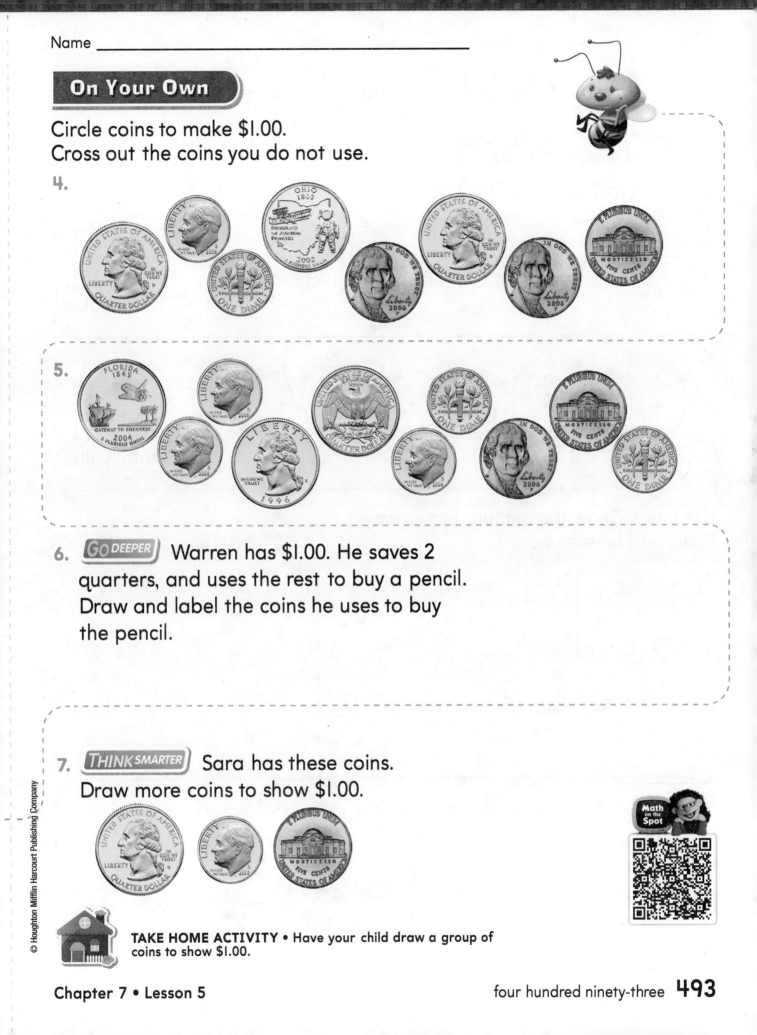

5.

6. **GO DEEPER** Warren has $1.00. He saves 2
quarters, and uses the rest to buy a pencil.
Draw and label the coins he uses to buy
the pencil.

7. **THINK SMARTER** Sara has these coins.
Draw more coins to show $1.00.

TAKE HOME ACTIVITY • Have your child draw a group of
coins to show $1.00.

Name _____

Concepts and Skills

Count on to find the total value. (2.MD.C.8)

1.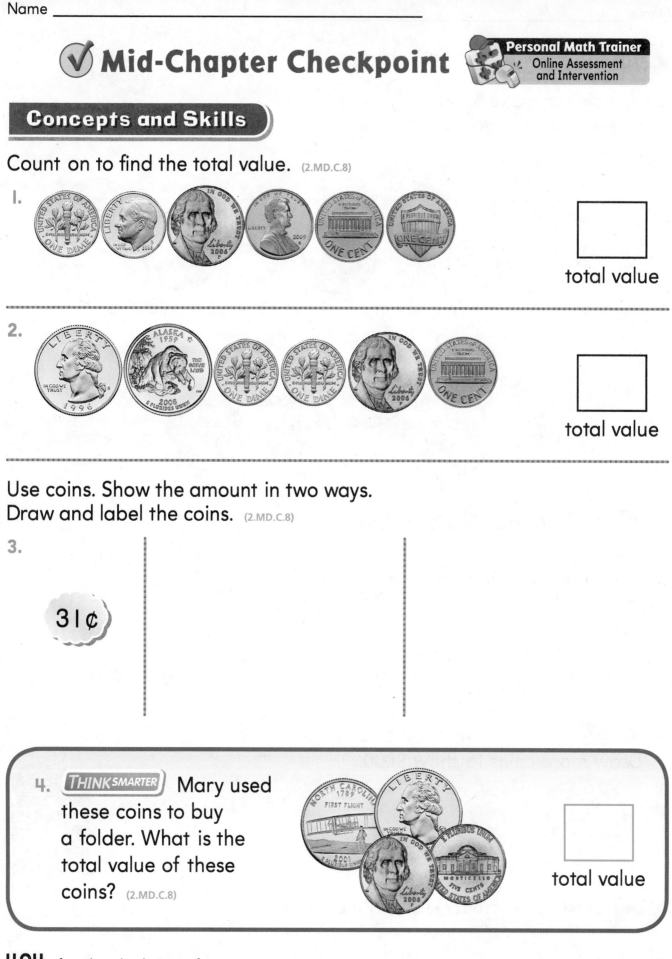

☐
total value

2.

☐
total value

Use coins. Show the amount in two ways.
Draw and label the coins. (2.MD.C.8)

3.

31¢

4. **THINKSMARTER** Mary used
these coins to buy
a folder. What is the
total value of these
coins? (2.MD.C.8)

☐
total value

One Dollar

COMMON CORE STANDARD—2.MD.C.8
Work with time and money.

Circle coins to make $1.00.
Cross out the coins you do not use.

1.

2.

Problem Solving *Real World*

3. Draw more coins to show $1.00 in all.

4. **WRITE** Math Draw coins to show
one way to make $1.00 using
only nickels and quarters.

Lesson Check (2.MD.C.8)

1. Which group of coins has a
value of $1.00?

Spiral Review (2.OA.C.3, 2.NBT.A.2, 2.NBT.A.3, 2.MD.C.8)

2. Write 692 using words.

_____

3. Keith ate 7 almonds, and then
ate 7 more. Is the total number
of almonds even or odd?

$7 + 7 =$ _____ almonds

_____

4. What is the total value of
1 quarter and 3 nickels?

_____

5. Kristin is counting by tens. What
numbers does she say next?

230, _____,

_____, _____

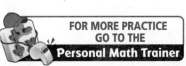

FOR MORE PRACTICE
GO TO THE
Personal Math Trainer

Amounts Greater Than $1

Essential Question How do you show money amounts greater than one dollar?

Common Core Measurement and Data—
2.MD.C.8
MATHEMATICAL PRACTICES
MP4, MP7

Listen and Draw (Real World)

Draw and label the coins.
Write the total value.

_____
total value

Math Talk

MATHEMATICAL PRACTICES 7

Look for Structure
Explain how you found the total value of the coins in the coin bank.

FOR THE TEACHER • Read the following problem: Dominic has 1 quarter, 2 dimes, 3 nickels, and 1 penny in his coin bank. How much money is in Dominic's bank? Have children draw and label coins to help them solve the problem.

Model and Draw

When you write amounts greater than one dollar, use a dollar sign and a decimal point.

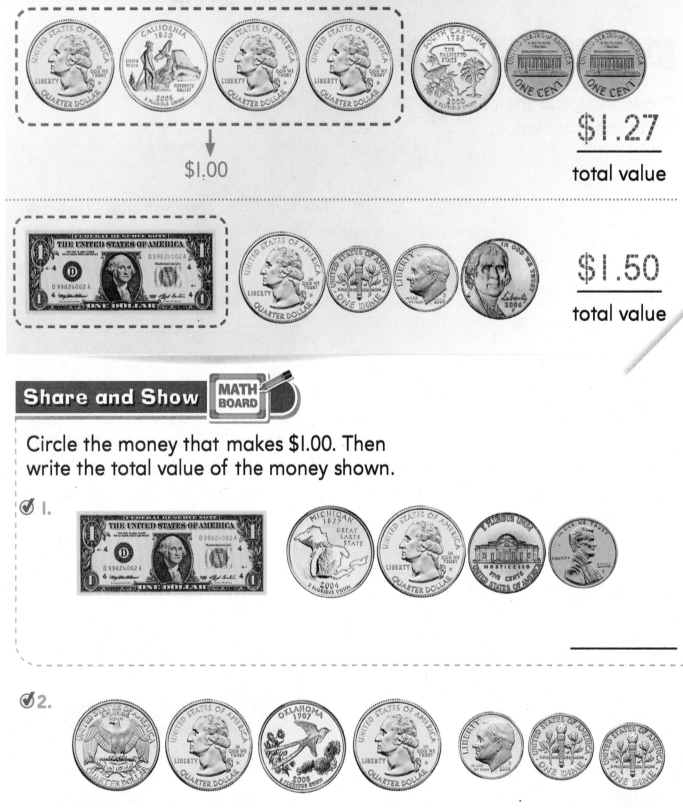

$1.00

$1.27
total value

$1.50
total value

Share and Show MATH BOARD

Circle the money that makes $1.00. Then write the total value of the money shown.

1.

_____

2.

_____

Name _____

Circle the money that makes $1.00. Then
write the total value of the money shown.

3.

_____

4.

_____

5.

_____

6. **THINK SMARTER** Martin used 3 quarters
and 7 dimes to pay for a kite.
How much money did he use?

_____

Math on the Spot

Problem Solving • Applications

Real World

WRITE Math

7. **GO DEEPER** Pam has fewer than 9 coins. The coins have a total value of $1.15. What coins could she have?

Draw the coins. Then write a list of her coins.

_____

_____

Personal Math Trainer

8. **THINK SMARTER +** Jason put this money in his bank.

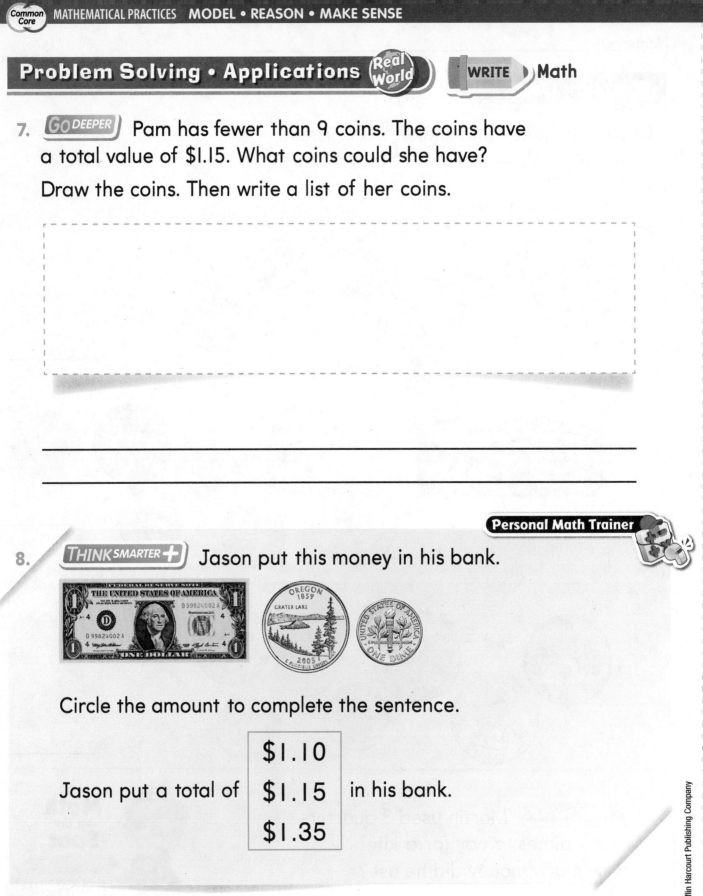

Circle the amount to complete the sentence.

Jason put a total of
| $1.10 |
| $1.15 |
| $1.35 |
in his bank.

🏠 **TAKE HOME ACTIVITY** • With your child, take turns drawing coins or a $1 bill and coins with a total value of $1.23.

Name _____

Amounts Greater Than $1

COMMON CORE STANDARD—2.MD.C.8
Work with time and money.

Circle the money that makes $1.00. Then
write the total value of the money shown.

1.

_____

2.

_____

Problem Solving *Real World*

Solve. Write or draw to explain.

3. Grace has $1.10. She spends 75¢
on a toy. How much change did
she get back?

_____

4. WRITE Math Write about how to use the
dollar sign and decimal point to show
the total value of 5 quarters.

_____

Lesson Check (2.MD.C.8)

1. Julie has this money in her bank. What is the total value of this money?

_____

Spiral Review (2.OA.B.2, 2.NBT.B.5, 2.NBT.B.8)

2. There are 79 squash plants and 42 pepper plants in Julia's garden. How many vegetable plants are in Julia's garden altogether?

$$\begin{array}{r} 7\,9 \\ +\ 4\,2 \\ \hline \end{array}$$

3. What is the difference?

$$\begin{array}{r} 6\,1 \\ -\,2\,7 \\ \hline \end{array}$$

4. What number is 100 less than 694?

_____

5. Write an addition fact that has the same sum as 6 + 5.

$10 +$ _____

FOR MORE PRACTICE
GO TO THE
Personal Math Trainer

Name _____

Problem Solving • Money

Essential Question How does acting it out help when solving problems about money?

Common Core Measurement and Data—
2.MD.C.8
MATHEMATICAL PRACTICES
MP1, MP4, MP6

Kendra gave 2 dimes, 2 nickels, I quarter, and two $1 bills to her sister. How much money did Kendra give her sister?

Unlock the Problem Real World

What do I need to find?	**What information do I need to use?**
how much money Kendra gave her sister	Kendra gave her sister 2 dimes, _____

Show how to solve the problem.
Draw to show the money that Kendra used.

Kendra gave her sister _____.

HOME CONNECTION • Your child used play money to act out the problem. Representing problems with materials can be a useful strategy for children to use to solve problems.

Use play coins and bills to solve.
Draw to show what you did.

> - What do I need to find?
> - What information do I need to use?

1. Jacob has two $1 bills, 2 dimes, and 3 pennies in his pocket. How much money does Jacob have in his pocket?

   _____

2. Amber used 2 quarters, I nickel, and three $1 bills to buy a toy. The toy costs $1.05. How much money does Amber have left?

   _____

Math Talk

MATHEMATICAL PRACTICES 6

Explain how you found the amount of money in Jacob's pocket.

Name _____

Use play coins and bills to solve.
Draw to show what you did.

☑ 3. Val used 3 quarters, 2 nickels, 2 pennies, and
one $1 bill to buy a book. How much money
did Val use to buy the book?

_____

☑ 4. Derek has two $1 bills, 2 quarters, and
6 dimes. How much money does he have?

_____

5. **THINK SMARTER** Katy has 3 quarters, 2 nickels,
2 dimes, and 3 pennies. How many more
pennies does she need to have $1.10?

_____ more pennies

Problem Solving • Applications  WRITE ▶ Math

6. **MATHEMATICAL PRACTICE ①** **Make Sense of Problems**
Victor saves 75¢ on Monday and $1.25 on Tuesday. Then he spends $1.00 to rent a movie. Draw and label how much money Victor has left.

7. **THINK SMARTER** Ross used 3 quarters, 4 dimes, 3 nickels, and 5 pennies to buy a card. How much money did Ross use to buy the card? Draw to show how you solve the problem.

TAKE HOME ACTIVITY • Ask your child to explain how he or she solved one problem in this lesson.

Problem Solving • Money

 COMMON CORE STANDARD—2.MD.C.8
Work with time and money.

Use play coins and bills to solve.
Draw to show what you did.

1. Sara has 2 quarters, 1 nickel, and two $1 bills. How much money does Sara have?

_____

2. Brad has $1.65. He spends 75¢ to buy a card. How much change does he get back?

_____

3. Mr. Morgan gives 1 quarter, 3 nickels, 4 pennies, and one $1 bill to the clerk. How much money does Mr. Morgan give the clerk?

_____

4. **WRITE** Math Write or draw to explain how you would find the total value of two $1 bills and 3 quarters.

_____

Lesson Check (2.MD.C.8)

1. Lee has two $1 bills and 4 dimes. How much money does Lee have?

_____

2. Dawn has 2 quarters, 1 nickel, and one $1 bill. How much money does Dawn have?

_____

Spiral Review (2.OA.B.2, 2.NBT.A.3, 2.NBT.A.4, 2.NBT.B.8)

3. What is the value of the underlined digit?

5<u>6</u>

____

4. Cecilia collected 342 pennies for her class's penny drive. Marked collected 243 pennies. Use <, >, or = to compare. Who collected more?

342 ____ 243

_____ collected more.

5. Brooke's dog has 15 treats. Then he ate 8 of them. How many treats does he have left?

15 − 8 = _____

6. What is the next number in this pattern?

225, 325, 425, 525, _____

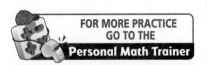
FOR MORE PRACTICE
GO TO THE
Personal Math Trainer

Time to the Hour and Half Hour

Essential Question How do you tell time to the hour and half hour on a clock?

Common Core **Measurement and Data—**
2.MD.C.7
MATHEMATICAL PRACTICES
MP5, MP6, MP8

Listen and Draw Real World

Draw the hour hand to show each time.

Math Talk

MATHEMATICAL PRACTICES 5

Communicate Describe where the hour hand points to show half past 4:00.

FOR THE TEACHER • Call out times to the hour and to the half hour. Begin with 3:00. Have children draw the hour hand to show the time. Repeat the activity for half past 5:00, 11:00, and half past 8:00.

Model and Draw

It takes 5 **minutes** for the minute hand to move from one number to the next number on a clock face.

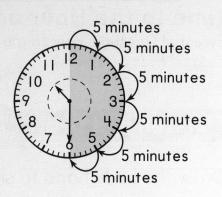

The clock hands on these clocks show 4:00 and 4:30. Write the times below the clocks.

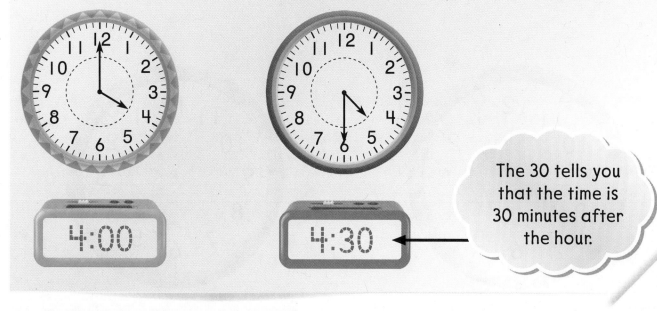

4:00

4:30

The 30 tells you that the time is 30 minutes after the hour.

Share and Show MATH BOARD

Look at the clock hands. Write the time.

1.

✓ 2.

✓ 3.

Name _____

On Your Own

Look at the clock hands. Write the time.

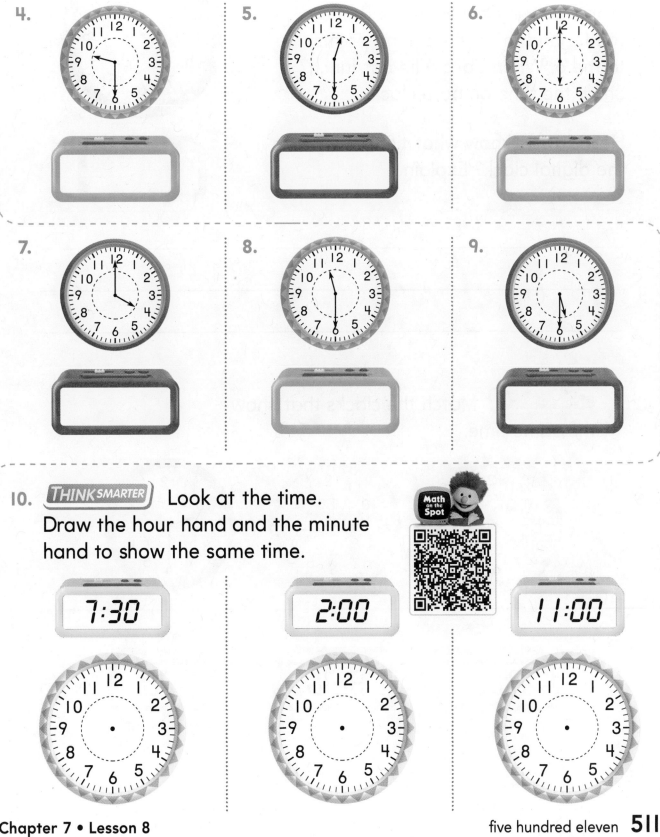

10. **THINK SMARTER** Look at the time.
Draw the hour hand and the minute hand to show the same time.

© Houghton Mifflin Harcourt Publishing Company

Problem Solving · Applications Real World | WRITE Math

11. **MATHEMATICAL PRACTICE 6** **Make Connections**

Allie eats lunch when the hour hand points halfway between the 11 and the 12, and the minute hand points to the 6. When does Allie eat lunch? Show the time on both clocks.

How do you know what time to write in the digital clock? Explain.

_____

_____

_____

12. **THINK SMARTER** Match the clocks that show the same time.

8:00   9:30   7:30

TAKE HOME ACTIVITY · Have your child describe what he or she knows about a clockface.

512 five hundred twelve

Time to the Hour and Half Hour

 **COMMON CORE STANDARD—2.MD.C.7**
Work with time and money.

Look at the clock hands. Write the time.

1.   **2.**   **3.**

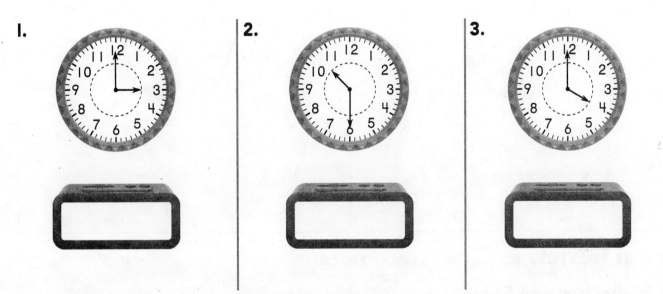

Problem Solving Real World

4. Amy's music lesson begins at 4:00. Draw hands on the clock to show this time.

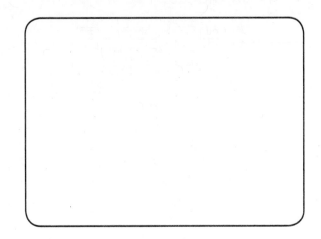

5. WRITE Math Draw a clock to show the time as 2:30. Describe how you decided where the clock hands should point.

_____

_____

_____

Lesson Check (2.MD.C.7)

1. What is the time on this clock?

_____

2. What is the time on this clock?

_____

Spiral Review (2.OA.C.3, 2.NBT.A.1, 2.NBT.A.4, 2.MD.C.8)

3. Rachel has one $1 bill, 3 quarters, and 2 pennies. How much money does Rachel have?

_____

4. Write <, >, or = to compare 260 and 362.

260 _____ 362

5. What number is shown with these blocks?

_____

6. Circle any even numbers.

1   3   4   5

**FOR MORE PRACTICE
GO TO THE
Personal Math Trainer**

Name _____

Time to 5 Minutes

Essential Question How do you tell and show time to five minutes?

Common Core Measurement and Data—2.MD.C.7
MATHEMATICAL PRACTICES
MP4, MP6, MP8

 **Listen and Draw** Real World

Draw the hour hand and the minute hand to show the time.

FOR THE TEACHER • Read the following story and have children draw the hour and minute hands to show each time. Sofia goes to music at 10:30. She goes to the playground at 11:00. She eats lunch at 11:30. Show the times Sofia does these things.

Math Talk MATHEMATICAL PRACTICES 6

Describe where the minute hand points to show half past the hour.

Chapter 7

Model and Draw

What does it mean when the minute hand points to the 7?

Count by fives until you reach the 7.

Remember:
The minute hand moves from one number to the next in 5 minutes.

The hour hand points between the 10 and the 11. The minute hand points to the 7.

The time is ___10:35___.

There are 60 minutes in 1 **hour**.

Share and Show   MATH BOARD

Look at the clock hands. Write the time.

1.

2.

3.

4.

✔ 5.

✔ 6.

516 five hundred sixteen

© Houghton Mifflin Harcourt Publishing Company

Name _____

On Your Own

Look at the clock hands. Write the time.

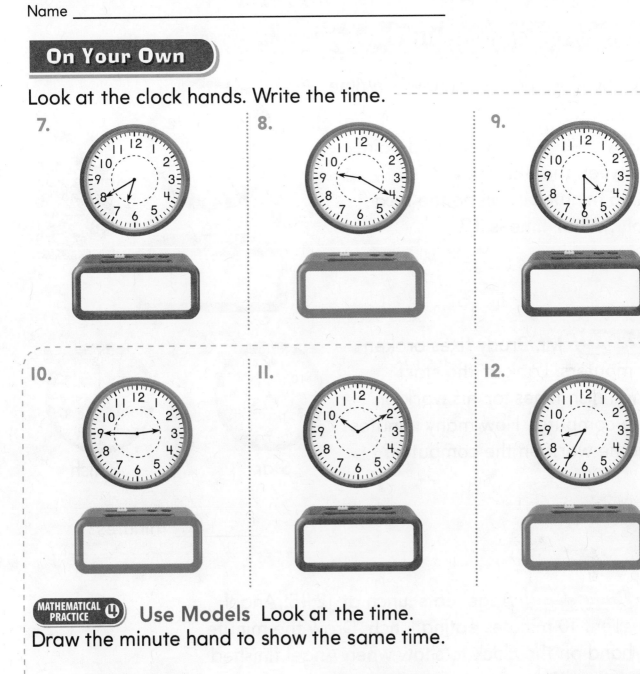

7.

8.

9.

10.

11.

12.

MATHEMATICAL PRACTICE 4 Use Models Look at the time.
Draw the minute hand to show the same time.

13.

7:25

14.

1:50

15.

5:05

Chapter 7 • Lesson 9

five hundred seventeen **517**

Problem Solving • Applications (Real World)

WRITE Math

Draw the clock hands to show the time. Then write the time.

16. **THINK SMARTER** My hour hand points between the 8 and the 9. In 35 minutes it will be the next hour. What time is it?

17. **GO DEEPER** Mr. Brady fixes broken computers. Look at the start and finish times for his work on one computer. How many minutes did he work on the computer?

Start   Finish

_____ minutes

18. **THINK SMARTER** Angel eats lunch at 12:45. Angel spent 10 minutes eating lunch. Draw the minute hand on the clock to show when Angel finished eating. Write the time.

_____ : _____

TAKE HOME ACTIVITY • Have your child draw a large blank clock face and use two pencils as clock hands to show some different times.

Time to 5 Minutes

Common Core

COMMON CORE STANDARD—2.MD.C.7
Work with time and money.

Look at the clock hands. Write the time.

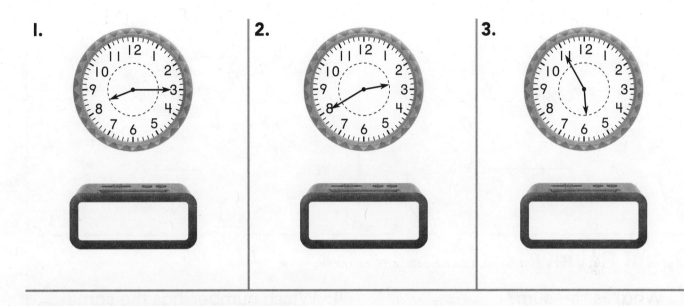

1.

2.

3.

Problem Solving Real World

Draw the minute hand to show the time.
Then write the time.

4. My hour hand points between the
4 and the 5. My minute hand points
to the 9. What time do I show?

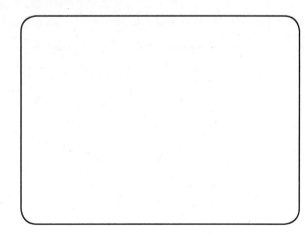

5. **WRITE** Math Draw a clock showing
2:50. Explain how you know where
the clock hands point.

_____

_____

_____

Lesson Check (2.MD.C.7)

1. What is the time on this clock?

_____

2. What is the time on this clock?

_____

Spiral Review (2.OA.A.1, 2.OA.B.2, 2.NBT.A.1a, 2.NBT.A.1b)

3. What is the sum?

$$1 + 6 + 8 = \underline{\quad}$$

4. Which number has the same value as 30 tens?

_____

5. Steven has 3 rows of toys. There are 4 toys in each row. How many toys are there?

____ toys

6. Jill has 14 buttons. She buys 8 more buttons. How many buttons does Jill have?

$$\begin{array}{r} 14 \\ + 8 \\ \hline \end{array}$$

buttons

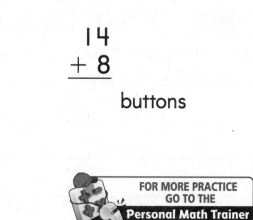

FOR MORE PRACTICE
GO TO THE
Personal Math Trainer

Practice Telling Time

Essential Question What are the different ways you can read the time on a clock?

Common Core **Measurement and Data—2.MD.C.7**
MATHEMATICAL PRACTICES
MP1, MP6, MP8

 **Listen and Draw** Real World

Write the times on the digital clocks.
Then label the clocks with the children's names.

© Houghton Mifflin Harcourt Publishing Company

FOR THE TEACHER • First have children write the time for each analog clock. Then write *Luke, Beth, Ivy,* and *Rohan* on the board. Tell children to listen for each name to label the different times with. Luke plays football at 3:25. Beth eats lunch at 11:45. Ivy reads a book at 6:10. Rohan eats breakfast at 7:15.

Math Talk MATHEMATICAL PRACTICES
Where would the minute hand point to show 15 minutes after the hour? **Explain**.

Chapter 7

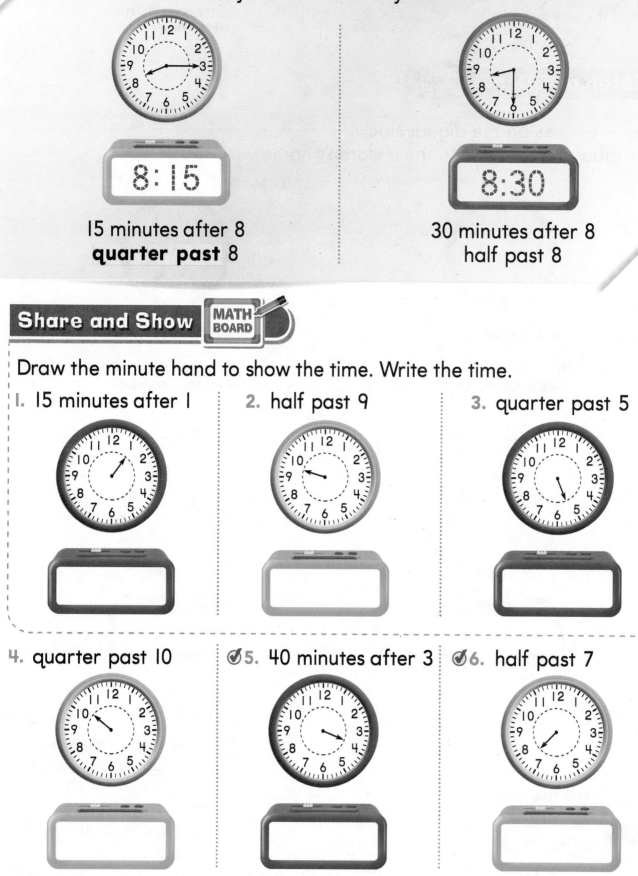

Model and Draw

These are different ways to write and say the time.

8:15

15 minutes after 8
quarter past 8

8:30

30 minutes after 8
half past 8

Share and Show MATH BOARD

Draw the minute hand to show the time. Write the time.

1. 15 minutes after 1

2. half past 9

3. quarter past 5

4. quarter past 10

☑5. 40 minutes after 3

☑6. half past 7

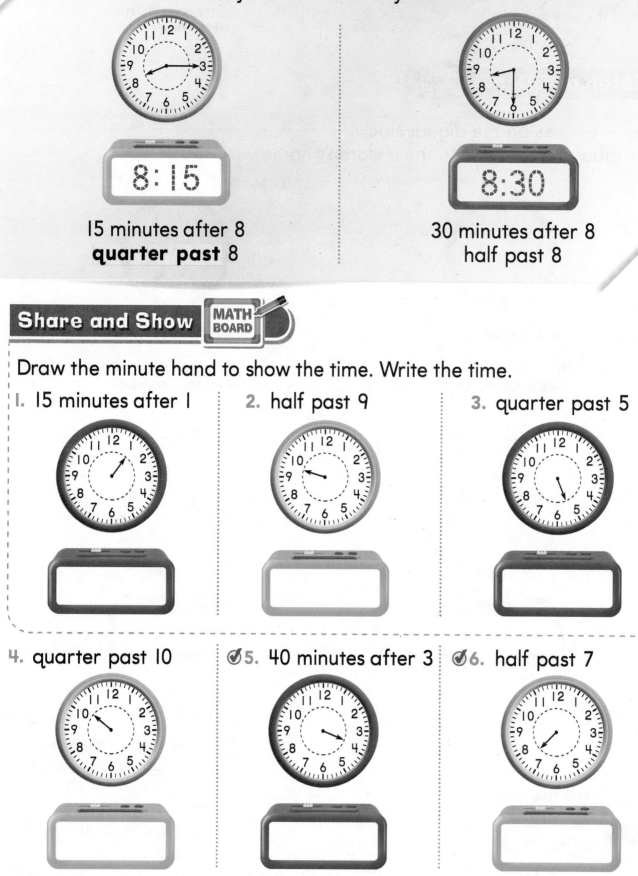

© Houghton Mifflin Harcourt Publishing Company

On Your Own

Draw the minute hand to show the time.
Write the time.

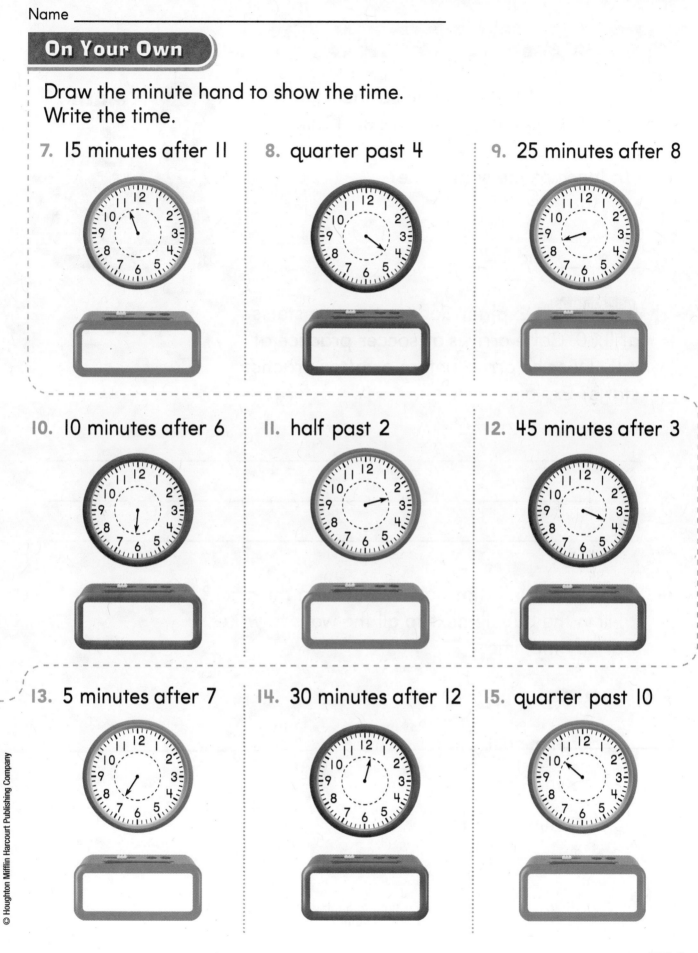

7. 15 minutes after 11

8. quarter past 4

9. 25 minutes after 8

10. 10 minutes after 6

11. half past 2

12. 45 minutes after 3

13. 5 minutes after 7

14. 30 minutes after 12

15. quarter past 10

Problem Solving • Applications (Real World)   WRITE ▸ Math

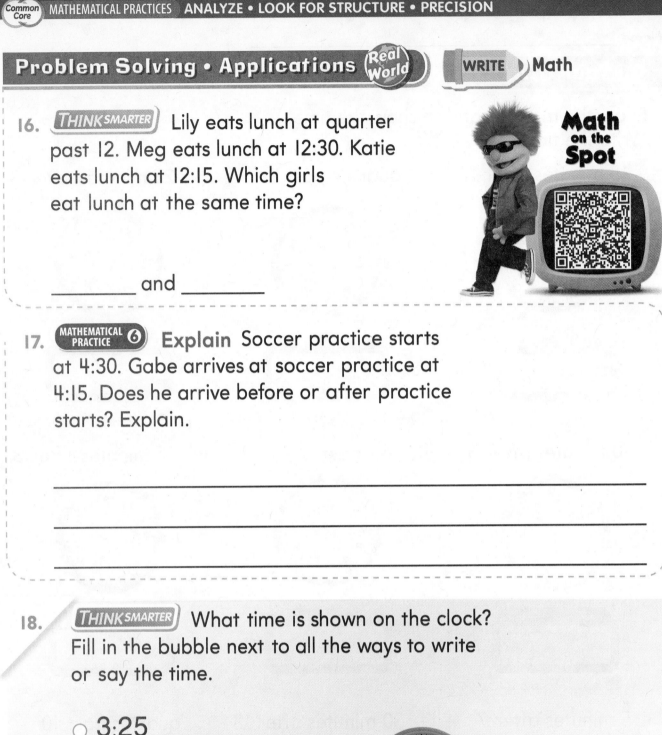

16. **THINK SMARTER** Lily eats lunch at quarter past 12. Meg eats lunch at 12:30. Katie eats lunch at 12:15. Which girls eat lunch at the same time?

_____ and _____

17. **MATHEMATICAL PRACTICE 6** **Explain** Soccer practice starts at 4:30. Gabe arrives at soccer practice at 4:15. Does he arrive before or after practice starts? Explain.

_____

_____

_____

18. **THINK SMARTER** What time is shown on the clock? Fill in the bubble next to all the ways to write or say the time.

○ 3:25

○ quarter past 5

○ 5 minutes after 3

○ 25 minutes after 3

 TAKE HOME ACTIVITY • Name a time to 5 minutes. Ask your child to describe where the clock hands point at this time.

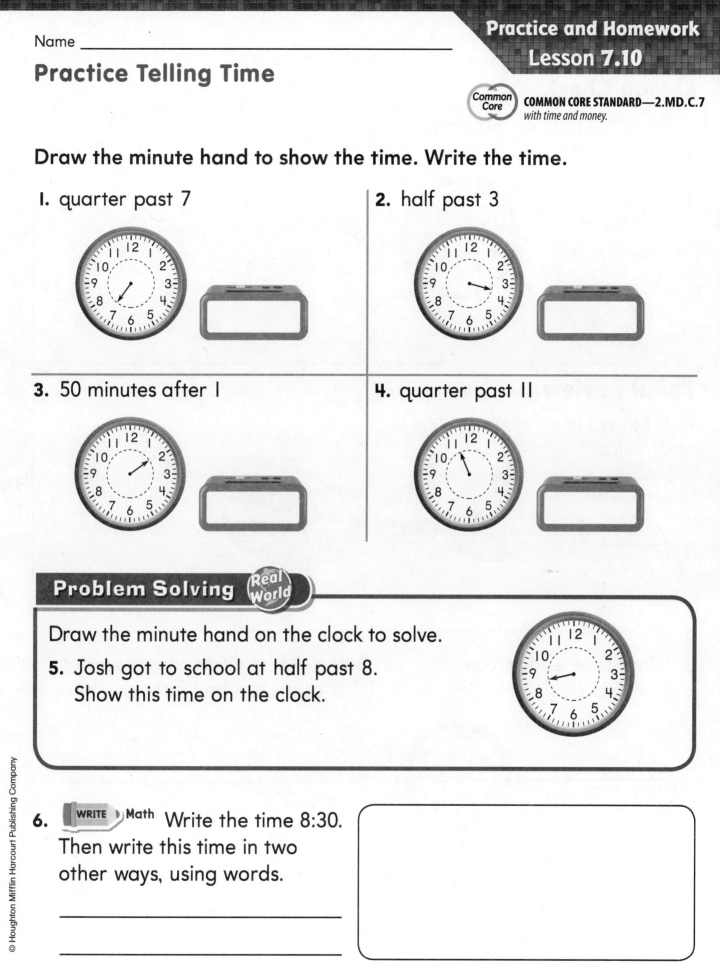

Practice Telling Time

Common Core **COMMON CORE STANDARD—2.MD.C.7**
with time and money.

Draw the minute hand to show the time. Write the time.

1. quarter past 7

2. half past 3

3. 50 minutes after 1

4. quarter past 11

Problem Solving Real World

Draw the minute hand on the clock to solve.

5. Josh got to school at half past 8.
Show this time on the clock.

6. **WRITE** Math Write the time 8:30.
Then write this time in two
other ways, using words.

_____

_____

Lesson Check (2.MD.C.7)

1. Write the time on this clock
   using words.

_____

Spiral Review (2.NBT.A.3, 2.MD.C.7, 2.MD.C.8)

2. What is the value of this group
   of coins?

_____

3. What time is shown on
   this clock?

_____

4. What number can be written
   as six hundred forty-seven?

_____

FOR MORE PRACTICE
GO TO THE
Personal Math Trainer

A.M. and P.M.

Essential Question How do you use a.m. and p.m. to describe times?

Common Core Measurement and Data—
2.MD.C.7
MATHEMATICAL PRACTICES
MP1, MP6, MP7

Draw the clock hands to show each time.
Then write each time.

Morning	Evening

Math Talk **MATHEMATICAL PRACTICES**

Describe some activities that you do in both the morning and in the evening.

FOR THE TEACHER • Have children draw a picture and write a label for the picture for an activity they do in the morning and for an activity they do in the evening. Then have them show the time they do each activity on the clocks.

Model and Draw

Noon is 12:00 in the daytime.

Midnight is 12:00 at night.

Times after midnight and before noon are written with **a.m.**	Times after noon and before midnight are written with **p.m.**
11:00 a.m. is in the morning.	11:00 p.m. is in the evening.

Share and Show MATH BOARD

Write the time. Then circle **a.m.** or **p.m.**

1. eat breakfast

 7:15   ~~a.m.~~

p.m.

2. go to art class

a.m.

p.m.

✓3. do homework

a.m.

p.m.

✓4. arrive at school

a.m.

p.m.

Name _____

On Your Own

Write the time. Then circle **a.m.** or **p.m.**

5. go to the library

a.m.

p.m.

6. go to science class

a.m.

p.m.

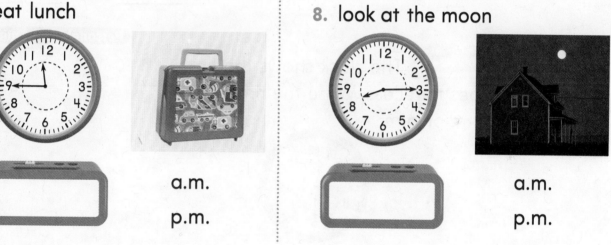

7. eat lunch

a.m.

p.m.

8. look at the moon

a.m.

p.m.

9. THINK SMARTER Use the times in the list to complete the story.

Don got to school at _____.

His class went to the library

at _____. After school,

Don read a book at _____.

10:15 a.m.

3:20 p.m.

8:30 a.m.

Math on the Spot

Problem Solving • Applications   Real World   WRITE) Math

10. GO DEEPER   Some times are shown on this time line. Write a label for each dot that names something you do at school during that part of the day.

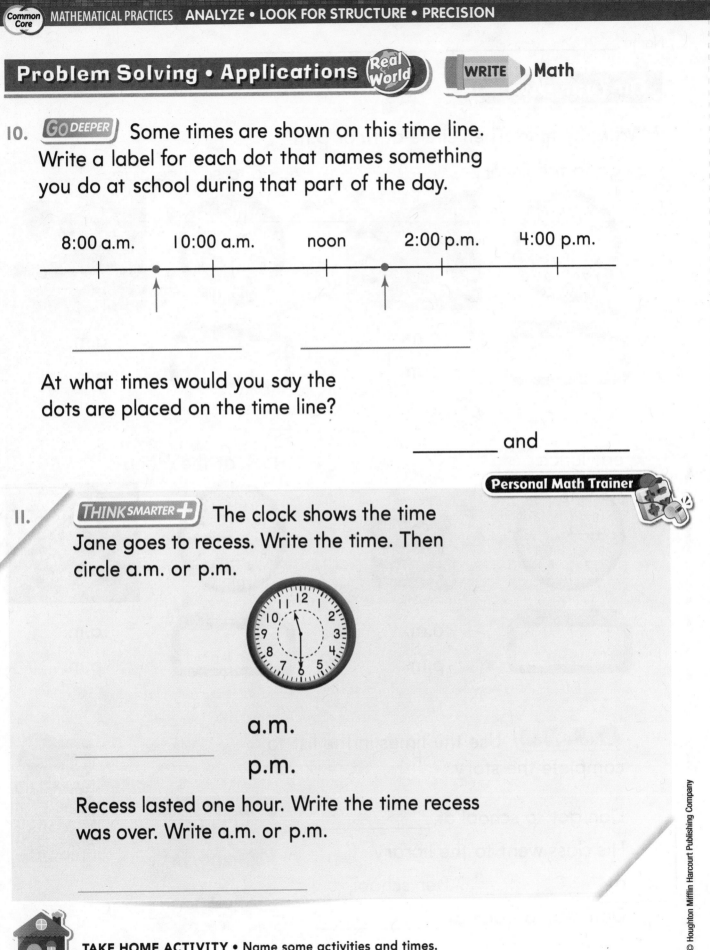

8:00 a.m.   10:00 a.m.   noon   2:00 p.m.   4:00 p.m.

_____   _____

At what times would you say the dots are placed on the time line?

_____ and _____

Personal Math Trainer

11. THINK SMARTER +   The clock shows the time Jane goes to recess. Write the time. Then circle a.m. or p.m.

a.m.

p.m.

_____

Recess lasted one hour. Write the time recess was over. Write a.m. or p.m.

_____

TAKE HOME ACTIVITY • Name some activities and times. Have your child say a.m. or p.m. for the times.

A.M. and P.M.

Common Core
COMMON CORE STANDARD—2.MD.C.7
Work with time and money.

Write the time. Then circle a.m. or p.m.

1. walk the dog

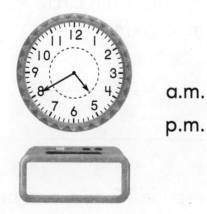

a.m.

p.m.

2. finish breakfast

a.m.

p.m.

Problem Solving Real World

Use the list of times. Complete the story.

3. Jess woke up at _____. She got on
the bus at _____ and went to school.
She left school at _____.

| 3:15 p.m. |
| 8:30 a.m. |
| 7:00 a.m. |

4. WRITE Math List two school
activities that you do in the
morning and two school
activities that you do in the
afternoon. Write times for
these activities using a.m.
and p.m.

_____

_____

_____

_____

_____

_____

Lesson Check

1. The clock shows when the soccer game ended. Write the time. Then circle a.m. or p.m.

_____ a.m.

p.m.

2. The clock shows when Jeff gets up for school. Write the time. Then circle a.m. or p.m.

_____ a.m.

p.m.

Spiral Review

3. What coin has the same value as 25 pennies? Draw your answer.

4. Describe 72 as a sum of tens and ones.

___ + ___

5. At the beginning of the school year there were 437 students at Woods Elementary. Over the course of the year, 24 students joined. How many students were there at the end of the year?

```
  4 3 7
+   2 4
```

_____ students

6. What time is quarter past 3?

_____

FOR MORE PRACTICE
GO TO THE
Personal Math Trainer

✓ Chapter 7 Review/Test

1. Andrea pays $2.15 for a jump rope.

   Fill in the bubble next to all the ways that show $2.15.

   ○ two $1 bills, 1 dime, and 1 nickel

   ○ one $1 bill, 4 quarters, and 1 dime

   ○ two $1 bills and 1 quarter

   ○ one $1 bill, 3 quarters, and 4 dimes

---

2. The clock shows the time Michael eats breakfast.

   Write the time. Circle a.m. or p.m.

   _____   a.m.

                      p.m

   Tell how you knew whether to select a.m. or p.m.

   _____

   _____

   _____

3. Does the group of coins have a total value of 60¢?
Choose Yes or No.

2 quarters and I dime.	○ Yes	○ No
I quarter, 2 dimes, and 3 nickels.	○ Yes	○ No
5 dimes, I nickel, and 6 pennies.	○ Yes	○ No
4 nickels and 20 pennies.	○ Yes	○ No

4. **GO DEEPER** Tess gave Raul these coins. Tess says she gave
Raul $1.00. Is Tess correct? Explain.

_____

_____

5. Write the time that is shown on this clock.

_____ : _____

6. What time is shown on the clock? Fill in the bubble
next to all the ways to write or say the time.

○ 4:35   ○ 35 minutes after 4

○ 7:20   ○ quarter past 4

Name _____

7. **THINK SMARTER** ✦ Alicia has this money in her pocket.

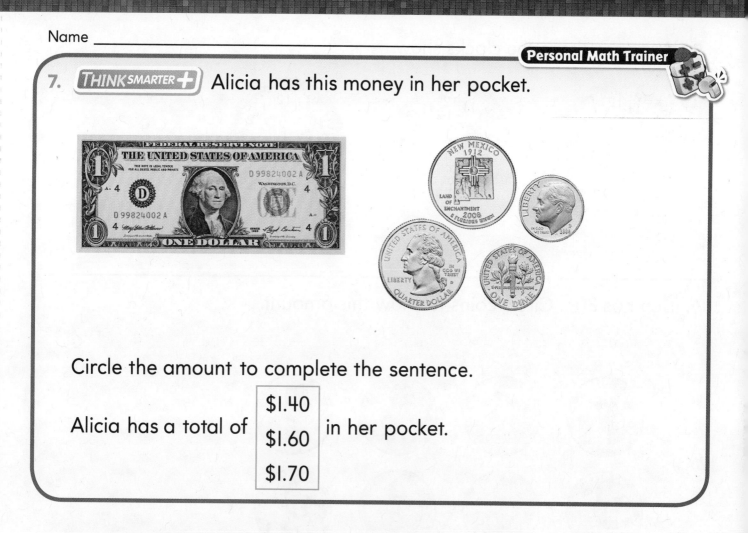

Circle the amount to complete the sentence.

Alicia has a total of | $1.40 |
| $1.60 |
| $1.70 | in her pocket.

8. Kate's father gave her these coins. Write the value of the coins. Explain how you found the the total value.

_____

_____

_____

_____

9. Write the times the clocks show.

_____   _____   _____

---

10. Ben has 30¢. Circle coins to show this amount.

---

11. Mia buys apples that cost 76¢.

Draw and label coins to show a total value of 76¢.

Chapter 8
Length in Customary Units

Curious about Math

The Missouri River is the longest river in the United States.

What is the longest piece of furniture in your classroom? How would you find out?

✓ Show What You Know

Personal Math Trainer
Online Assessment
and Intervention

Compare Lengths

1. Order the pencils from shortest to longest. (1.MD.A.1)
Write 1, 2, 3.

_____

_____

_____

Use Nonstandard Units to Measure Length

Use real objects and ▢ to measure. (1.MD.A.2)

2.

about _____ ▢

3. Crayon

about _____ ▢

Measure Length Twice: Nonstandard Units

Use 🖇 first. Then use ▫.
Measure the length of the pencil. (1.MD.A.2)

4. about _____ 🖇

5. about _____ ▫

This page checks understanding of important skills needed
for success in Chapter 8.

Vocabulary Builder

Review Words
length
longer
shorter
longest
shortest

Visualize It

Fill in the graphic organizer to describe the lengths of different objects.

```
           length
     ┌────────┴────────┐
┌─────────┐      ┌─────────┐
│         │      │         │
│         │      │         │
│         │      │         │
└─────────┘      └─────────┘
```

Understand Vocabulary

Use review words. Complete the sentences.

1. The blue pencil is the _____ pencil.

2. The red pencil is the _____ pencil.

3. The red pencil is _____ than the yellow pencil.

4. The blue pencil is _____ than the yellow pencil.

Game

Longer or Shorter?

Materials

• 9 ▣   • 9 ▣   • ◑

Play with a partner.

① Each player chooses a picture on the board and then finds a real object that matches that picture.

② Place the objects next to each other to find which is longer and which is shorter. If the objects are the same length, choose another object.

③ Spin the pointer on the spinner. The player with the object that matches the spinner puts a cube on that picture on the board.

④ Take turns until all the pictures have cubes. The player with more cubes on the board wins.

Longer | Shorter

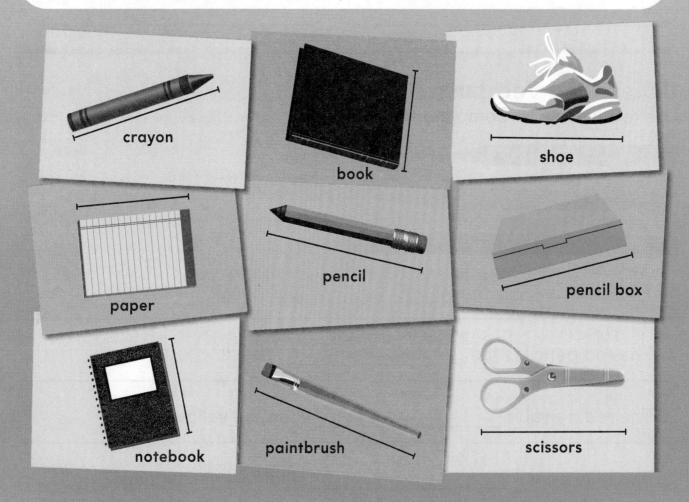

crayon

book

shoe

paper

pencil

pencil box

notebook

paintbrush

scissors

Chapter 8 Vocabulary

data datos 12	**estimate** estimación 21
foot pie 24	**inch** pulgada 32
line plot diagrama de puntos 37	**measuring tape** cinta métrica 38
sum suma o total 59	**yardstick** regla de 1 yarda 66

An **estimate** is an amount that tells about how many.

Favorite Lunch	
Lunch	Tally
pizza	IIII
sandwich	‖‖ I
salad	III
pasta	‖‖

The information in this chart is called **data**.

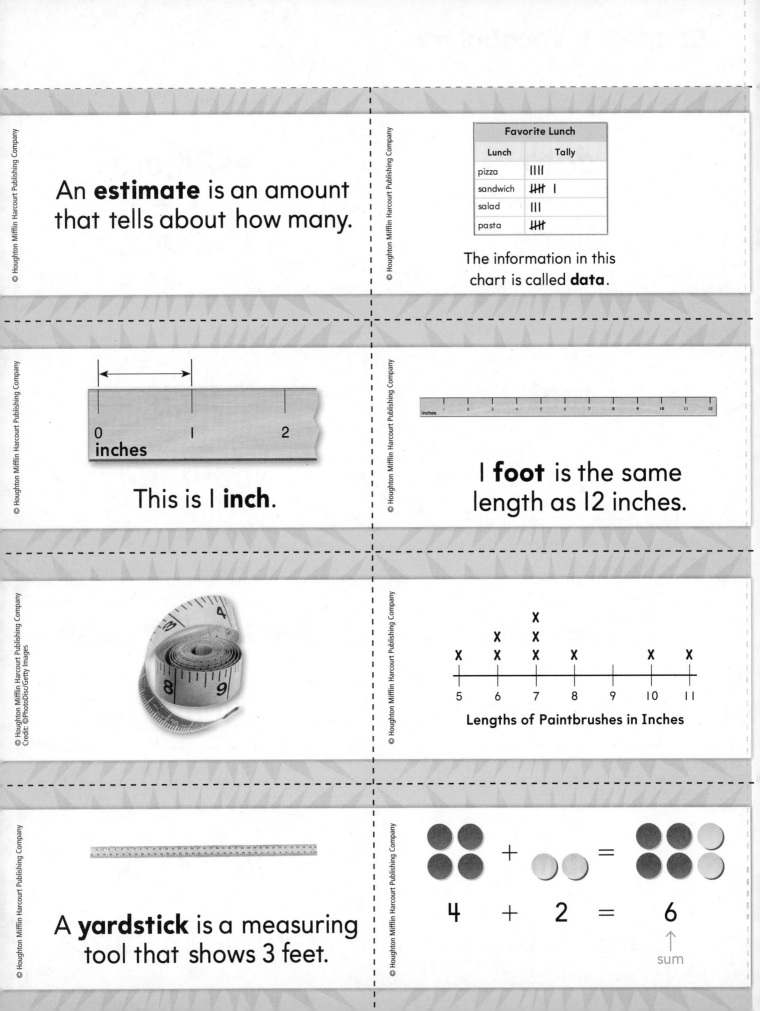

This is I **inch**.

I **foot** is the same length as 12 inches.

Lengths of Paintbrushes in Inches

A **yardstick** is a measuring tool that shows 3 feet.

4 + 2 = 6

↑
sum

Guess the Word

Word Box
data
estimate
foot
inch
line plot
measuring tape
sum
yardstick

For 3 to 4 players

Materials

* timer

How to Play

1. Take turns to play.
2. Choose a math word, but do not say it aloud.
3. Set the timer for 1 minute.
4. Give a one-word clue about your word. Give each player one chance to guess your word.
5. If nobody guesses correctly, repeat Step 4 with a different clue. Repeat until a player guesses the word or time runs out. Give a different one-word clue each time.
6. The first player to guess the word gets 1 point. If the player can use the word in a sentence, he or she gets 1 more point. Then that player gets the next turn.
7. The first player to score 5 points wins.

The Write Way

Reflect

Choose one idea. Write about it in the space below.

- When would you measure the length of an object? When would you estimate its length? Write 2–3 sentences to explain.

- Explain when you would use each measuring tool.

 measuring tape   yardstick   inch ruler

- Tell at least **two** things you know about a line plot.

Name _____

Measure with Inch Models

Essential Question How can you use inch models to measure length?

Common Core   **Measurement and Data—**
2.MD.A.1
MATHEMATICAL PRACTICES
MP2, MP5, MP6, MP8

Listen and Draw Real World

Use color tiles to measure the length.

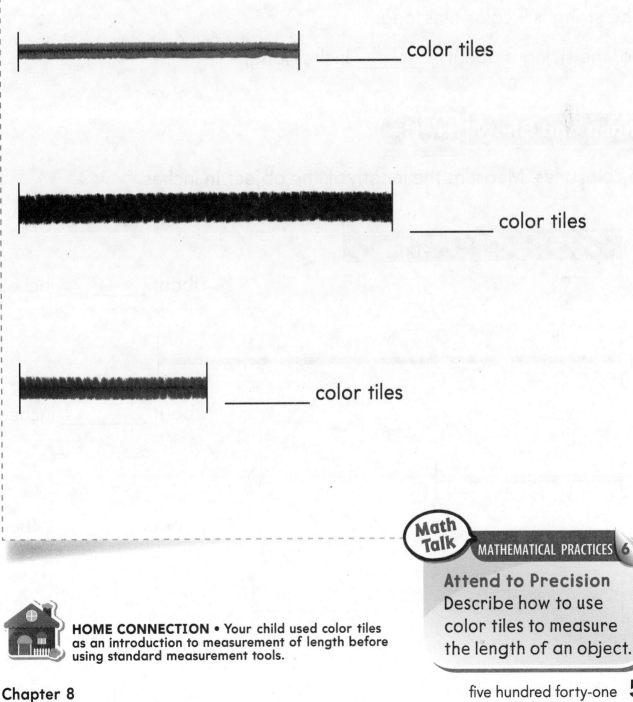

_____ color tiles

_____ color tiles

_____ color tiles

HOME CONNECTION • Your child used color tiles as an introduction to measurement of length before using standard measurement tools.

Math Talk MATHEMATICAL PRACTICES 6

Attend to Precision Describe how to use color tiles to measure the length of an object.

Chapter 8

five hundred forty-one **541**

A color tile is about 1 **inch** long.

About how many inches long is this string?

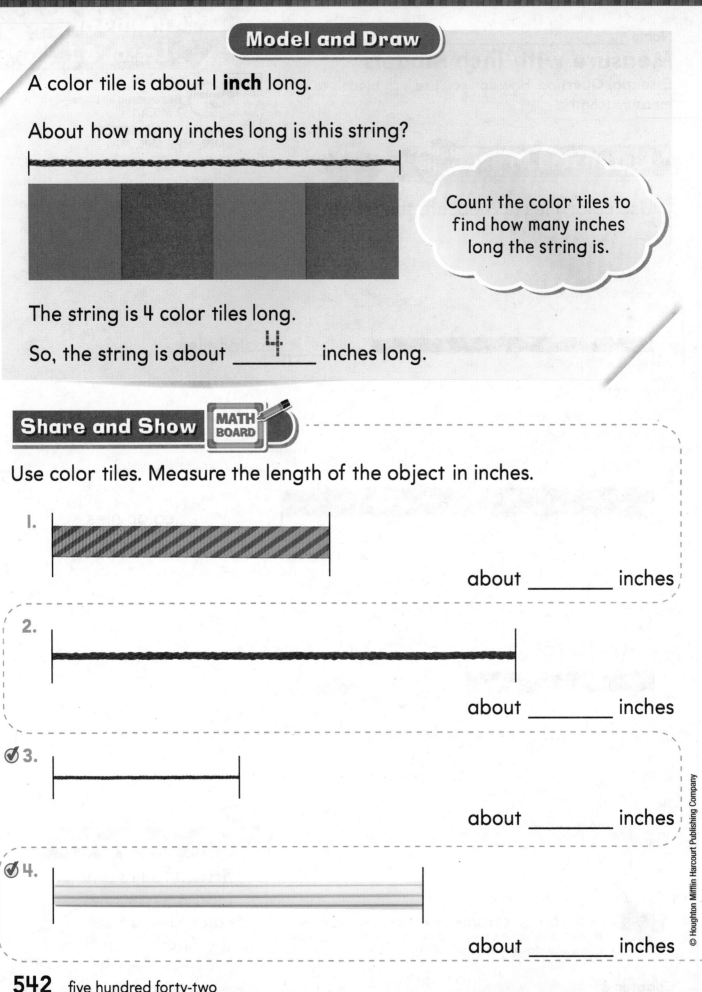

Count the color tiles to find how many inches long the string is.

The string is 4 color tiles long.

So, the string is about _____4_____ inches long.

Share and Show MATH BOARD

Use color tiles. Measure the length of the object in inches.

1.

about _____ inches

2.

about _____ inches

3.

about _____ inches

4.

about _____ inches

Name _____

Use color tiles. Measure the length of the object in inches.

5.

about _____ inches

6.

about _____ inches

7.

about _____ inches

8.

about _____ inches

9.

about _____ inches

10. **GO DEEPER** Blue paper chains are 4 inches long.
Red paper chains are 3 inches long. How many
are needed to have 10 inches of paper chains?

_____ blue paper chain   _____ red paper chains

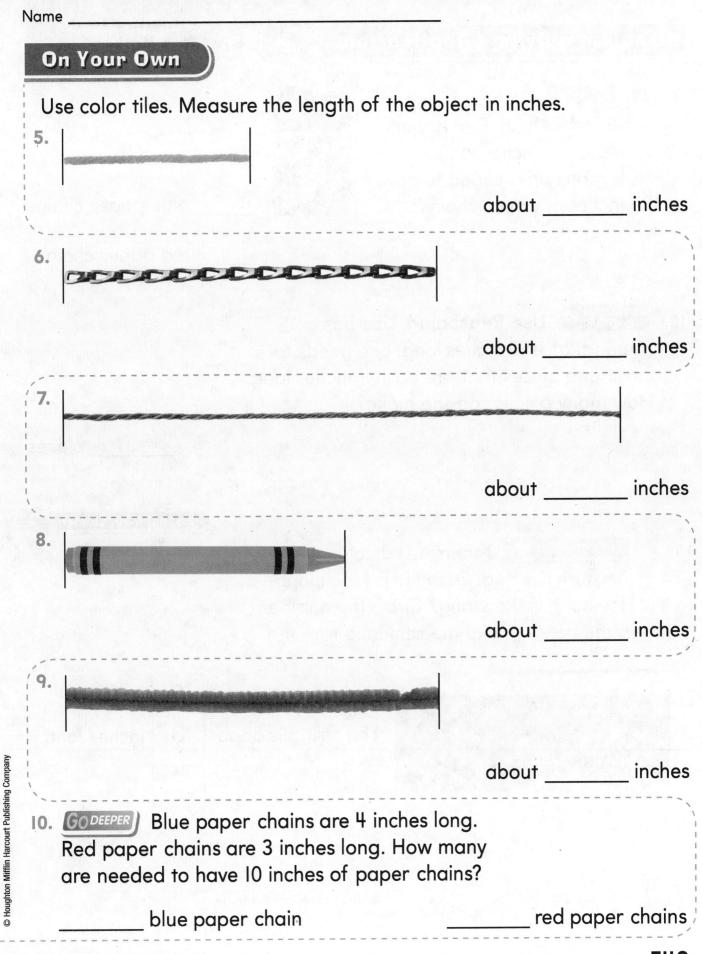

Problem Solving • Applications (Real World)   WRITE Math

11. **THINK SMARTER** Blue paper chains are 8 inches long. Red paper chains are 6 inches long. How many are needed to have 22 inches of paper chains?

Math on the Spot

_____ blue paper chains

_____ red paper chain

12. **MATHEMATICAL PRACTICE 2** **Use Reasoning** Liza has a ribbon that is 12 inches long. She needs to cut it into pieces that are each 4 inches long. How many pieces can she make?

_____ pieces

Personal Math Trainer

13. **THINK SMARTER +** Jeremy used color tiles to measure a string. Each tile is 1 inch long. How long is the string? Circle the number in the box to make the sentence true.

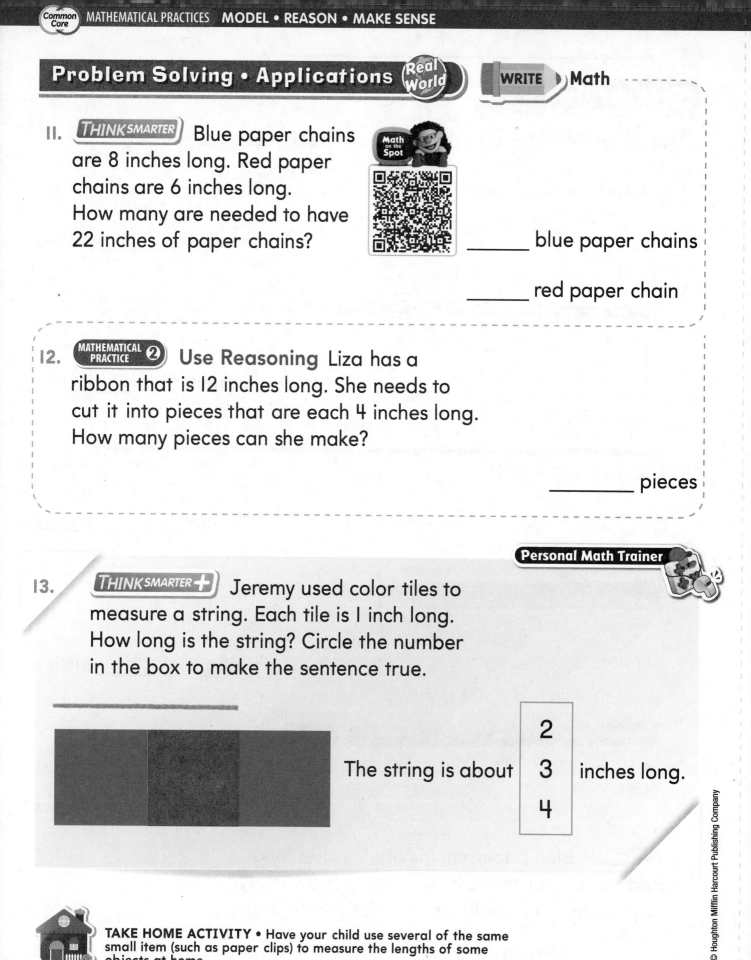

The string is about | 2 3 4 | inches long.

🏠 **TAKE HOME ACTIVITY** • Have your child use several of the same small item (such as paper clips) to measure the lengths of some objects at home.

Measure with Inch Models

Common Core COMMON CORE STANDARD—2.MD.A.1
Measure and estimate lengths in standard units.

Use color tiles. Measure the length of the object in inches.

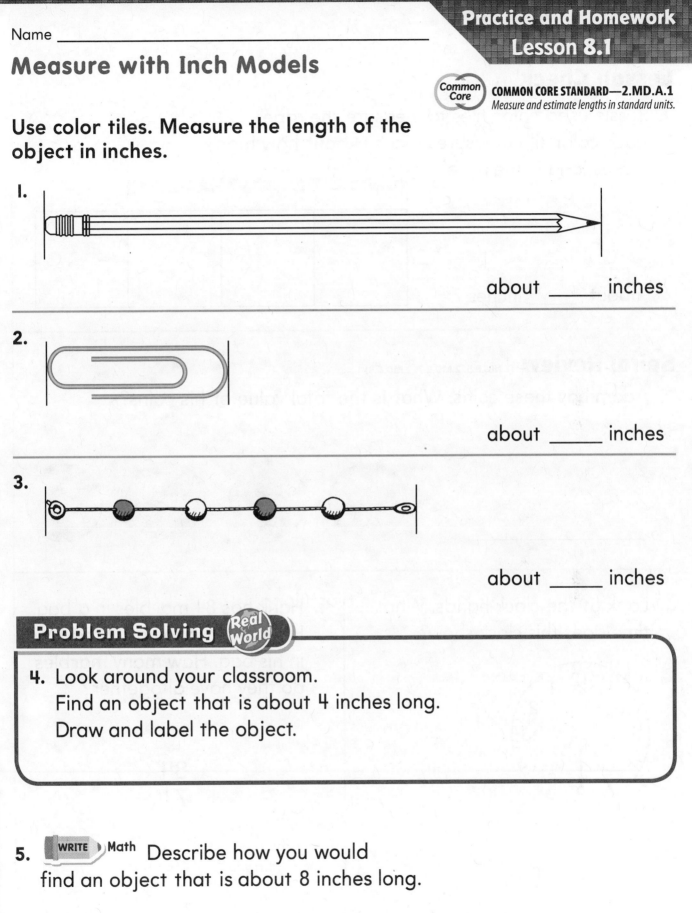

1.

about _____ inches

2.

about _____ inches

3.

about _____ inches

Problem Solving Real World

4. Look around your classroom.
   Find an object that is about 4 inches long.
   Draw and label the object.

5. WRITE Math Describe how you would
   find an object that is about 8 inches long.

_____

Lesson Check (2.MD.A.1)

1. Jessie used color tiles to measure the rope. Each color tile measures 1 inch. About how many inches long is the rope?

about _____ inches

Spiral Review (2.NBT.B.5, 2.MD.C.7, 2.MD.C.8)

2. Adam has these coins. What is the total value of his coins?

_____

---

3. Look at the clock hands. What time does this clock show?

___ : ___

4. Hank has 84 marbles in a bag. His friend Mario has 71 marbles in his bag. How many marbles do they have altogether?

$$\begin{array}{r} 84 \\ + 71 \\ \hline \end{array}$$

FOR MORE PRACTICE
GO TO THE
Personal Math Trainer

Name _____

Make and Use a Ruler

Essential Question Why is using a ruler similar to using a row of color tiles to measure length?

Common Core **Measurement and Data—**
2.MD.A.1
MATHEMATICAL PRACTICES
MP5, MP6

Listen and Draw

Use color tiles. Make the given length. Trace along the edge to show the length.

4 inches

2 inches

3 inches

Math Talk

MATHEMATICAL PRACTICES 6

Describe how you knew how many color tiles to use for each length.

HOME CONNECTION • Your child used color tiles as 1-inch models to show different lengths. This activity helps to make inch units a more familiar concept.

Use a color tile to make a ruler on a paper strip.
Color 6 parts that are each about 1 inch long.

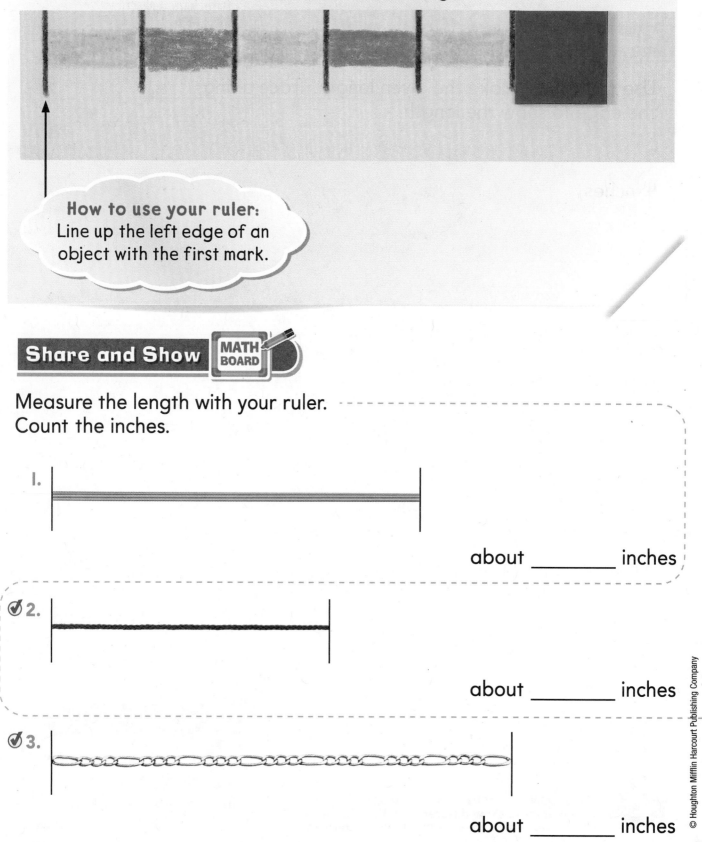

How to use your ruler:
Line up the left edge of an
object with the first mark.

Share and Show MATH BOARD

Measure the length with your ruler.
Count the inches.

1.

about _____ inches

✓2.

about _____ inches

✓3.

about _____ inches

Name _____

Measure the length with your ruler.
Count the inches.

4.

about _____ inches

5.

about _____ inches

6.

about _____ inches

7.

about _____ inches

8.

about _____ inches

© Houghton Mifflin Harcourt Publishing Company • Image Credits: (t) ©FEV/Shutterstock

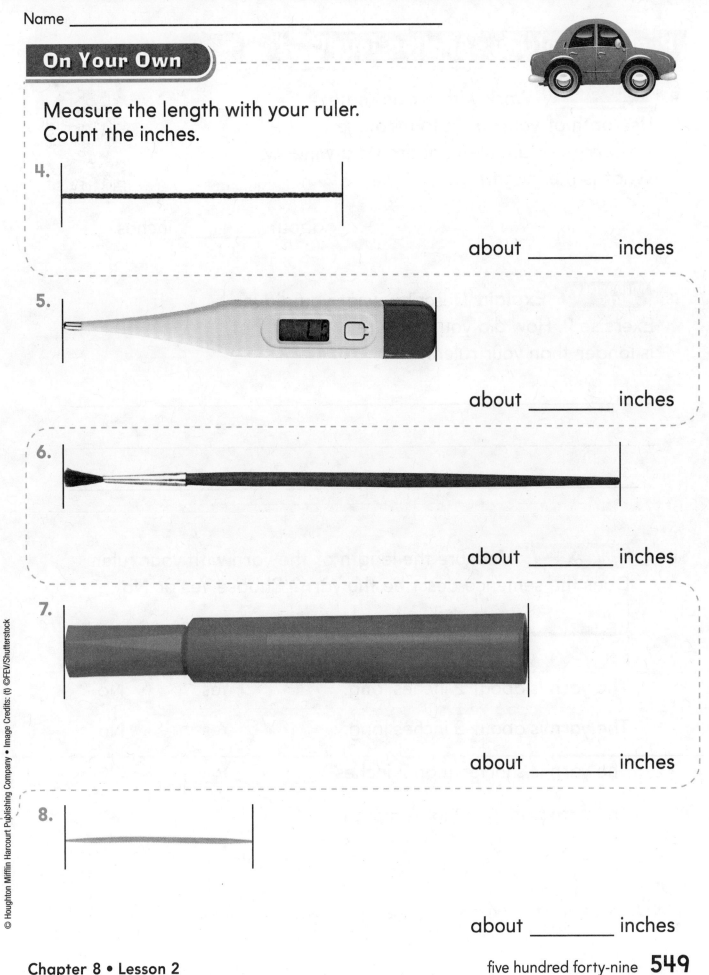

Problem Solving • Applications (Real World)   WRITE ▸ Math

9. **THINK SMARTER** Work with a classmate.
Use both of your rulers to measure
the length of a bulletin board or a window.
What is the length?

about _____ inches

10. **MATHEMATICAL PRACTICE ⑥ Explain** Describe what you did in
Exercise 9. How did you measure a length that
is longer than your rulers?

_____

_____

_____

11. **THINK SMARTER** Measure the length of the yarn with your ruler.
Does the sentence describe the yarn? Choose Yes or No.

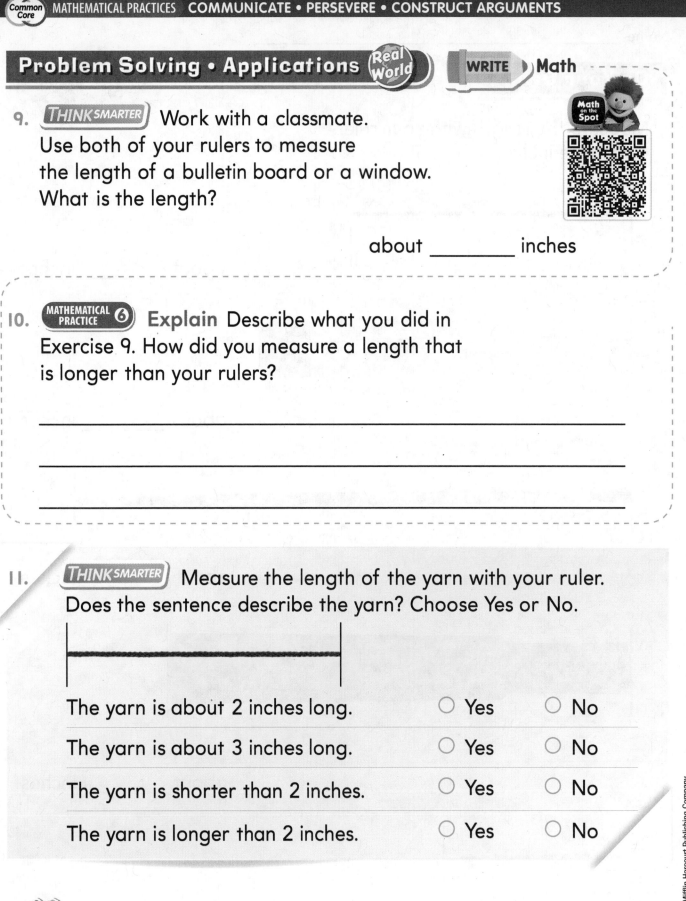

The yarn is about 2 inches long.	○ Yes	○ No
The yarn is about 3 inches long.	○ Yes	○ No
The yarn is shorter than 2 inches.	○ Yes	○ No
The yarn is longer than 2 inches.	○ Yes	○ No

TAKE HOME ACTIVITY • Choose one object in this lesson. Have your
child find objects that are longer, about the same length, and shorter.

Make and Use a Ruler

Common Core

COMMON CORE STANDARD—2.MD.A.1
Measure and estimate lengths in standard units.

Measure the length with your ruler.
Count the inches.

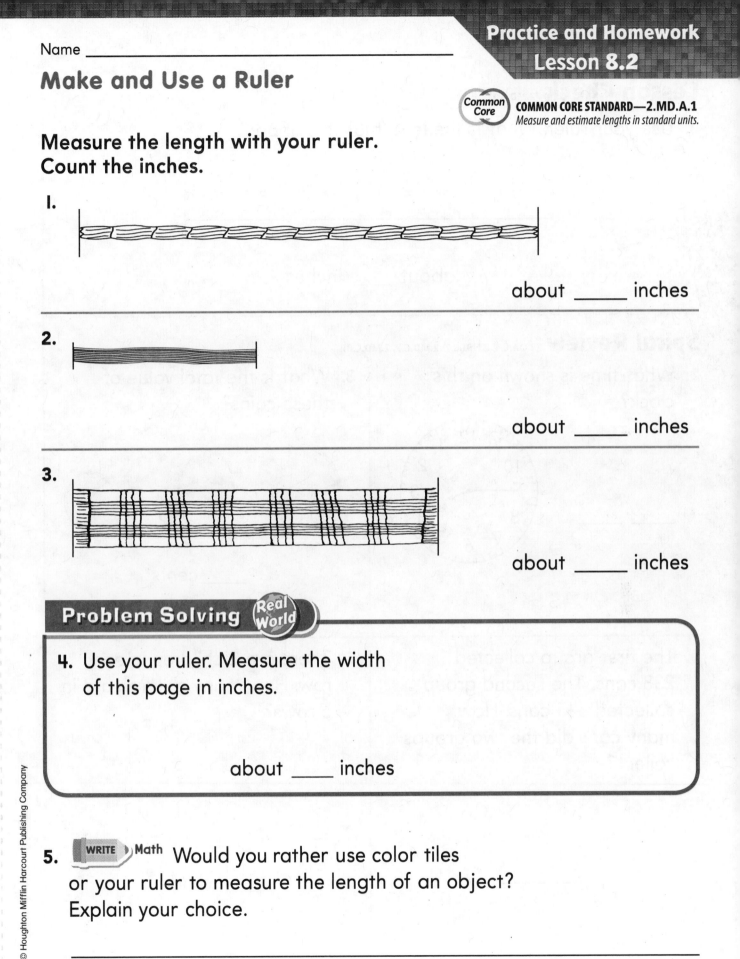

1.

about _____ inches

2.

about _____ inches

3.

about _____ inches

Problem Solving Real World

4. Use your ruler. Measure the width
   of this page in inches.

   about _____ inches

5. **WRITE** **Math** Would you rather use color tiles
   or your ruler to measure the length of an object?
   Explain your choice.

_____

Lesson Check (2.MD.A.1)

1. Use your ruler. What is the length of this ribbon?

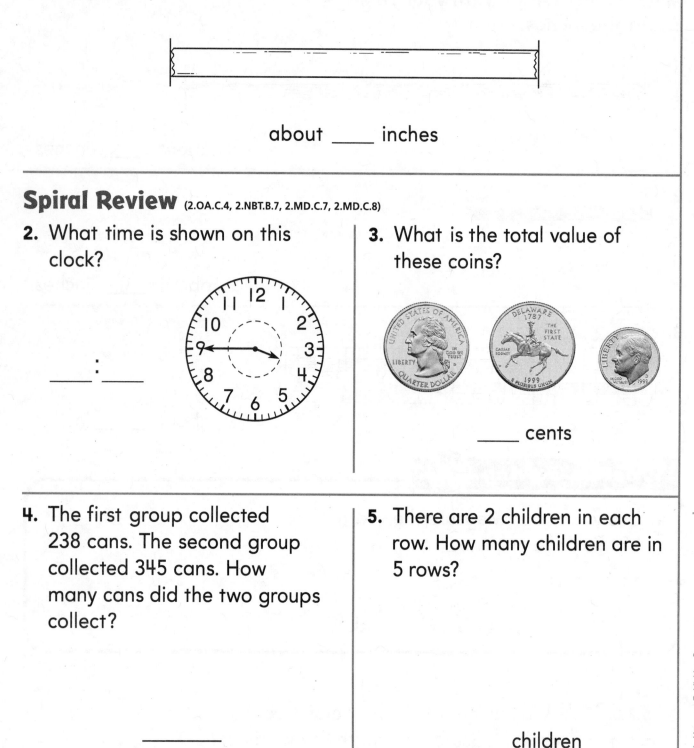

about _____ inches

Spiral Review (2.OA.C.4, 2.NBT.B.7, 2.MD.C.7, 2.MD.C.8)

2. What time is shown on this clock?

_____ : _____

3. What is the total value of these coins?

_____ cents

4. The first group collected 238 cans. The second group collected 345 cans. How many cans did the two groups collect?

_____

5. There are 2 children in each row. How many children are in 5 rows?

_____ children

FOR MORE PRACTICE
GO TO THE
Personal Math Trainer

Estimate Lengths in Inches

Essential Question How do you estimate the lengths of objects in inches?

Common Core **Measurement and Data—2.MD.A.3**
MATHEMATICAL PRACTICES
MP1, MP6, MP7

Listen and Draw Real World • Hands On

Choose three objects. Measure their lengths with your ruler. Draw the objects and write their lengths.

about _____ inches

about _____ inches

about _____ inches

Math Talk MATHEMATICAL PRACTICES 6

Describe how the three lengths compare. Which is the longest object?

FOR THE TEACHER • Provide a collection of small objects, 2 to 6 inches in length, for children to measure. Have them select one object, measure it, and return it before selecting another object.

© Houghton Mifflin Harcourt Publishing Company

The bead is 1 inch long. Use this bead to help find how many beads will fit on the string. Which is the best estimate for the length of the string?

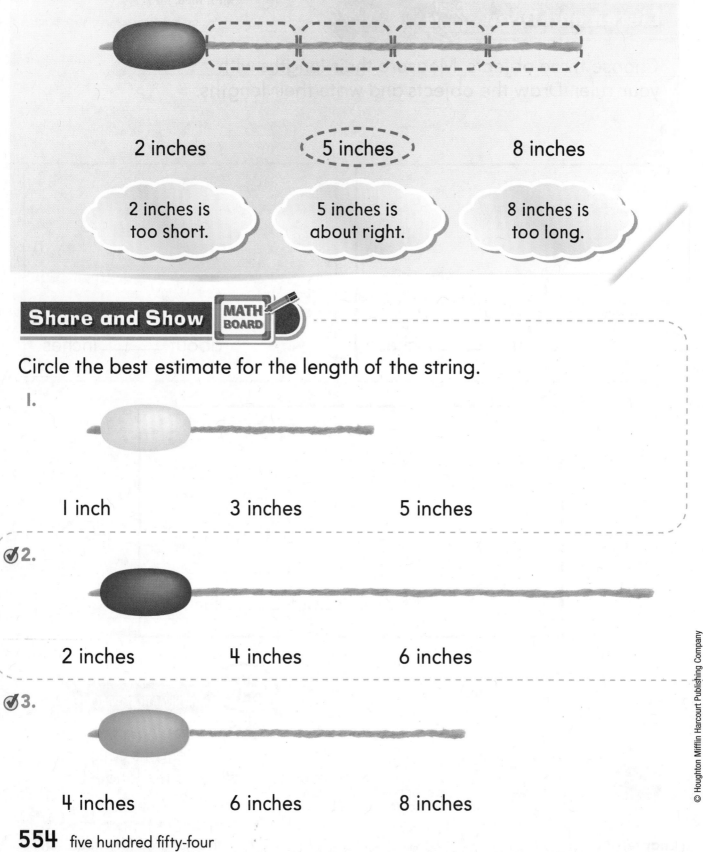

2 inches   5 inches   8 inches

2 inches is too short.

5 inches is about right.

8 inches is too long.

Share and Show MATH BOARD

Circle the best estimate for the length of the string.

1.

1 inch   3 inches   5 inches

2.

2 inches   4 inches   6 inches

3.

4 inches   6 inches   8 inches

On Your Own

Circle the best estimate for the length of the string.

4.

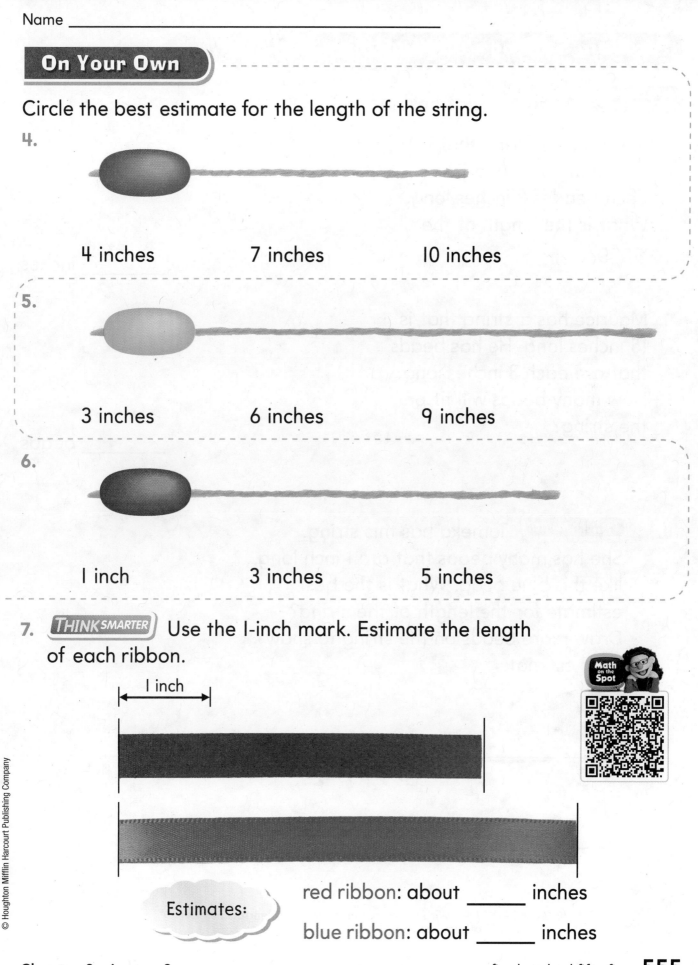

4 inches   7 inches   10 inches

5.

3 inches   6 inches   9 inches

6.

1 inch   3 inches   5 inches

7. **THINK SMARTER** Use the 1-inch mark. Estimate the length of each ribbon.

1 inch

Estimates:

red ribbon: about _____ inches

blue ribbon: about _____ inches

Problem Solving • Applications (Real World) WRITE Math

MATHEMATICAL PRACTICE ① **Analyze Relationships**

8. Sasha has a string that is the length of 5 beads. Each bead is 2 inches long. What is the length of the string?

_____ inches

9. Maurice has a string that is 15 inches long. He has beads that are each 3 inches long. How many beads will fit on the string?

_____ beads

10. THINK SMARTER Tameka has this string. She has many beads that are 1 inch long, like this blue bead. What is the best estimate for the length of the string? Draw more beads on the string to show your estimate.

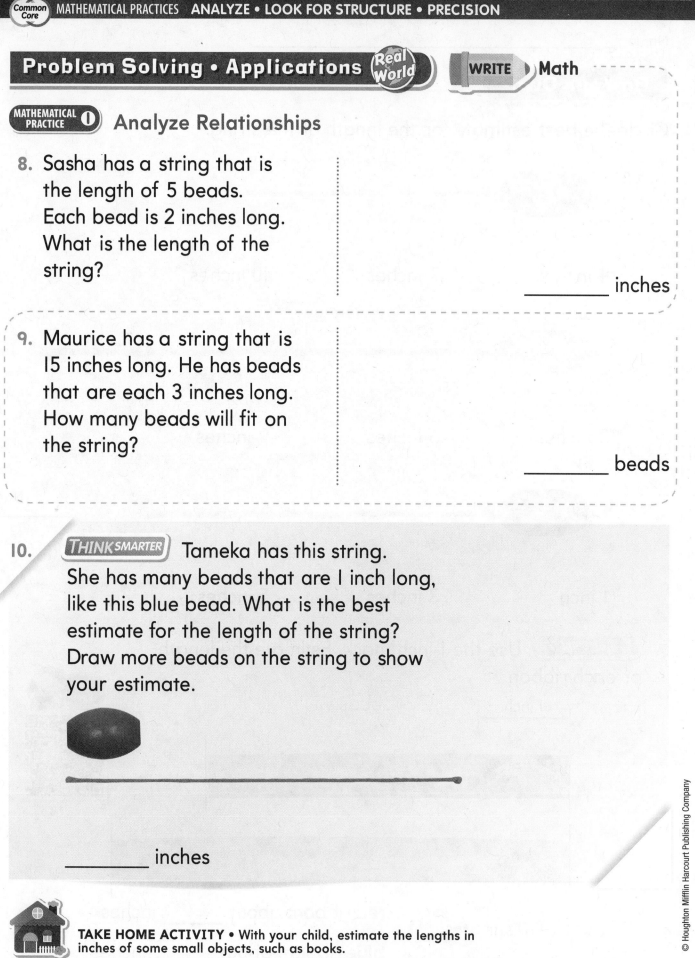

_____ inches

TAKE HOME ACTIVITY • With your child, estimate the lengths in inches of some small objects, such as books.

Estimate Lengths in Inches

Common Core   **COMMON CORE STANDARD—2.MD.A.3**
Measure and estimate lengths in standard units.

The bead is I inch long.
Circle the best estimate for the length
of the string.

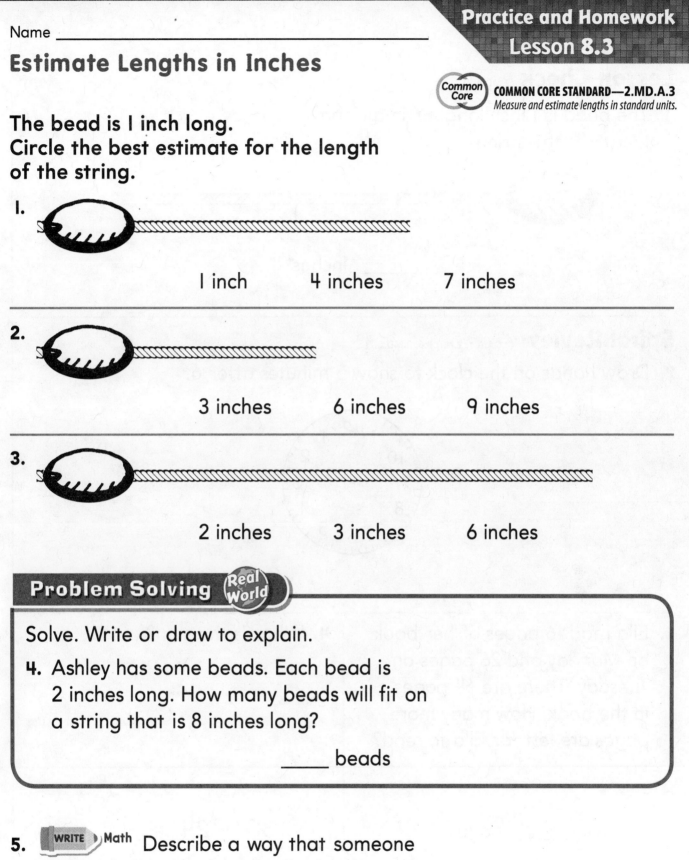

I.

        I inch   4 inches   7 inches

2.

        3 inches   6 inches   9 inches

3.

        2 inches   3 inches   6 inches

Problem Solving *Real World*

Solve. Write or draw to explain.

4. Ashley has some beads. Each bead is
   2 inches long. How many beads will fit on
   a string that is 8 inches long?

   _____ beads

5. **WRITE** Math Describe a way that someone
   could estimate the length of a book.

Lesson Check (2.MD.A.3)

I. The bead is I inch long. Estimate the
length of the string.

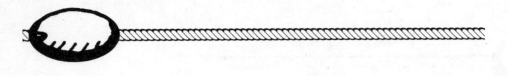

_____ inches

Spiral Review (2.OA.A.1, 2.NBT.B.6, 2.MD.C.7)

2. Draw hands on the clock to show 5 minutes after 6.

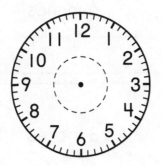

3. Ella read 16 pages of her book
on Monday and 26 pages on
Tuesday. There are 64 pages
in the book. How many more
pages are left for Ella to read?

_____ pages

4. What is the sum?

$38 + 24 = $ _____

FOR MORE PRACTICE
GO TO THE
Personal Math Trainer

Name _____

Measure with an Inch Ruler

Essential Question How do you use an inch ruler to measure lengths?

Common Core **Measurement and Data—
2.MD.A.1**
MATHEMATICAL PRACTICES
MP2, MP5, MP6

Draw each worm to match the given length.

Math Talk
MATHEMATICAL PRACTICES 2

Use Reasoning Describe how you decided how long to draw the 2-inch and 3-inch worms.

FOR THE TEACHER • Have children use the rulers that they made in Lesson 8.2 to draw a worm that is 1 inch long. Have children use the 1-inch-long worm as a guide to draw a worm that is 2 inches long and a worm that is 3 inches long, without using their rulers.

Chapter 8

Model and Draw

What is the length of the string to the nearest inch?

Step 1
Line up the end of the string with the zero mark on the ruler.

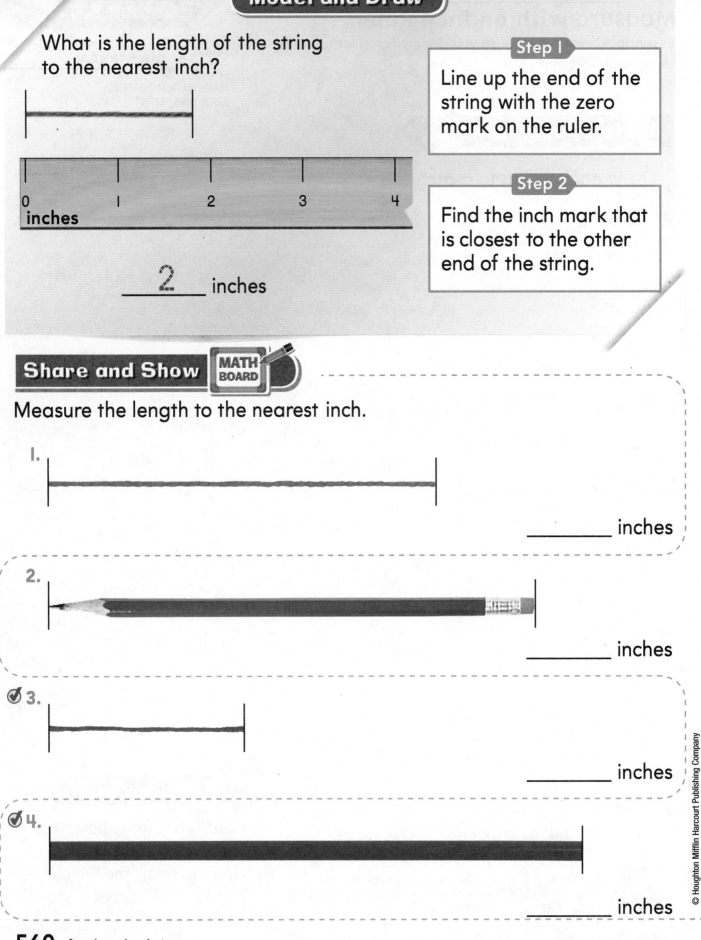

Step 2
Find the inch mark that is closest to the other end of the string.

__2__ inches

Share and Show MATH BOARD

Measure the length to the nearest inch.

1.

_____ inches

2.

_____ inches

✓ 3.

_____ inches

✓ 4.

_____ inches

Name _____

Measure the length to the nearest inch.

5.

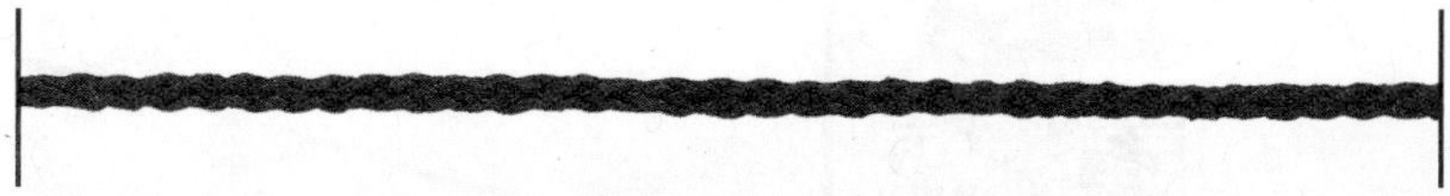

_____ inches

6.

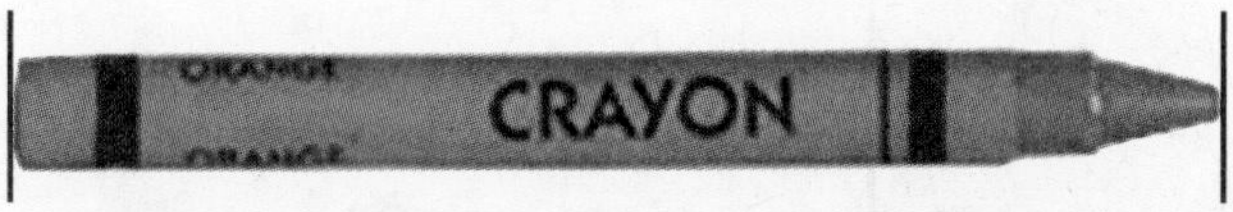

CRAYON

_____ inches

7.

_____ inches

8.

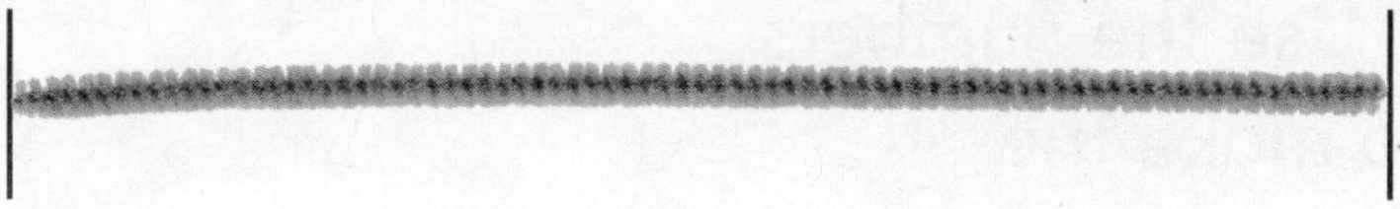

_____ inches

9. **GO DEEPER** Measure the lengths to the nearest inch. How much shorter is the ribbon than the yarn?

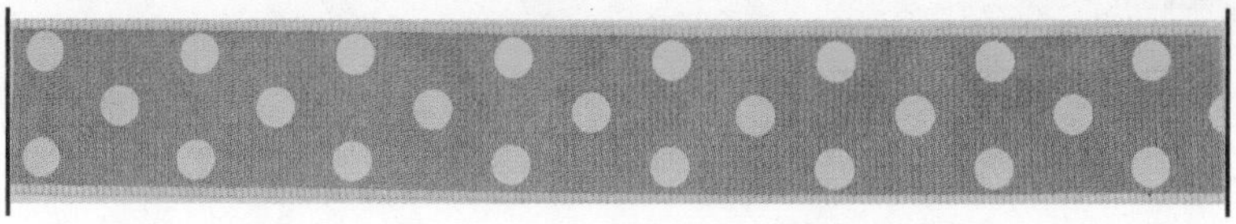

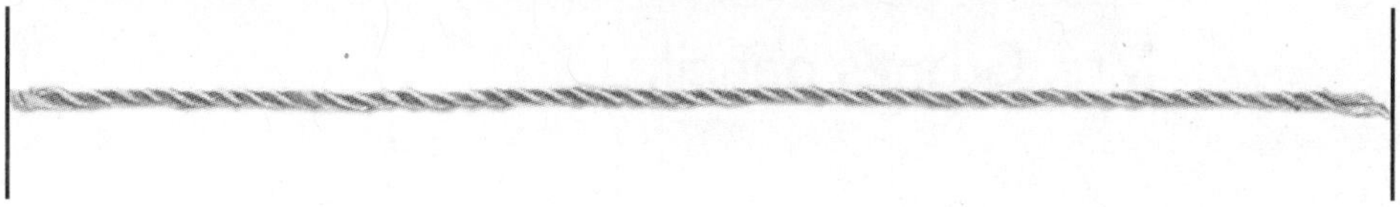

_____ inch shorter

Problem Solving • Applications (Real World)   WRITE › Math

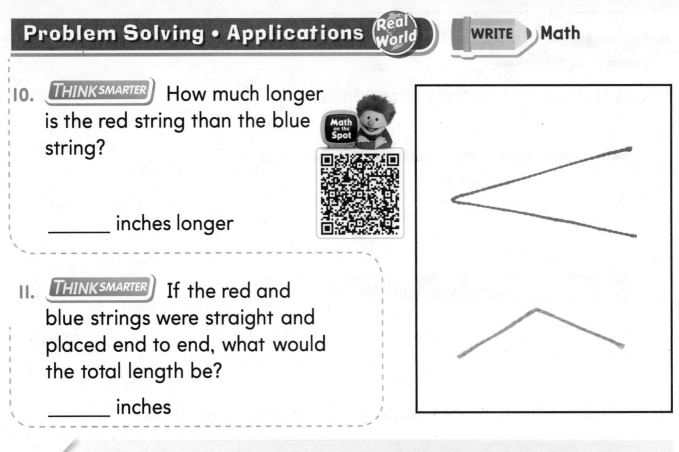

10. **THINK SMARTER** How much longer is the red string than the blue string?

_____ inches longer

11. **THINK SMARTER** If the red and blue strings were straight and placed end to end, what would the total length be?

_____ inches

12. **THINK SMARTER** Mrs. Grant's pencil is 5 inches long. Is this Mrs. Grant's pencil? Use an inch ruler to find out. Use the numbers and words on the tiles to make the sentences true.

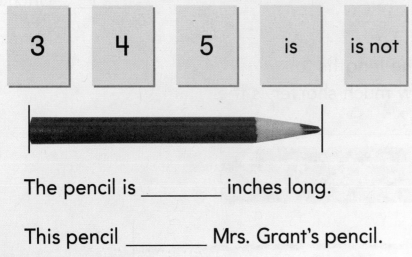

| 3 | 4 | 5 | is | is not |

The pencil is _____ inches long.

This pencil _____ Mrs. Grant's pencil.

TAKE HOME ACTIVITY • Have your child measure the lengths of some objects to the nearest inch using a ruler or a similar measuring tool.

Measure with an Inch Ruler

Common Core
COMMON CORE STANDARD—2.MD.A.1
Measure and estimate lengths in standard units.

Measure the length to the nearest inch.

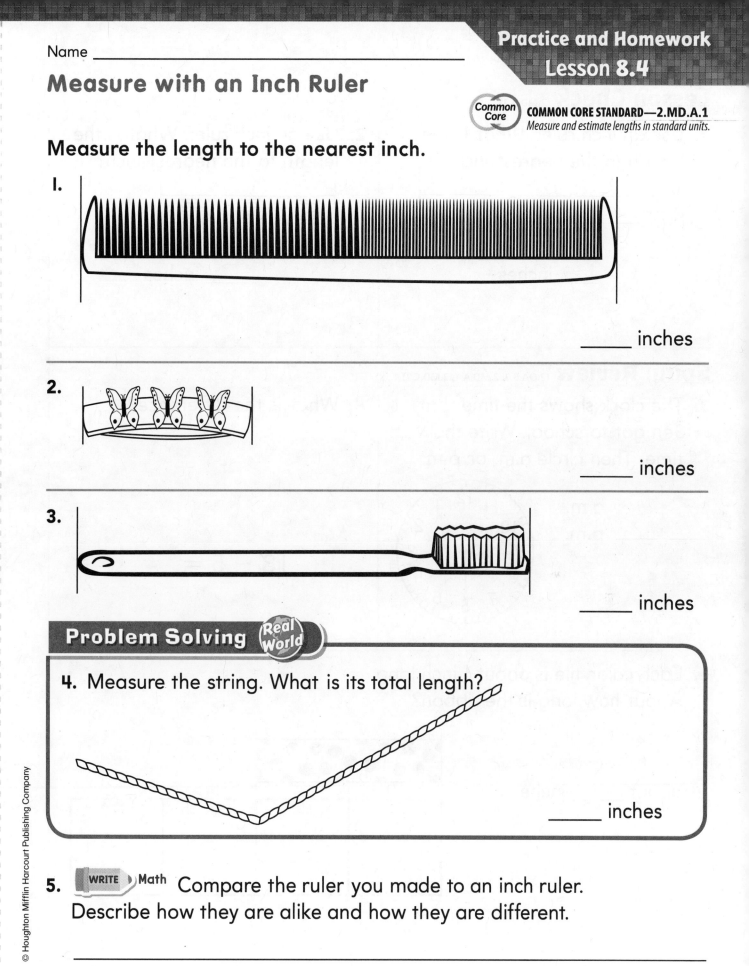

1.

_____ inches

2.

_____ inches

3.

_____ inches

Problem Solving *Real World*

4. Measure the string. What is its total length?

_____ inches

5. **WRITE** Math Compare the ruler you made to an inch ruler.
Describe how they are alike and how they are different.

_____

Lesson Check (2.MD.A.1)

I. Use an inch ruler. What is the length to the nearest inch?

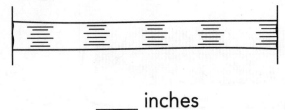

_____ inches

2. Use an inch ruler. What is the length to the nearest inch?

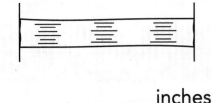

_____ inches

Spiral Review (2.OA.B.2, 2.MD.A.1, 2.MD.C.7)

3. The clock shows the time that Jen got to school. Write the time. Then circle a.m. or p.m.

_____ : _____
a.m.
p.m.

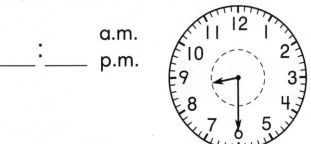

4. What is the difference?

$13 - 5 =$ _____

5. Each color tile is about 1 inch long. About how long is the ribbon?

about _____ inches

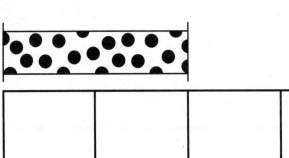

FOR MORE PRACTICE
GO TO THE
Personal Math Trainer

Problem Solving • Add and Subtract in Inches

Essential Question How can drawing a diagram help when solving problems about length?

Common Core — Measurement and Data—
2.MD.B.5, 2.MD.B.6
MATHEMATICAL PRACTICES
MP1, MP2, MP4, MP6

There is a paper clip chain that is 16 inches long. Aliyah removes 9 inches of paper clips from the chain. How long is the paper clip chain now?

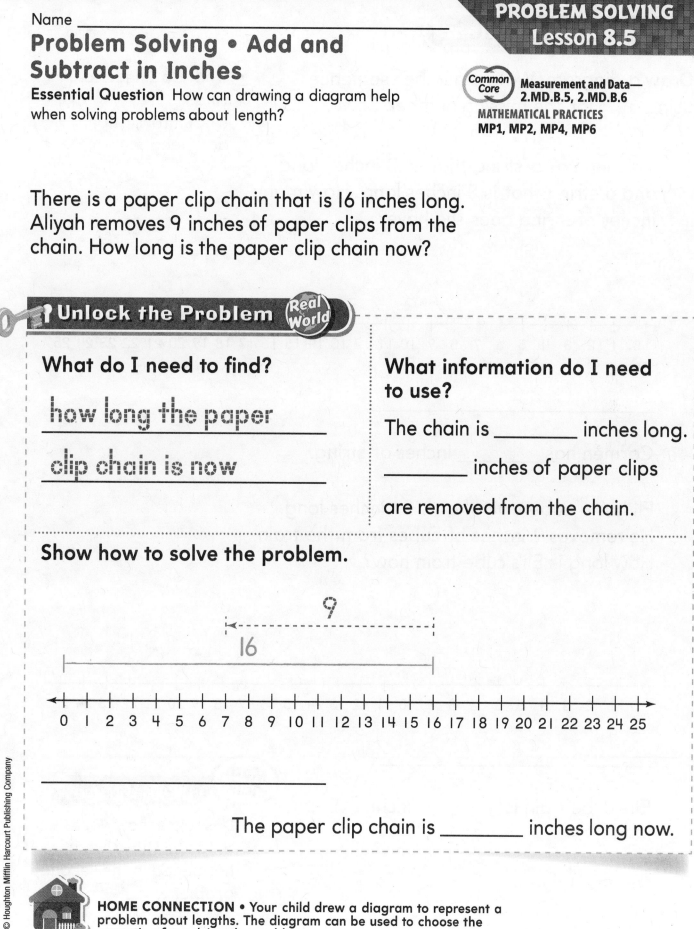

Unlock the Problem Real World

What do I need to find?

how long the paper

clip chain is now

What information do I need to use?

The chain is _____ inches long.

_____ inches of paper clips

are removed from the chain.

Show how to solve the problem.

9

16

0 1 2 3 4 5 6 7 8 9 10 11 12 13 14 15 16 17 18 19 20 21 22 23 24 25

_____

The paper clip chain is _____ inches long now.

HOME CONNECTION • Your child drew a diagram to represent a problem about lengths. The diagram can be used to choose the operation for solving the problem.

Try Another Problem

Draw a diagram. Write a number sentence using a ■ for the missing number. Solve.

- What do I need to find?
- What information do I need to use?

1. Carmen has a string that is 13 inches long and a string that is 8 inches long. How many inches of string does she have?

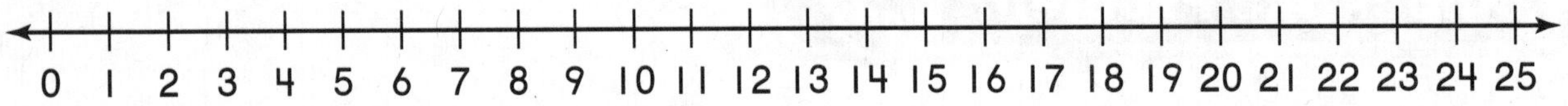
0 1 2 3 4 5 6 7 8 9 10 11 12 13 14 15 16 17 18 19 20 21 22 23 24 25

____

Carmen has ________ inches of string.

2. Eli has a cube train that is 24 inches long. He removes 9 inches of cubes from the train. How long is Eli's cube train now?

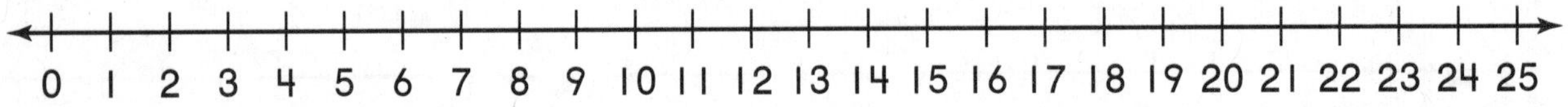
0 1 2 3 4 5 6 7 8 9 10 11 12 13 14 15 16 17 18 19 20 21 22 23 24 25

____

Eli's cube train is ________ inches long now.

Math Talk MATHEMATICAL PRACTICES 6

Describe how your diagram shows what happened in the second problem.

Name _____

Share and Show MATH BOARD

Draw a diagram. Write a number sentence using a ▨ for the missing number. Solve.

☑ **3.** Lee has a paper strip chain that is 25 inches long. He unhooks 13 inches from the chain. How long is Lee's paper strip chain now?

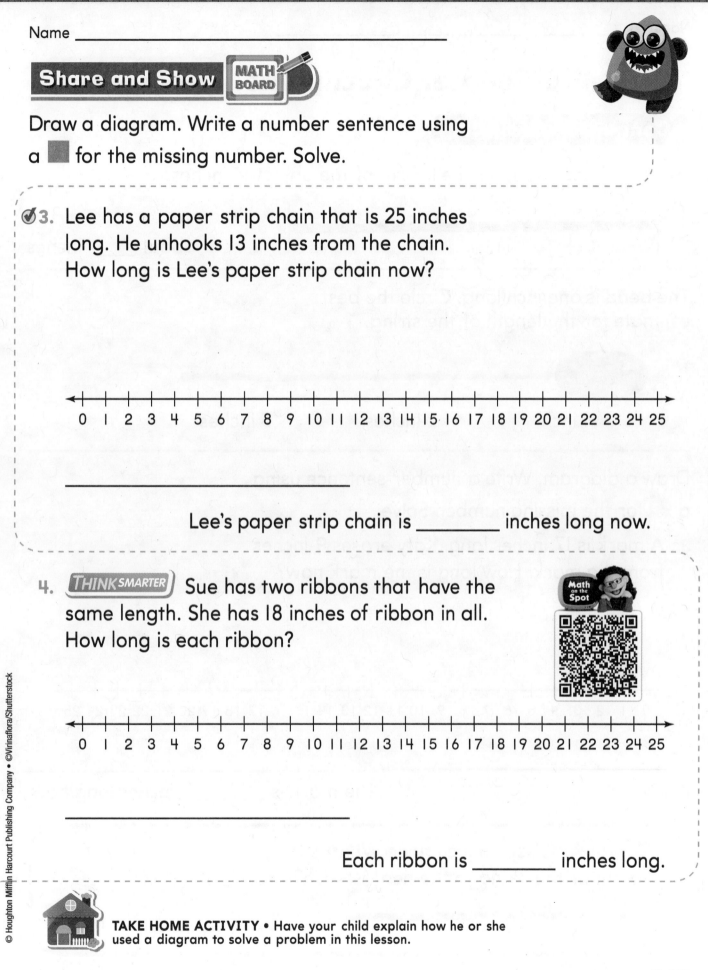

0 1 2 3 4 5 6 7 8 9 10 11 12 13 14 15 16 17 18 19 20 21 22 23 24 25

_____

Lee's paper strip chain is _____ inches long now.

4. **THINK SMARTER** Sue has two ribbons that have the same length. She has 18 inches of ribbon in all. How long is each ribbon?

Math on the Spot

0 1 2 3 4 5 6 7 8 9 10 11 12 13 14 15 16 17 18 19 20 21 22 23 24 25

_____

Each ribbon is _____ inches long.

TAKE HOME ACTIVITY • Have your child explain how he or she used a diagram to solve a problem in this lesson.

Name _____

✓ Mid-Chapter Checkpoint

Personal Math Trainer
Online Assessment and Intervention

Concepts and Skills

Use color tiles. Measure the length of the object in inches. (2.MD.A.1)

1. about _____ inches

The bead is one inch long. Circle the best
estimate for the length of the string. (2.MD.A.3)

2.

         1 inch   2 inches   5 inches

Draw a diagram. Write a number sentence using

a ▮ for the missing number. Solve.

3. A mark is 17 inches long. Katy erases 9 inches
from the mark. How long is the mark now? (2.MD.B.5, 2.MD.B.6)

← + →
0 1 2 3 4 5 6 7 8 9 10 11 12 13 14 15 16 17 18 19 20 21 22 23 24 25

_____

The mark is _____ inches long now.

4. **THINK SMARTER** Use an inch ruler. What is the
length of the string to the nearest inch? (2.MD.A.1)

_____ inches

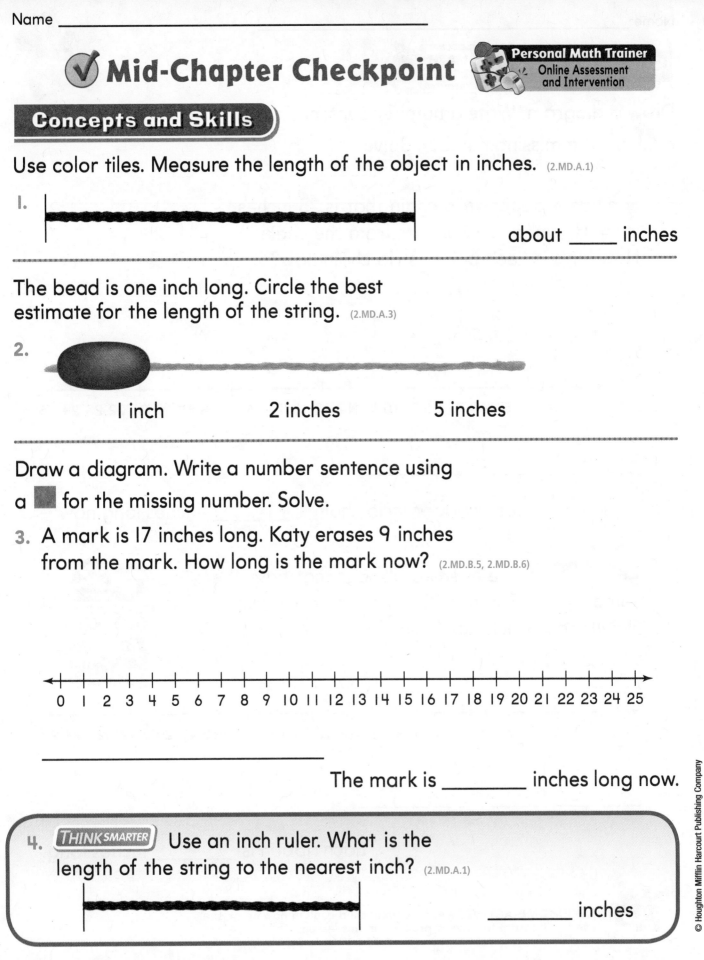

Problem Solving • Add and Subtract in Inches

COMMON CORE STANDARDS—2.MD.B.5,
2.MD.B.6 *Relate addition and subtraction to length.*

Draw a diagram. Write a number sentence using a ▢ for the missing number. Solve.

1. Molly had a ribbon that was 23 inches long. She cut 7 inches off the ribbon. How long is her ribbon now?

```
←─┼─┼─┼─┼─┼─┼─┼─┼─┼─┼─┼─┼─┼─┼─┼─┼─┼─┼─┼─┼─┼─┼─┼─┼─┼─→
  0 1 2 3 4 5 6 7 8 9 10 11 12 13 14 15 16 17 18 19 20 21 22 23 24 25
```

_____

Molly's ribbon is _____ inches long now.

2. **WRITE** Math Describe how you could draw a diagram for a problem about finding the total length for two strings, 15 inches long and 7 inches long.

_____
_____
_____
_____
_____
_____

Lesson Check (2.MD.B.5, 2.MD.B.6)

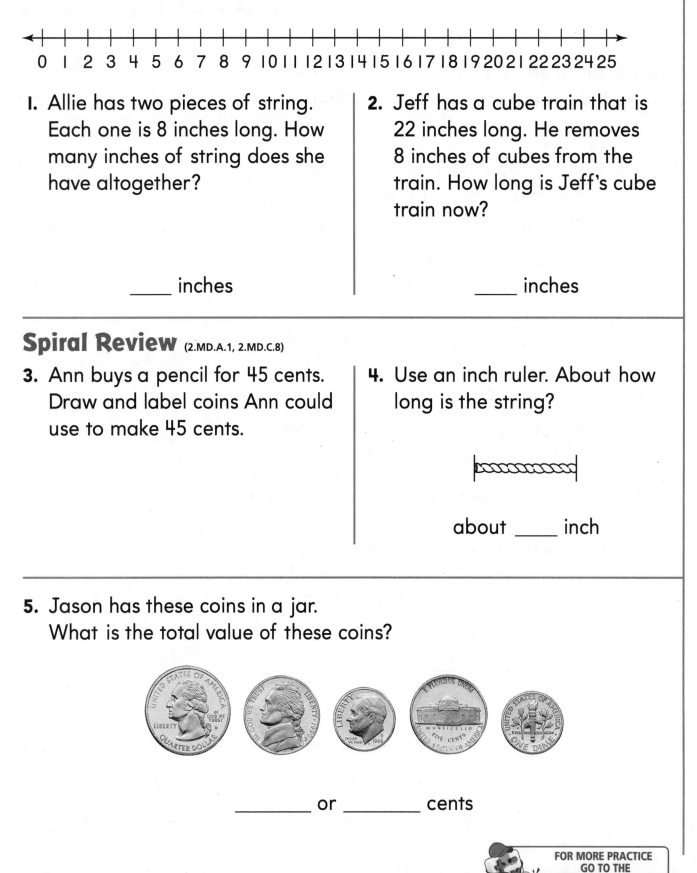

0 1 2 3 4 5 6 7 8 9 10 11 12 13 14 15 16 17 18 19 20 21 22 23 24 25

1. Allie has two pieces of string. Each one is 8 inches long. How many inches of string does she have altogether?

_____ inches

2. Jeff has a cube train that is 22 inches long. He removes 8 inches of cubes from the train. How long is Jeff's cube train now?

_____ inches

Spiral Review (2.MD.A.1, 2.MD.C.8)

3. Ann buys a pencil for 45 cents. Draw and label coins Ann could use to make 45 cents.

4. Use an inch ruler. About how long is the string?

about _____ inch

5. Jason has these coins in a jar. What is the total value of these coins?

_____ or _____ cents

FOR MORE PRACTICE
GO TO THE
Personal Math Trainer

Name _____

Measure in Inches and Feet

Essential Question Why is measuring in feet different from measuring in inches?

 Common Core Measurement and Data—
2.MD.A.2
MATHEMATICAL PRACTICES
MP2, MP5, MP6

Listen and Draw **Real World**  Hands On

Draw or write to describe how you did each measurement.

First measurement

Second measurement

Math Talk MATHEMATICAL PRACTICES 2

Use Reasoning
Describe how the length of a sheet of paper and the length of a paper clip are different.

FOR THE TEACHER • Have pairs of children stand apart and measure the distance between them with sheets of paper folded in half lengthwise. Then have them measure the same distance using large paper clips.

Chapter 8

12 inches is the same as 1 **foot**.
A 12-inch ruler is 1 foot long.
You can measure lengths in inches
and also in feet.

The real table is about 60 inches long.
The real table is also about 5 feet long.

Share and Show MATH BOARD

Measure to the nearest inch.
Then measure to the nearest foot.

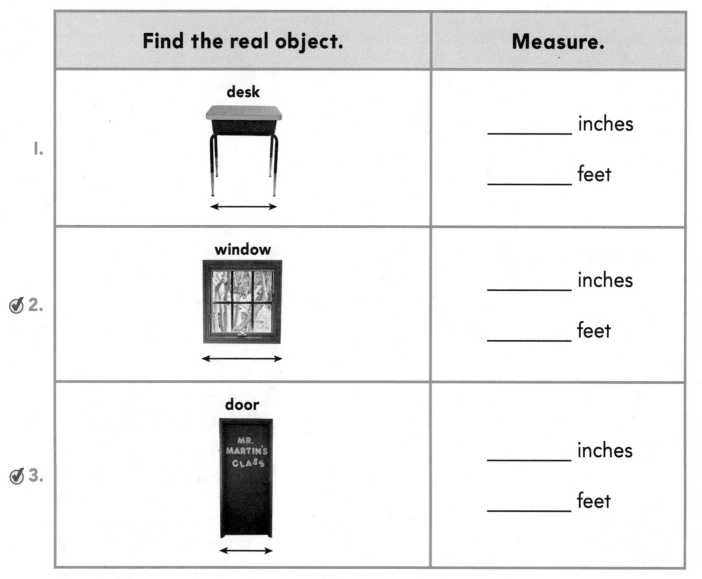

Find the real object.	Measure.
desk 1.	_____ inches _____ feet
window 2.	_____ inches _____ feet
door MR. MARTIN'S CLASS 3.	_____ inches _____ feet

Name _____

Measure to the nearest inch.
Then measure to the nearest foot.

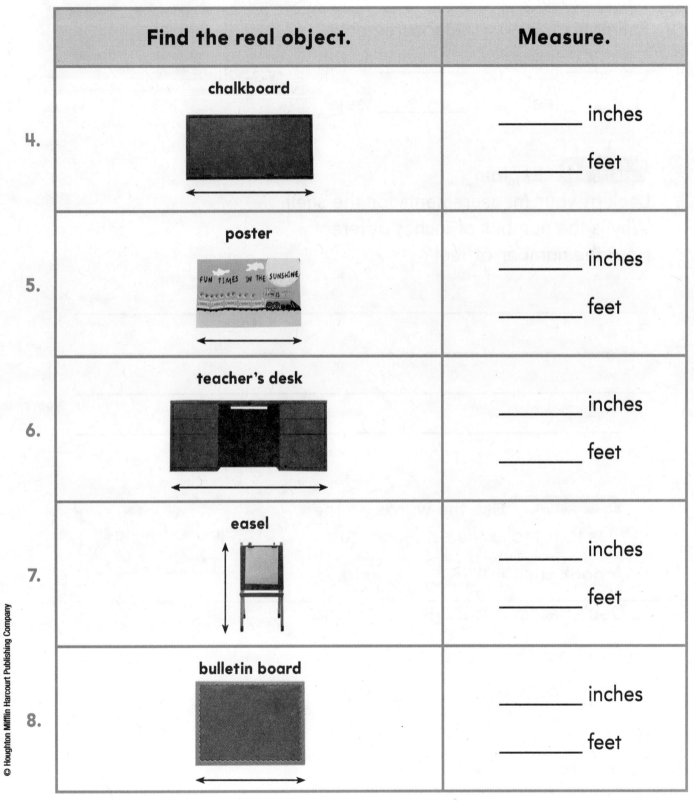

Find the real object.	Measure.
chalkboard 4.	_____ inches _____ feet
poster FUN TIMES IN THE SUNSHINE 5.	_____ inches _____ feet
teacher's desk 6.	_____ inches _____ feet
easel 7.	_____ inches _____ feet
bulletin board 8.	_____ inches _____ feet

Problem Solving • Applications (Real World)   WRITE ⟩ Math

9. THINK SMARTER Estimate the length of a real shelf in inches and in feet. Then measure.

Estimates: Measurements:

_____ inches   _____ inches

_____ feet   _____ feet

10. MATHEMATICAL PRACTICE ⑥ **Explain**

Look at your measurements for the shelf. Why is the number of inches different from the number of feet?

_____

_____

_____

_____

11. THINK SMARTER Use the words on the tiles that make the sentence true.

| inches | feet |

A book shelf is 4 _____ long.

Deb's necklace is 20 _____ long.

A marker is 3 _____ long.

Jim's bicycle is 4 _____ long.

TAKE HOME ACTIVITY • Have your child measure the distance of a few footsteps in inches and then in feet.

Name _____

Measure in Inches and Feet

 COMMON CORE STANDARD—2.MD.A.2
Measure and estimate lengths in standard units.

Measure to the nearest inch.
Then measure to the nearest foot.

Find the real object.	Measure.
1. bookcase	_____ inches _____ feet
2. window	_____ inches _____ feet

Problem Solving Real World

3. Jake has a piece of yarn that is 4 feet long.
Blair has a piece of yarn that is 4 inches long.
Who has the longer piece of yarn? Explain.

_____

_____

4. WRITE Math Would you measure the length of a
jump rope in inches or in feet? Explain your choice.

_____

Lesson Check (2.MD.A.2)

1. Larry is telling his sister about using a ruler to measure length. Write **inch** or **foot** in each blank to make the sentence true.

   One _____ is longer than one _____.

Spiral Review (2.NBT.B.5, 2.NBT.B.7, 2.MD.C.7, 2.MD.C.8)

2. Matt put this money in his pocket. What is the total value of this money?

   $ _____

3. What time is shown on this clock?

   ____ : ____

4. Ali had 38 game cards. Her friend gave her 15 more game cards. How many game cards does Ali have now?

   ____ cards

FOR MORE PRACTICE
GO TO THE
Personal Math Trainer

Name _____

Estimate Lengths in Feet

Essential Question How do you estimate the lengths of objects in feet?

Common Core   Measurement and Data—
2.MD.A.3
MATHEMATICAL PRACTICES
MP6, MP7

Listen and Draw

Look for 3 classroom objects that are about the same length as a 12-inch ruler. Draw and label the objects.

Math Talk

MATHEMATICAL PRACTICES 6

Which objects have a greater length than the ruler? **Explain.**

FOR THE TEACHER • Provide a collection of objects for children to choose from. Set a 12-inch ruler on the table with the objects for children to use as a visual comparison.

Estimate how many 12-inch rulers will be about the same length as this bulletin board.

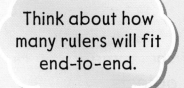

Think about how many rulers will fit end-to-end.

_____ rulers, or _____ feet

Share and Show MATH BOARD

Find each object. Estimate how many 12-inch rulers will be about the same length as the object.

✓ 1. bookshelf

Estimate: _____ rulers, or _____ feet

✓ 2. chair

Estimate: _____ rulers, or _____ feet

Name _____

Find each object. Estimate how many 12-inch rulers will be about the same length as the object.

3. desktop

Estimate: _____ rulers, or _____ feet

4. wall map

Estimate: _____ rulers, or _____ feet

5. window

Estimate: _____ rulers, or _____ feet

6. teacher's desk

Estimate: _____ rulers, or _____ feet

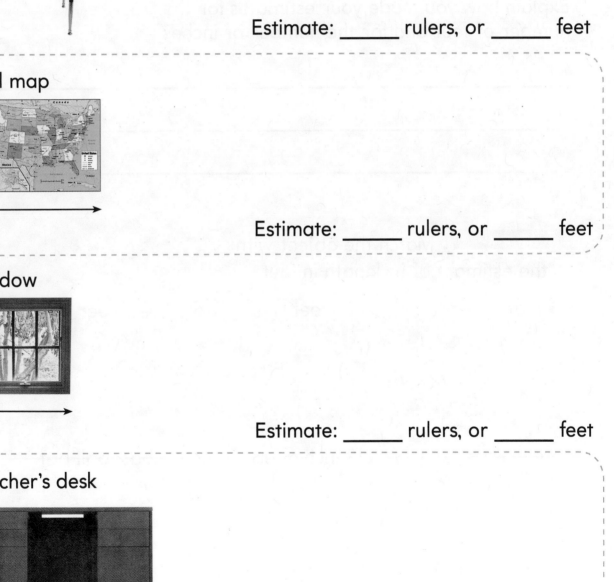

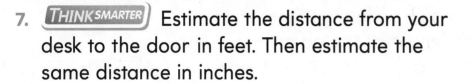

Problem Solving • Applications

WRITE ▸ Math

7. **THINK SMARTER** Estimate the distance from your desk to the door in feet. Then estimate the same distance in inches.

_____ feet

_____ inches

Explain how you made your estimates for the number of feet and for the number of inches.

_____

_____

_____

8. **THINK SMARTER** Match the object with the estimate of its length in feet.

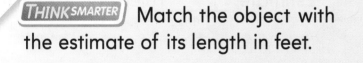

1 foot	3 feet	7 feet
•	•	•

•	•	•
jump rope	12-inch ruler	baseball bat

 TAKE HOME ACTIVITY • With your child, estimate the lengths of some objects in feet.

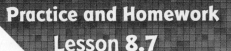

Estimate Lengths in Feet

COMMON CORE STANDARD—2.MD.A.3
Measure and estimate lengths in standard units.

Find each object.
Estimate how many 12-inch rulers will
be about the same length as the object.

1. door

   Estimate: _____ rulers, or _____ feet

2. flag

   Estimate: _____ rulers, or _____ feet

Problem Solving Real World

Solve. Write or draw to explain.

3. Mr. and Mrs. Baker place 12-inch rulers end-to-end
   along the entire length of a rug. They each use
   3 rulers. About how many feet long is the rug?

   about _____ feet

4. **WRITE** Math Choose an object that is about the
   same length as a real baseball bat. Explain how
   to estimate its length in feet.

   _____

   _____

Lesson Check (2.MD.A.3)

1. Estimate how many 12-inch rulers will be about the same length as a bike.

_____ rulers, or _____ feet

2. Estimate how many 12-inch rulers will be about the same length as a window.

_____ rulers, or _____ feet

Spiral Review (2.NBT.B.5, 2.NBT.B.7, 2.MD.C.8)

3. What is the total value of 2 quarters, 3 dimes, and 4 nickels?

$ _____

4. What is the total value of 2 dimes, 3 nickels, and 2 pennies?

_____ or _____ cents

5. There are 68 children in the school. There are 19 children on the playground. How many more children are in the school than on the playground?

_____ children

6. What is the sum?

$$\begin{array}{r} 548 \\ + \ 436 \\ \hline \end{array}$$

FOR MORE PRACTICE
GO TO THE
Personal Math Trainer

Choose a Tool

Essential Question How do you choose a measuring tool to use when measuring lengths?

Common Core Measurement and Data—2.MD.A.1
MATHEMATICAL PRACTICES
MP3, MP5, MP6, MP8

Listen and Draw Real World Hands On

Draw or write to describe how you measured the distances with the yarn.

Distance 1

Distance 2

Math Talk
MATHEMATICAL PRACTICES 6
Which distance was longer? **Explain** how you know.

FOR THE TEACHER • Have each small group use a 1-yard piece of yarn to measure a distance marked on the floor with masking tape. Have groups repeat the activity to measure another distance that is different from the first one.

Model and Draw

You can use different tools to measure lengths and distances.

inch ruler	yardstick	measuring tape
An inch ruler can be used to measure shorter lengths.	A **yardstick** shows 3 feet. It can be used to measure greater lengths and distances.	A **measuring tape** can be used to measure lengths and distances that are not flat or straight.

Share and Show   MATH BOARD

> inch ruler
> yardstick
> measuring tape

Choose the best tool for measuring the real object. Then measure and record the length or distance.

☑ 1. the length of a book

Tool: _____

Length: _____

☑ 2. the distance around a cup

Tool: _____

Distance: _____

Name _____

inch ruler
yardstick
measuring tape

Choose the best tool for measuring the real object.
Then measure and record the length or distance.

3. the length of a chalkboard

Tool: _____

Length: _____

4. the length of a marker

Tool: _____

Length: _____

5. the distance around a globe

Tool: _____

Distance: _____

6. the length of a classroom wall

Tool: _____

Length: _____

Problem Solving • Applications Real World   WRITE Math

7. **THINK SMARTER** Rachel wants to measure the length of a sidewalk. Should she use an inch ruler or a yardstick? Explain.

Rachel should use _____ because

_____

_____

_____

8. **MATHEMATICAL PRACTICE ③ Apply**

What is an object that you would measure with a measuring tape? Explain why you would use this tool.

_____

_____

_____

Personal Math Trainer

9. **THINK SMARTER +** Jim measures the length of a picnic table with an inch ruler. Is Jim using the best tool for measuring? Explain.

_____

_____

_____

TAKE HOME ACTIVITY • Have your child name some objects that he or she would measure using a yardstick.

Choose a Tool

Common Core   **COMMON CORE STANDARD—2.MD.A.1**
Measure and estimate lengths in standard units.

Choose the best tool for measuring the real object. Then measure and record the length or distance.

| inch ruler |
| yardstick |
| measuring tape |

1. the length of your desk

Tool: _____

Length: _____

_____

2. the distance around a basket

Tool: _____

Length: _____

Problem Solving (Real World)

Choose the better tool for measuring.
Explain your choice.

3. Mark wants to measure the length of his room.
Should he use an inch ruler or a yardstick?

Mark should use _____ because

_____

_____

4. WRITE Math Describe how you would use a
yardstick to measure the length of a rug.

_____

Lesson Check (2.MD.A.1)

1. Kim wants to measure the distance around her bike tire. Circle the best tool for her to use.

   cup   yardstick

   color tiles   measuring tape

2. Ben wants to measure the length of a seesaw. Circle the best tool for him to use.

   cup   yardstick

   color tiles   paper clips

Spiral Review (2.MD.A.2, 2.MD.A.3, 2.MD.B.5, 2.MD.B.6)

3. Estimate how many 12-inch rulers will be about the same length as a sheet of paper.

   _____ ruler, or _____ foot

4. Andy has a rope that is 24 inches long. He cuts off 7 inches from the rope. How long is the rope now?

   _____ inches

5. Jan is telling her friend about using a ruler to measure length. Write **inches** or **foot** in each blank to make the sentence true.

   12 _____ is the same length as 1 _____.

FOR MORE PRACTICE
GO TO THE
Personal Math Trainer

Name _____

Display Measurement Data

Essential Question How can a line plot be used to show measurement data?

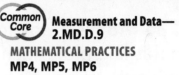

Common Core Measurement and Data—
2.MD.D.9
MATHEMATICAL PRACTICES
MP4, MP5, MP6

Use an inch ruler. Measure and record each length.

_____ inches

_____ inches

_____ inches

Math Talk MATHEMATICAL PRACTICES 6

Describe how the lengths of the three strings are different.

HOME CONNECTION • Your child practiced measuring different lengths in inches in preparation for collecting measurement data in this lesson.

Model and Draw

A **line plot** is a way to show data. On this line plot, each **X** stands for the length of one pencil in inches.

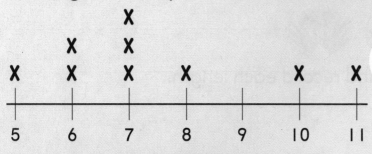

Lengths of Pencils in Inches

How many pencils are just 6 inches long? How many different pencils are shown in this data?

1. Use an inch ruler. Measure and record the lengths of 5 books in inches.

1st book: _____ inches	
2nd book: _____ inches	
3rd book: _____ inches	
4th book: _____ inches	
5th book: _____ inches	

2. Write a title for the line plot. Then write the numbers and draw the **X**s.

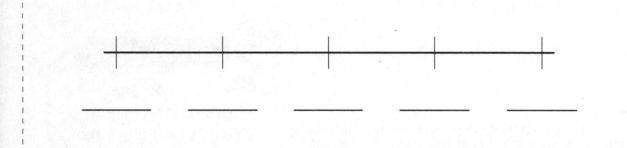

© Houghton Mifflin Harcourt Publishing Company

Name _____

3. Use an inch ruler. Measure and record the lengths of 5 pencils in inches.

4. Write a title for the line plot. Then write the numbers and draw the **X**s.

| 1st pencil: _____ inches |
| 2nd pencil: _____ inches |
| 3rd pencil: _____ inches |
| 4th pencil: _____ inches |
| 5th pencil: _____ inches |

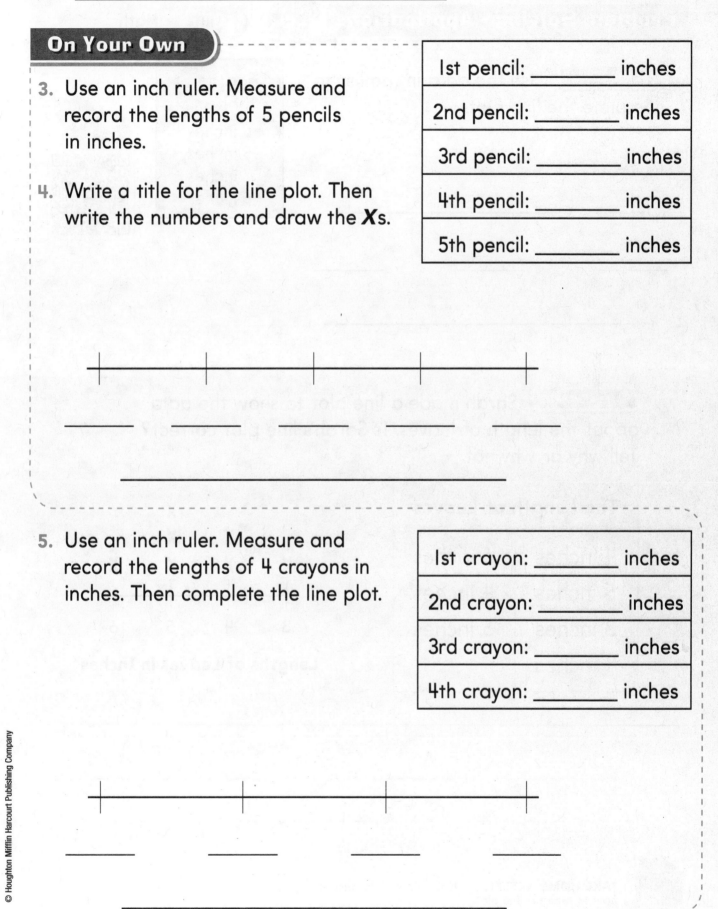

5. Use an inch ruler. Measure and record the lengths of 4 crayons in inches. Then complete the line plot.

| 1st crayon: _____ inches |
| 2nd crayon: _____ inches |
| 3rd crayon: _____ inches |
| 4th crayon: _____ inches |

© Houghton Mifflin Harcourt Publishing Company

Problem Solving • Applications (Real World)   WRITE Math

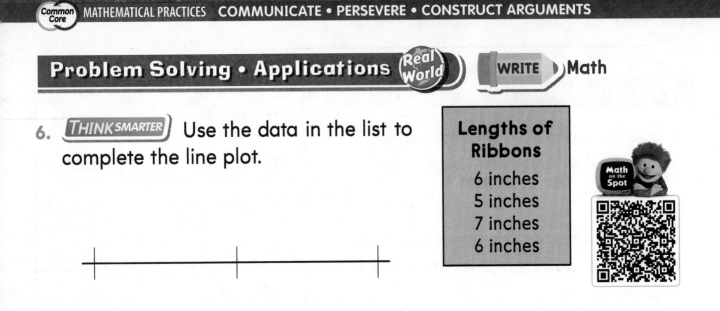

6. **THINK SMARTER** Use the data in the list to complete the line plot.

Lengths of Ribbons

6 inches
5 inches
7 inches
6 inches

7. **THINK SMARTER** Sarah made a line plot to show the data about the length of leaves. Is Sarah's line plot correct? Tell why or why not.

The Length of Leaves	
4 inches	6 inches
5 inches	4 inches
3 inches	5 inches
4 inches	

```
                              X
                     X        X
            X        X   X        X
            |_____|____|_____|
            3        4    5        6
```

Lengths of Leaves in Inches

_____

_____

_____

TAKE HOME ACTIVITY • Have your child describe how to make a line plot.

Display Measurement Data

Common Core **COMMON CORE STANDARD—2.MD.D.9**
Represent and interpret data.

1. Use an inch ruler. Measure and record the lengths of 4 different books in inches.

1st book: _____ inches	
2nd book: _____ inches	
3rd book: _____ inches	
4th book: _____ inches	

2. Write a title for the line plot. Then write the numbers and draw the **X**s.

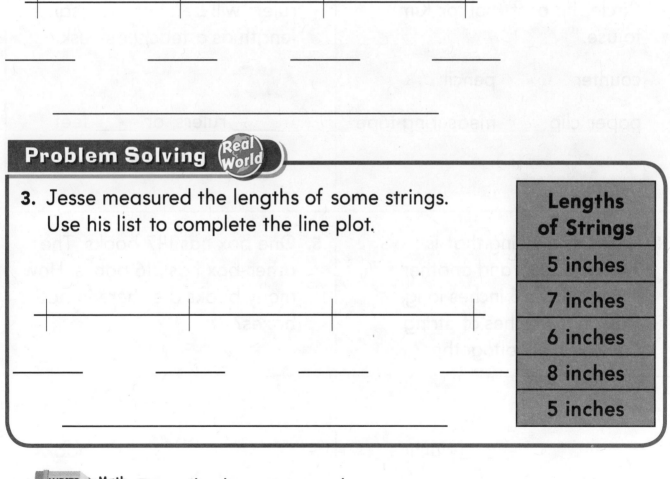

Problem Solving Real World

3. Jesse measured the lengths of some strings. Use his list to complete the line plot.

Lengths of Strings
5 inches
7 inches
6 inches
8 inches
5 inches

4. WRITE Math Describe how you made a line plot in this lesson.

_____

Lesson Check (2.MD.D.9)

1. Use the line plot. How many sticks are 4 inches long?

```
                              X
          X         X         X
          X         X         X         X
          +---------+---------+---------+
          2         3         4         5
```

Lengths of Sticks in Inches

_____ sticks

Spiral Review (2.NBT.B.7, 2.MD.A.1, 2.MD.A.3, 2.MD.B.5, 2.MD.B.6)

2. Kim wants to measure a ball. Circle the best tool for Kim to use.

counter   pencil

paper clip   measuring tape

3. Estimate how many 12-inch rulers will be about the same length as a teacher's desk.

_____ rulers, or _____ feet

4. Kurt has a string that is 12 inches long and another string that is 5 inches long. How many inches of string does he have altogether?

_____ inches

5. One box has 147 books. The other box has 216 books. How many books are there in both boxes?

_____ books

FOR MORE PRACTICE
GO TO THE
Personal Math Trainer

Name ______________________________

Chapter 8 Review/Test

Personal Math Trainer
Online Assessment and Intervention

Personal Math Trainer

1. THINK SMARTER + Josh wants to measure the distance around a soccer ball.

Circle the best choice of tool.

inch ruler   yardstick   measuring tape

Explain your choice of tool.

____

____

2. GO DEEPER Luke has a string that is 6 inches long and a string that is 11 inches long. How many inches of string does Luke have?

Draw a diagram. Write a number sentence using a ☐ for the missing number. Solve.

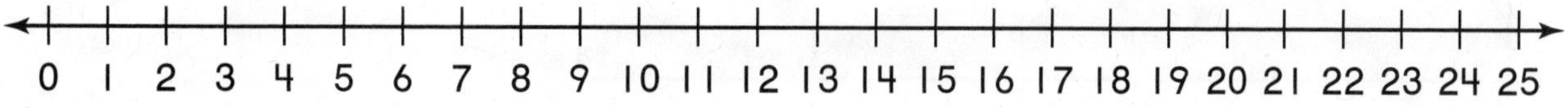

____

Luke has ________ inches of string.

GO DIGITAL Assessment Options Chapter Test

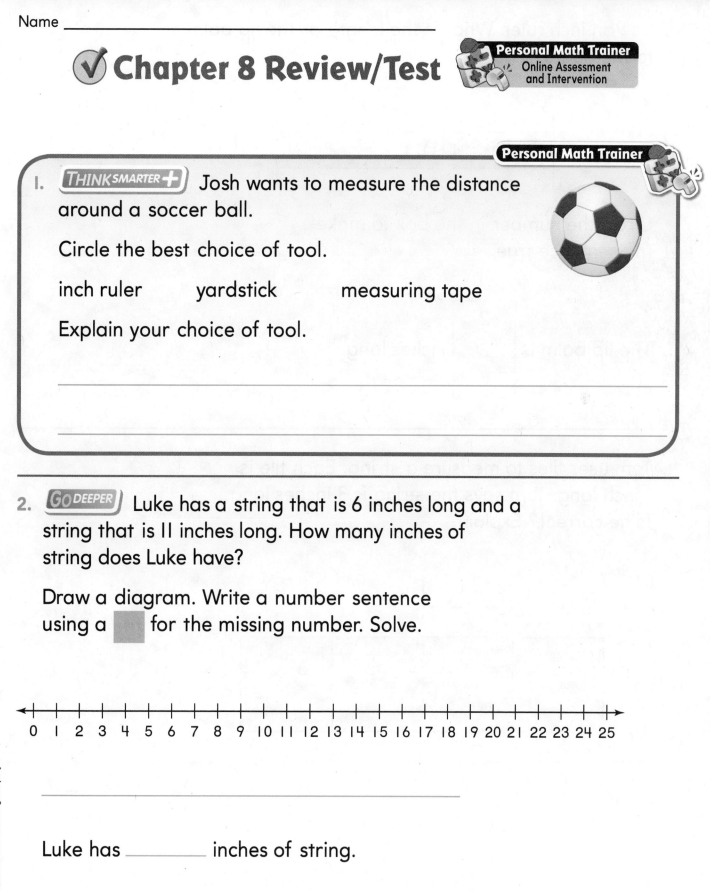

3. Use an inch ruler. What is the length of the lip balm to the nearest inch?

Circle the number in the box to make the sentence true.

The lip balm is
| 2 |
| 3 |
| 4 |
inches long.

4. Tom uses tiles to measure a string. Each tile is 1 inch long. Tom says the string is 3 inches long. Is he correct? Explain.

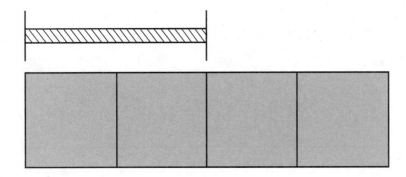

_____

_____

Name _____

5. Dalia made a line plot to show the lengths of her ribbons.

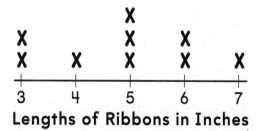

Lengths of Ribbons in Inches

How many ribbons are shown in the line plot?

The line plot shows _____ ribbons.

How many ribbons are 6 inches long?

_____ ribbons

6. Use the words on the tiles to make the sentence true.

The table is 3 _____ long.

The belt is 30 _____ long.

The hallway is 15 _____ long.

| inches | feet |

7. Use the 1-inch mark. Estimate the length of each object.

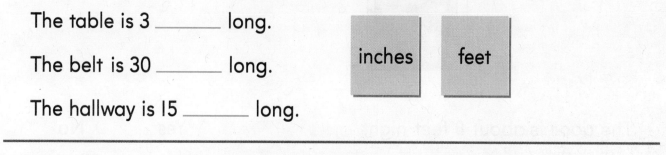

about _____ inches

about _____ inches

8. Use an inch ruler. What is the length of the paper clip to the nearest inch?

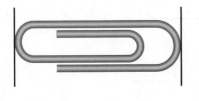

_____ inches

---

9. Estimate how many 12-inch rulers will be about the same height as a classroom door. Does the sentence describe the door? Choose Yes or No.

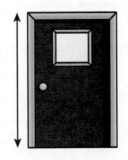

The door is about 8 feet high.	○ Yes	○ No
The door is less than 3 rulers high.	○ Yes	○ No
The door is more than 20 feet high.	○ Yes	○ No
The door is less than 15 rulers high.	○ Yes	○ No

Length in Metric Units

Curious about Math

A wind farm is a group of wind turbines used to make electricity. One way to measure the distance between two wind turbines is by counting footsteps. What is another way?

✓ Show What You Know

Personal Math Trainer
Online Assessment
and Intervention

Compare Lengths

1. Order the strings from shortest to longest.
   Write 1, 2, 3. (1.MD.A.1)

_____

_____

_____

Use Nonstandard Units to Measure Length

Use real objects and ■ to measure. (1.MD.A.2)

2.

about _____ ■

3.

about _____ ■

Measure Length Twice: Nonstandard Units

Use ■ first. Then use ⌐══⌐ .
Measure the length of the ribbon. (1.MD.A.2)

4. about _____ ■   5. about _____ ⌐══⌐

This page checks understanding of important
skills needed for success in Chapter 9.

Name _____

Vocabulary Builder

Visualize It

Fill in the graphic organizer. Think of an object and write about how you can **measure** the **length** of that object.

length

Understand Vocabulary

Use the color tile to **estimate** the length of each straw.

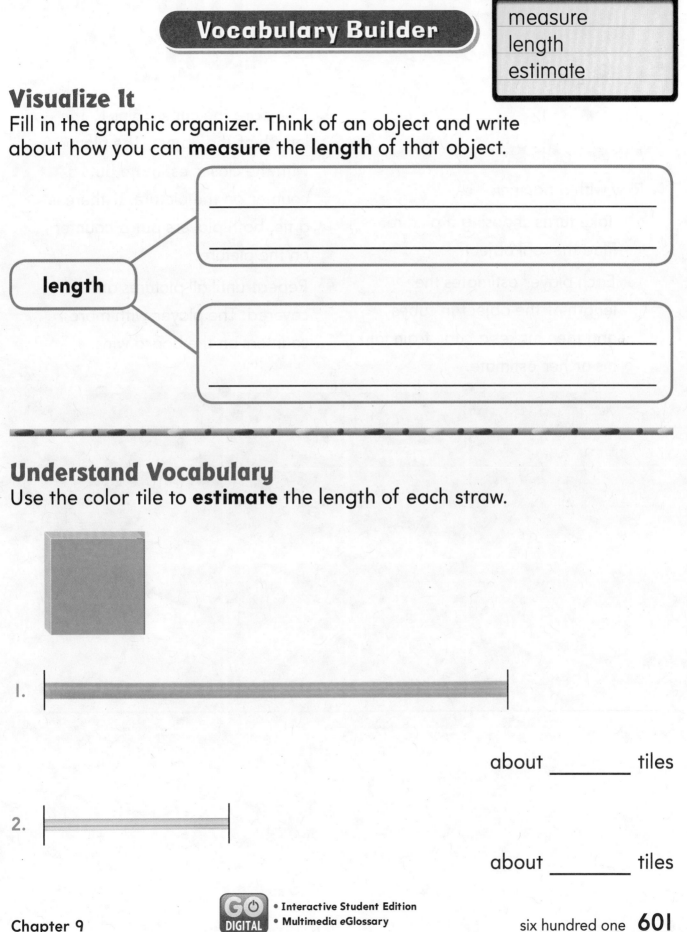

1.

about _____ tiles

2.

about _____ tiles

Chapter 9

GO DIGITAL • Interactive Student Edition • Multimedia eGlossary

 # Estimating Length

Materials

- 12 ●
- 12 ○
- 15 ◻
- 15 ◻

Play with a partner.

① Take turns choosing a picture. Find the real object.

② Each player estimates the length of the object in cubes and then makes a cube train for his or her estimate.

③ Compare the cube trains to the length of the object. The player with the closer estimate puts a counter on the picture. If there is a tie, both players put a counter on the picture.

④ Repeat until all pictures are covered. The player with more counters on the board wins.

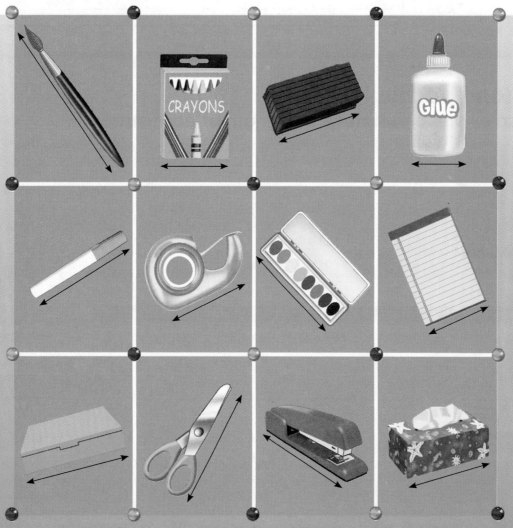

Chapter 9 Vocabulary

addend

sumando

1

centimeter

centímetro

6

compare

comparar

8

difference

diferencia

14

digit

dígito

15

estimate

estimación

21

meter (m)

metro (m)

39

sum

suma o total

59

This is 1 **centimeter**.

centimeters
0 1 2 3 4 5

---

5 + 3 = 8

addends

---

5 − 3 = 2

difference

Compare the lengths of the pencil and the crayon.

The pencil is longer than the crayon.
The crayon is shorter than the pencil.

An **estimate** is an amount that tells about how many.

0, 1, 2, 3, 4, 5, 6, 7, 8, and 9 are **digits**.

---

4 + 2 = 6

sum

---

1 **meter** is the same length as 100 centimeters.

Game

Make a Match

For 3 players

Materials

- 4 sets of word cards

How to Play

1. Every player is dealt 5 cards. Put the rest face-down in a draw pile.

2. Ask another player for a word card to match a word card you have.

   - If the player has the word card, he or she gives it to you. Put both cards in front of you. Take another turn.

   - If the player does not have the word card, take a card from the pile. If the word you get matches one you are holding, put both cards in front of you. Take another turn. If it does not match, your turn is over.

3. The game is over when one player has no cards left. The player with the most pairs wins.

The Write Way

Reflect

Choose one idea. Write about it in the space below.

- Compare a centimeter to a meter. Explain how they are alike and how they are different.
- Explain how you would find the length of this crayon in centimeters.

- How would you compare the length of a door to the length of a window in meters? Draw pictures and write to explain. Use another piece of paper for your drawing.

Name _____

Measure with a Centimeter Model

Essential Question How do you use a centimeter model to measure the lengths of objects?

Common Core **Measurement and Data—**
2.MD.A.1
MATHEMATICAL PRACTICES
MP5, MP6, MP8

Listen and Draw

Use ▪ to measure the length.

_____ _____ unit cubes

~~~~~~~~~~~~~~~~~ _____ unit cubes

~~~~~~~~~~~~~~~~~ _____ unit cubes

Math Talk
MATHEMATICAL PRACTICES 5

Use Tools Describe how to use unit cubes to measure an object's length.

HOME CONNECTION • Your child used unit cubes as an introduction to measurement of length before using metric measurement tools.

© Houghton Mifflin Harcourt Publishing Company

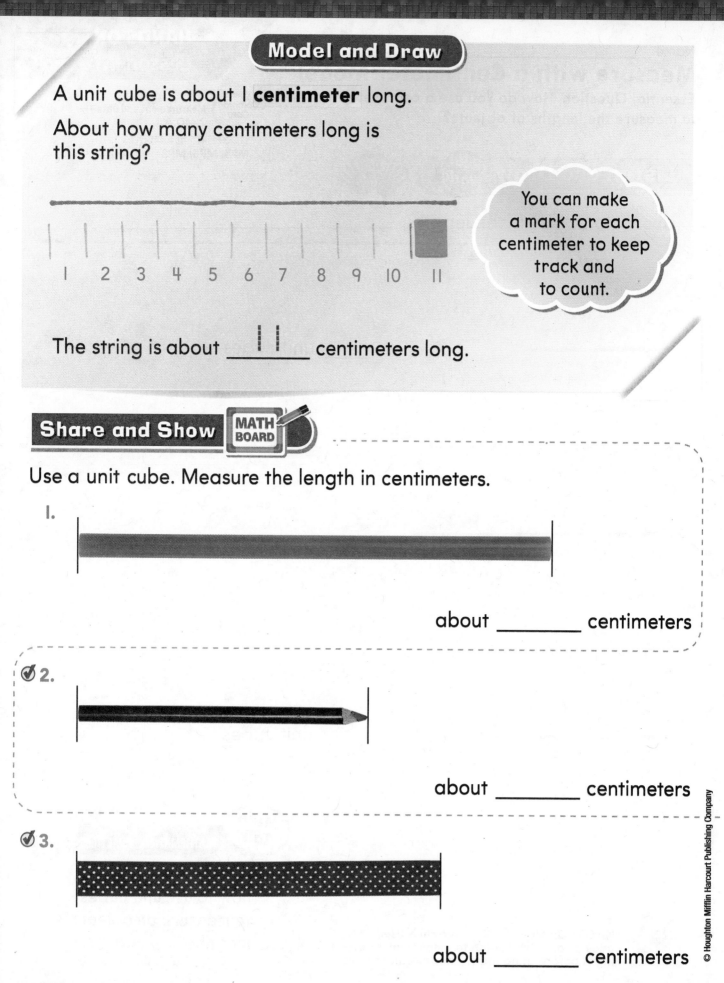

A unit cube is about 1 **centimeter** long.

About how many centimeters long is this string?

1 2 3 4 5 6 7 8 9 10 11

> You can make a mark for each centimeter to keep track and to count.

The string is about ____|||____ centimeters long.

Share and Show MATH BOARD

Use a unit cube. Measure the length in centimeters.

1.

about _____ centimeters

2.

about _____ centimeters

3.

about _____ centimeters

© Houghton Mifflin Harcourt Publishing Company

Name _____

Use a unit cube. Measure the length in centimeters.

4.

about _____ centimeters

5.

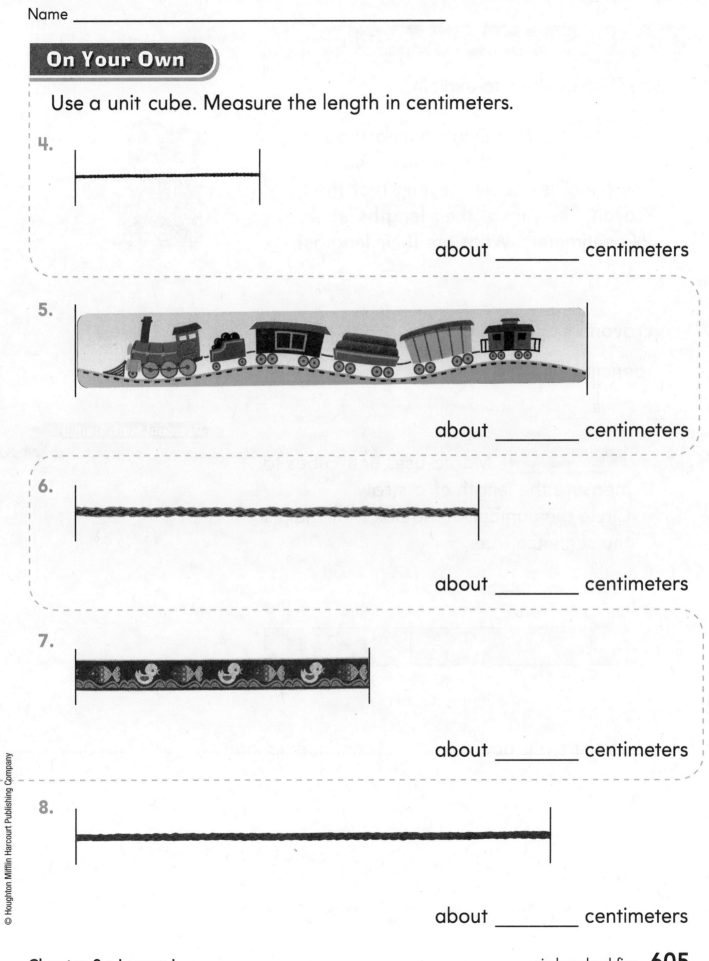

about _____ centimeters

6.

about _____ centimeters

7.

about _____ centimeters

8.

about _____ centimeters

Problem Solving • Applications

WRITE Math

Solve. Write or draw to explain.

9. **THINK SMARTER** Mrs. Duncan measured the lengths of a crayon and a pencil. The pencil is double the length of the crayon. The sum of their lengths is 24 centimeters. What are their lengths?

crayon: _____

pencil: _____

Personal Math Trainer

10. **THINK SMARTER +** Marita uses unit cubes to measure the length of a straw. Circle the number in the box that makes the sentence true.

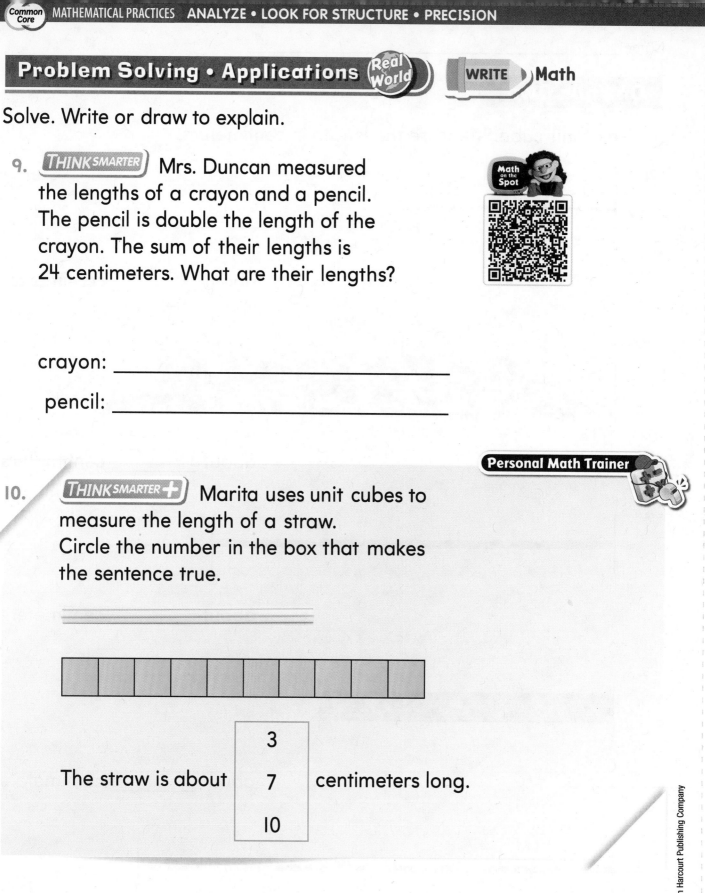

The straw is about
| 3 |
| 7 |
| 10 |
centimeters long.

TAKE HOME ACTIVITY • Have your child compare the lengths of other objects to those in this lesson.

Measure with a Centimeter Model

Common Core
COMMON CORE STANDARD—2.MD.A.1
Measure and estimate lengths in standard units.

Use a unit cube. Measure the length in centimeters.

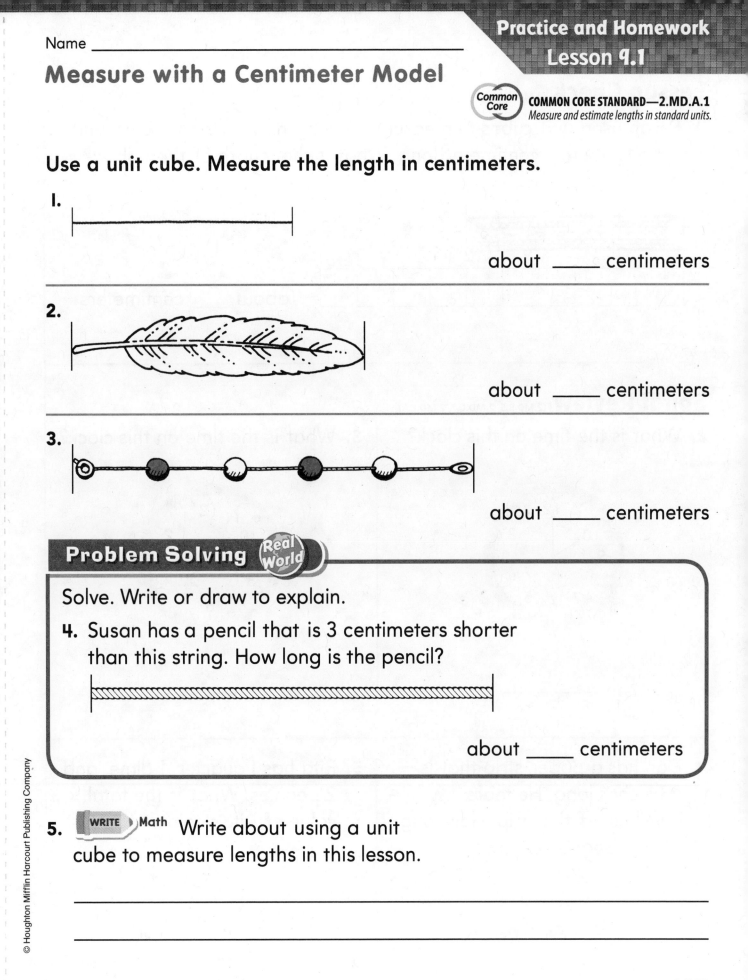

1.

about _____ centimeters

2.

about _____ centimeters

3.

about _____ centimeters

Problem Solving (Real World)

Solve. Write or draw to explain.

4. Susan has a pencil that is 3 centimeters shorter than this string. How long is the pencil?

about _____ centimeters

5. **WRITE** Math Write about using a unit cube to measure lengths in this lesson.

_____

_____

Lesson Check (2.MD.A.1)

1. Sarah used unit cubes to measure the length of a ribbon. Each unit cube is about 1 centimeter long. What is the length of the ribbon?

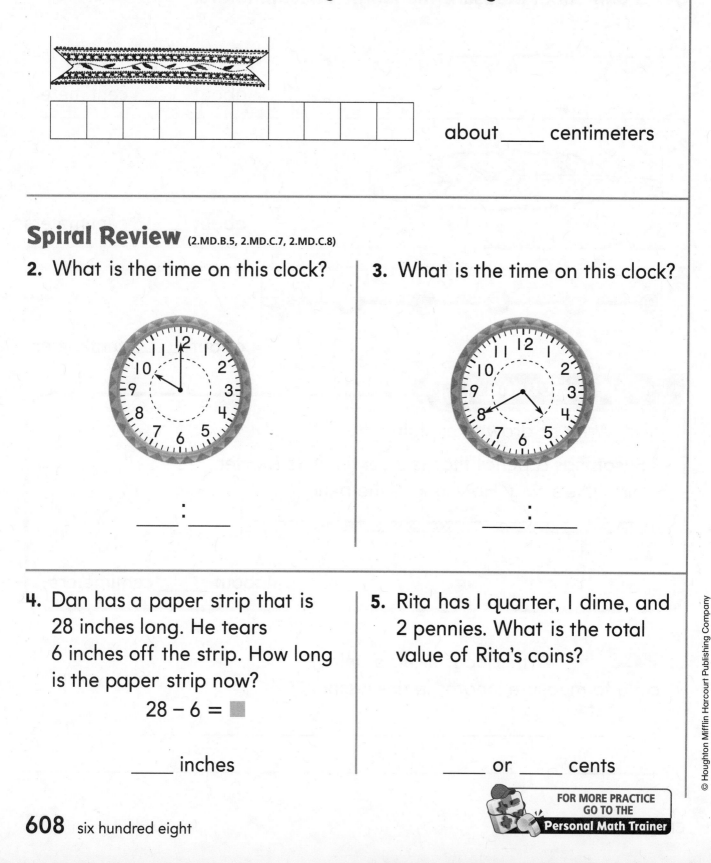

about _____ centimeters

Spiral Review (2.MD.B.5, 2.MD.C.7, 2.MD.C.8)

2. What is the time on this clock?

____ : ____

3. What is the time on this clock?

____ : ____

4. Dan has a paper strip that is 28 inches long. He tears 6 inches off the strip. How long is the paper strip now?

$$28 - 6 = \blacksquare$$

_____ inches

5. Rita has 1 quarter, 1 dime, and 2 pennies. What is the total value of Rita's coins?

_____ or _____ cents

FOR MORE PRACTICE
GO TO THE
Personal Math Trainer

Name _____

Estimate Lengths in Centimeters

Essential Question How do you use known lengths to estimate unknown lengths?

Common Core · **Measurement and Data— 2.MD.A.3**

MATHEMATICAL PRACTICES
MP1, MP6, MP7

Listen and Draw Real World — Hands On

Find three classroom objects that are shorter than your 10-centimeter strip. Draw the objects. Write estimates for their lengths.

about _____ centimeters

about _____ centimeters

about _____ centimeters

Math Talk

MATHEMATICAL PRACTICES 6

Which object has a length closest to 10 centimeters? **Explain.**

HOME CONNECTION • Your child used a 10-centimeter strip of paper to practice estimating the lengths of some classroom objects.

This pencil is about 10 centimeters long. Which is the most reasonable estimate for the length of the ribbon?

7 centimeters

13 centimeters

20 centimeters

> The ribbon is longer than the pencil. 7 centimeters is not reasonable.

> The ribbon is not twice as long as the pencil. 20 centimeters is not reasonable.

The ribbon is a little longer than the pencil. So, 13 centimeters is the most reasonable estimate.

Share and Show | MATH BOARD

1. The yarn is about 5 centimeters long. Circle the best estimate for the length of the crayon.

10 centimeters

15 centimeters

20 centimeters

2. The string is about 12 centimeters long. Circle the best estimate for the length of the straw.

3 centimeters

7 centimeters

11 centimeters

On Your Own

3. The rope is about 8 centimeters long. Circle the
best estimate for the length of the paper clip.

2 centimeters

4 centimeters

8 centimeters

4. The pencil is about 11 centimeters long.
Circle the best estimate for the length of the chain.

6 centimeters

10 centimeters

13 centimeters

5. The hair clip is about 7 centimeters long.
Circle the best estimate for the length of the yarn.

10 centimeters

17 centimeters

22 centimeters

6. The ribbon is about 13 centimeters long.
Circle the best estimate for the length of the string.

5 centimeters

11 centimeters

17 centimeters

Problem Solving • Applications

WRITE Math

7. **THINK SMARTER** For each question, circle the best estimate.

About how long is a new crayon?	About how long is a new pencil?
5 centimeters	20 centimeters
10 centimeters	40 centimeters
20 centimeters	50 centimeters

8. **MATHEMATICAL PRACTICE ①** Analyze Mr. Lott has 250 more centimeters of tape than Mrs. Sanchez. Mr. Lott has 775 centimeters of tape. How many centimeters of tape does Mrs. Sanchez have?

_____ centimeters

9. **THINK SMARTER** This feather is about 7 centimeters long. Rachel says the yarn is about 14 centimeters long. Is Rachel correct? Explain.

_____

_____

_____

🏠 **TAKE HOME ACTIVITY** • Give your child an object that is about 5 centimeters long. Have him or her use it to estimate the lengths of some other objects.

Estimate Lengths in Centimeters

Common Core **COMMON CORE STANDARD—2.MD.A.3**
Measure and estimate lengths in standard units.

1. The toothpick is about 6 centimeters long. Circle the best estimate for the length of the yarn.

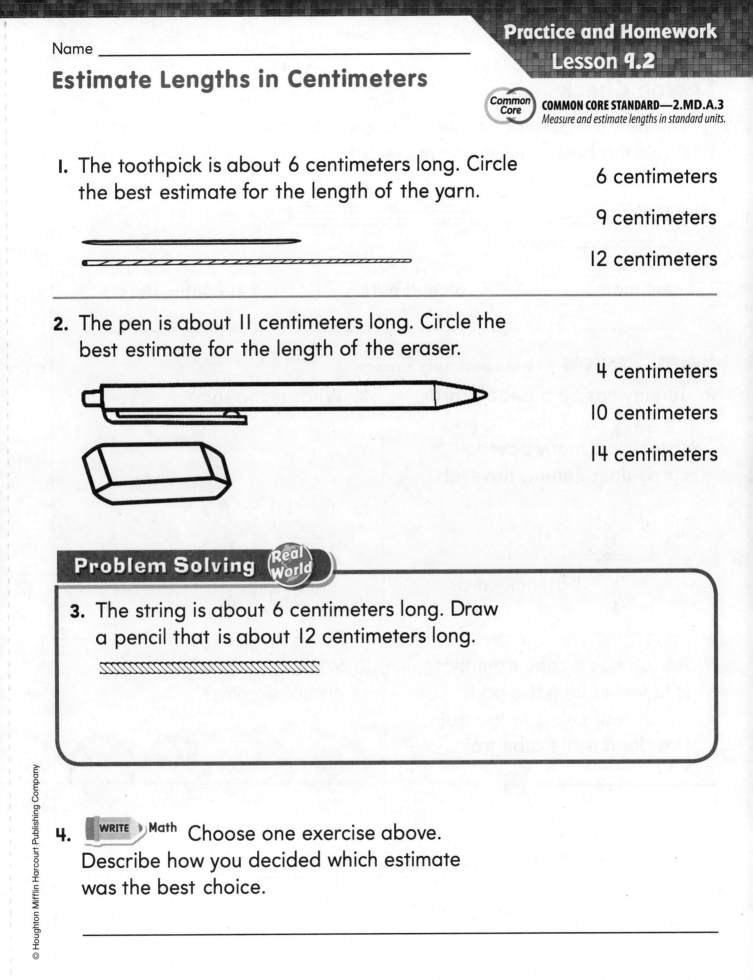

6 centimeters

9 centimeters

12 centimeters

2. The pen is about 11 centimeters long. Circle the best estimate for the length of the eraser.

4 centimeters

10 centimeters

14 centimeters

Problem Solving Real World

3. The string is about 6 centimeters long. Draw a pencil that is about 12 centimeters long.

4. WRITE Math Choose one exercise above. Describe how you decided which estimate was the best choice.

_____

Lesson Check (2.MD.A.3)

1. The pencil is about 12 centimeters long. Circle the best estimate for the length of the yarn.

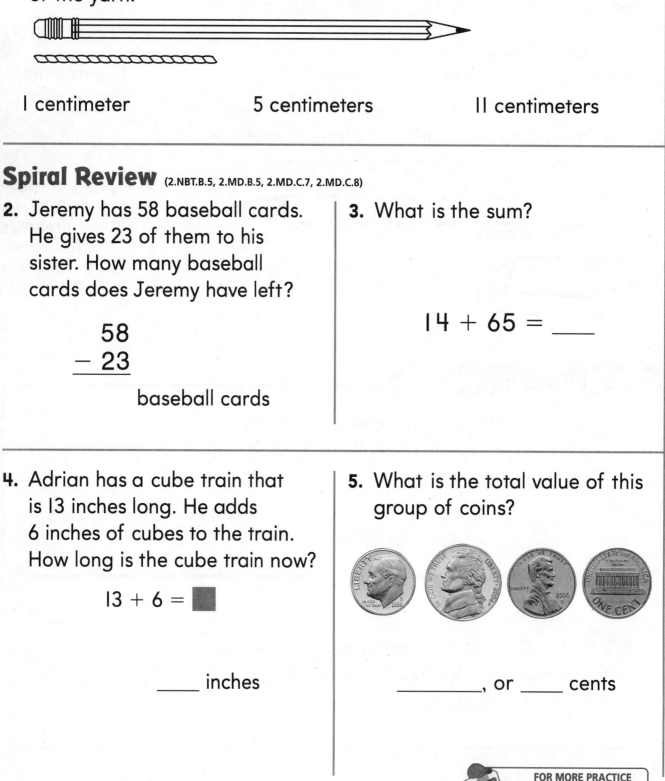

I centimeter   5 centimeters   II centimeters

Spiral Review (2.NBT.B.5, 2.MD.B.5, 2.MD.C.7, 2.MD.C.8)

2. Jeremy has 58 baseball cards. He gives 23 of them to his sister. How many baseball cards does Jeremy have left?

   58
   − 23

   _____ baseball cards

3. What is the sum?

   14 + 65 = _____

4. Adrian has a cube train that is 13 inches long. He adds 6 inches of cubes to the train. How long is the cube train now?

   13 + 6 = ▊

   _____ inches

5. What is the total value of this group of coins?

   _____, or _____ cents

FOR MORE PRACTICE
GO TO THE
Personal Math Trainer

Name _____

Measure with a Centimeter Ruler

Essential Question How do you use a centimeter ruler to measure lengths?

Common Core **Measurement and Data—2.MD.A.1**
MATHEMATICAL PRACTICES
MP3, MP5, MP6

Listen and Draw · Real World · Hands On

Find three small objects in the classroom.
Use unit cubes to measure their lengths.
Draw the objects and write their lengths.

about _____ centimeters

about _____ centimeters

about _____ centimeters

Math Talk · MATHEMATICAL PRACTICES 3

Apply
Describe how the three lengths compare. Which object is shortest?

HOME CONNECTION • Your child used unit cubes to measure the lengths of some classroom objects as an introduction to measuring lengths in centimeters.

What is the length of the crayon to the nearest centimeter?

> **Remember:** Line up the left edge of the object with the zero mark on the ruler.

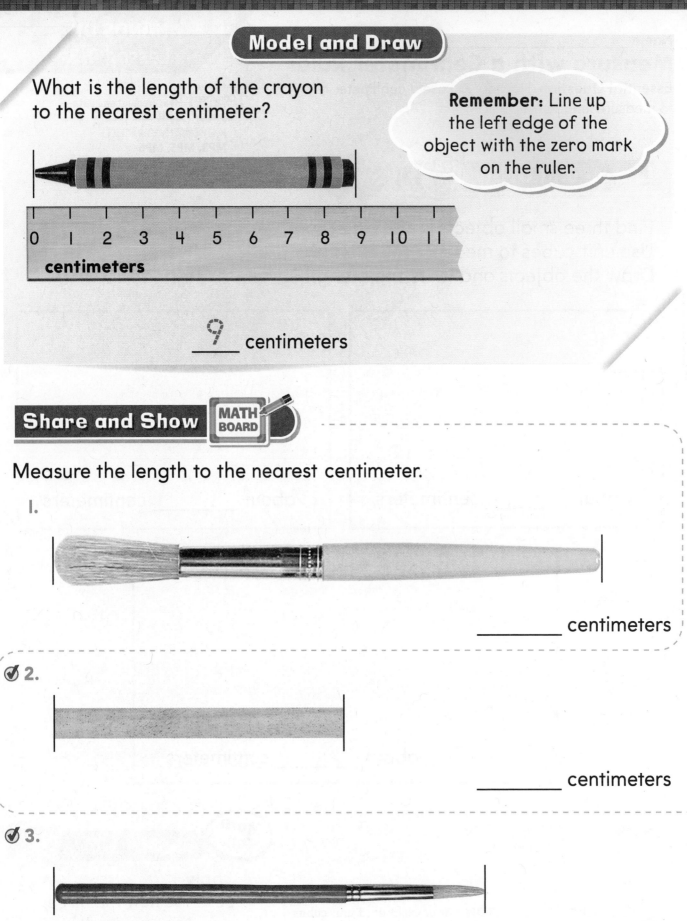

centimeters

_9_ centimeters

Share and Show MATH BOARD

Measure the length to the nearest centimeter.

1.

_____ centimeters

✓ 2.

_____ centimeters

✓ 3.

_____ centimeters

Name _____

Measure the length to the nearest centimeter.

4.

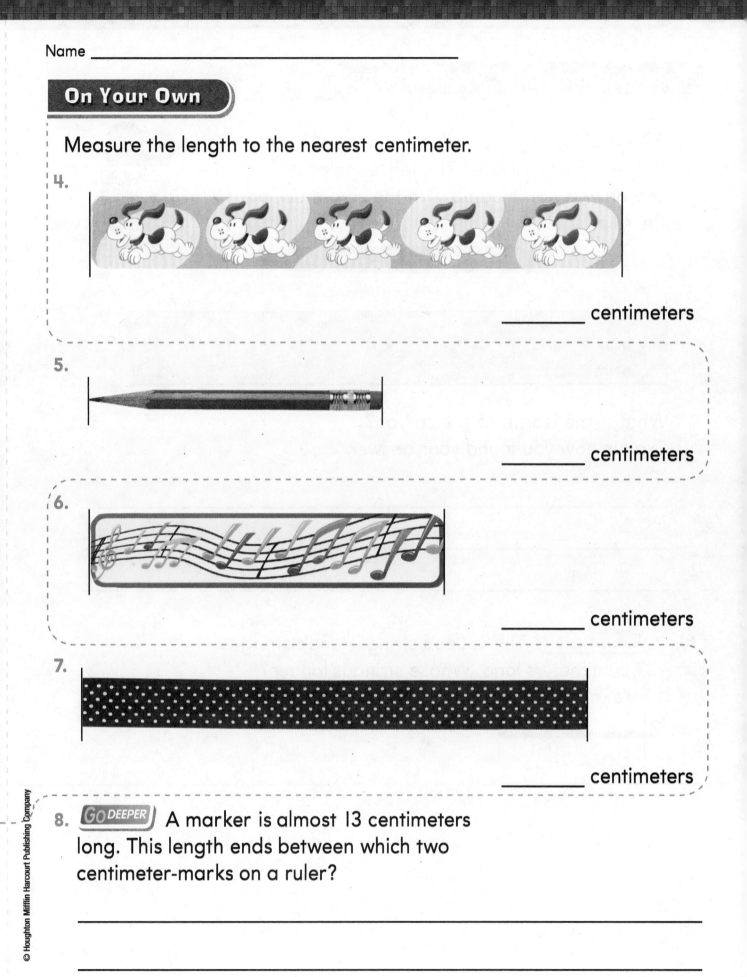

_____ centimeters

5.

_____ centimeters

6.

_____ centimeters

7.

_____ centimeters

8. **Go DEEPER** A marker is almost 13 centimeters long. This length ends between which two centimeter-marks on a ruler?

_____

_____

Problem Solving • Applications Real World   WRITE ▸ Math

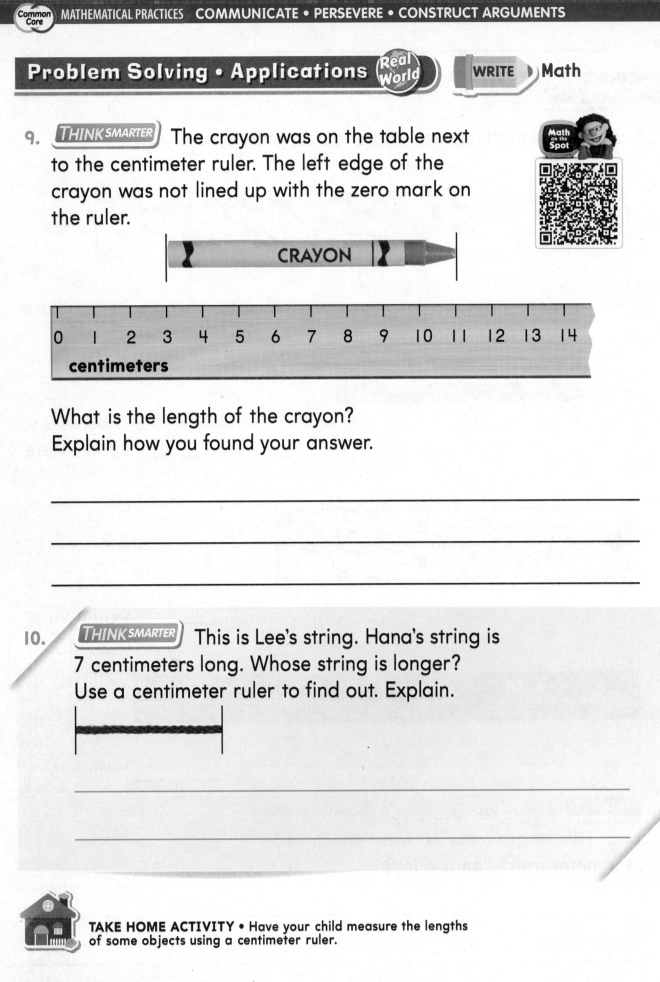

9. **THINK SMARTER** The crayon was on the table next to the centimeter ruler. The left edge of the crayon was not lined up with the zero mark on the ruler.

CRAYON

What is the length of the crayon?
Explain how you found your answer.

_____

_____

_____

10. **THINK SMARTER** This is Lee's string. Hana's string is 7 centimeters long. Whose string is longer? Use a centimeter ruler to find out. Explain.

_____

_____

TAKE HOME ACTIVITY • Have your child measure the lengths of some objects using a centimeter ruler.

Measure with a Centimeter Ruler

Common Core
COMMON CORE STANDARD—2.MD.A.1
Measure and estimate lengths in standard units.

Measure the length to the nearest centimeter.

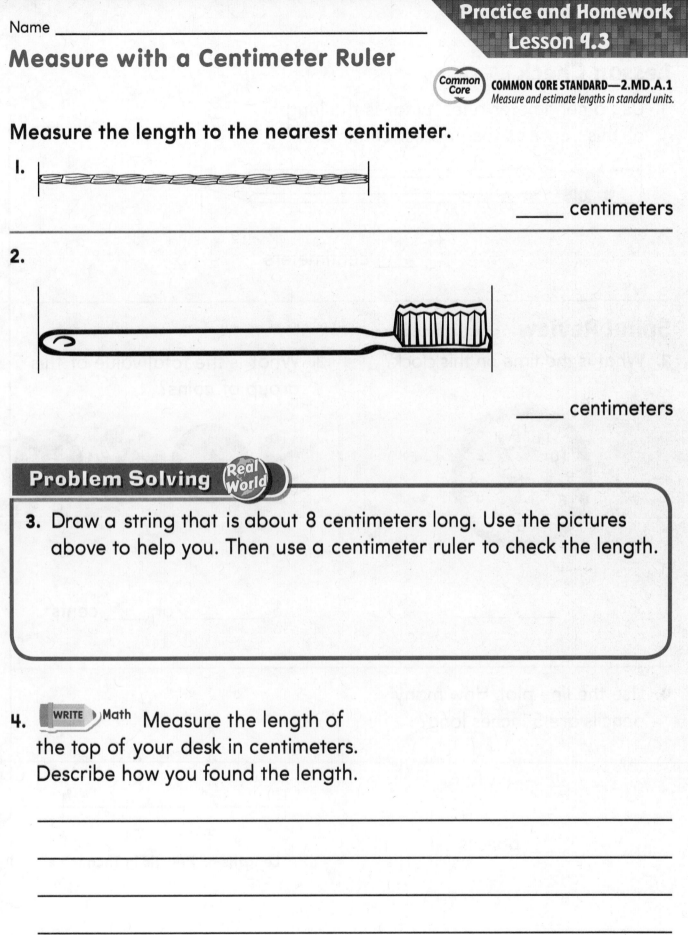

1. _____ centimeters

2. _____ centimeters

Problem Solving Real World

3. Draw a string that is about 8 centimeters long. Use the pictures above to help you. Then use a centimeter ruler to check the length.

4. WRITE Math Measure the length of the top of your desk in centimeters. Describe how you found the length.

_____

_____

_____

Lesson Check (2.MD.A.1)

1. Use a centimeter ruler. What is the length of this pencil to the nearest centimeter?

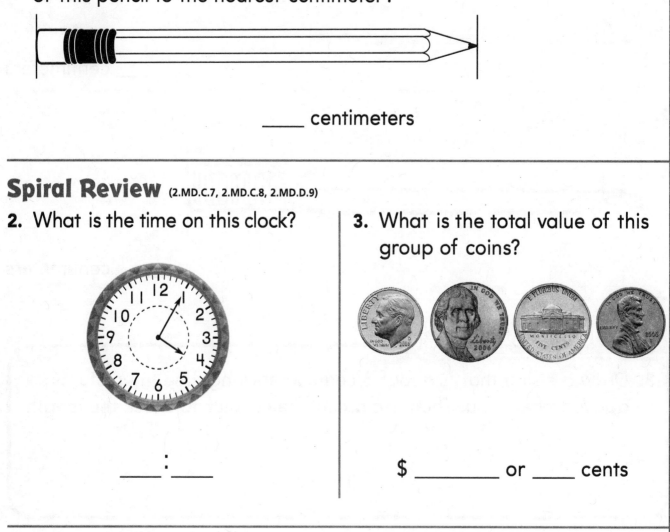

_____ centimeters

Spiral Review (2.MD.C.7, 2.MD.C.8, 2.MD.D.9)

2. What is the time on this clock?

_____ : _____

3. What is the total value of this group of coins?

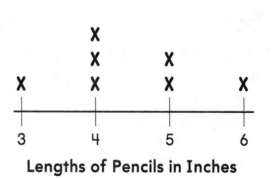

$ _____ or _____ cents

4. Use the line plot. How many pencils are 5 inches long?

_____ pencils

```
                X
                X          X
     X          X          X          X
     |          |          |          |
     3          4          5          6
```
Lengths of Pencils in Inches

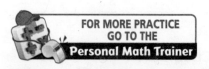
FOR MORE PRACTICE
GO TO THE
Personal Math Trainer

Name _____

Problem Solving • Add and Subtract Lengths

Essential Question How can drawing a diagram help when solving problems about lengths?

Common Core **Measurement and Data—**
2.MD.B.6, 2.MD.B.5
MATHEMATICAL PRACTICES
MP1, MP2, MP4

Nate had 23 centimeters of string.
He gave 9 centimeters of string to Myra.
How much string does Nate have now?

Unlock the Problem (Real World)

What do I need to find?

how much string

Nate has now

What information do I need to use?

Nate had _____ centimeters of string.

He gave _____ centimeters of string to Myra.

Show how to solve the problem.

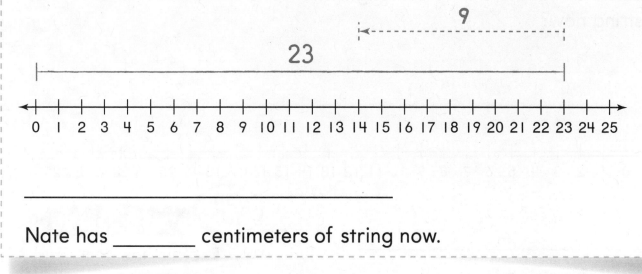

_____

Nate has _____ centimeters of string now.

HOME CONNECTION • Your child drew a diagram to represent a problem about lengths. The diagram can be used to choose the operation for solving the problem.

Draw a diagram. Write a number sentence using a ▇ for the unknown number. Then solve.

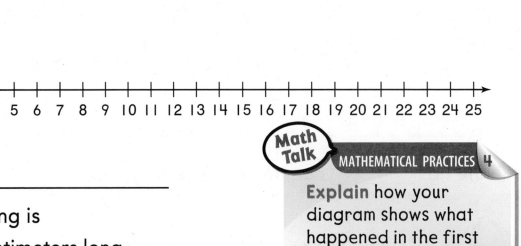
- What do I need to find?
- What information do I need to use?

1. Ellie has a ribbon that is 12 centimeters long. Gwen has a ribbon that is 9 centimeters long. How many centimeters of ribbon do they have?

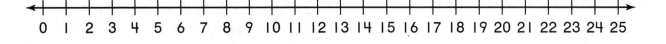

```
0  1  2  3  4  5  6  7  8  9  10 11 12 13 14 15 16 17 18 19 20 21 22 23 24 25
```

_____

They have _____ centimeters of ribbon.

2. A string is 24 centimeters long. Justin cuts 8 centimeters off. How long is the string now?

```
0  1  2  3  4  5  6  7  8  9  10 11 12 13 14 15 16 17 18 19 20 21 22 23 24 25
```

Math Talk

MATHEMATICAL PRACTICES 4

Explain how your diagram shows what happened in the first problem.

_____

Now the string is

_____ centimeters long.

Name _____

Draw a diagram. Write a number sentence using a ▪ for the unknown number. Then solve.

✓3. A chain of paper clips is 18 centimeters long. Sondra adds 6 centimeters of paper clips to the chain. How long is the chain now?

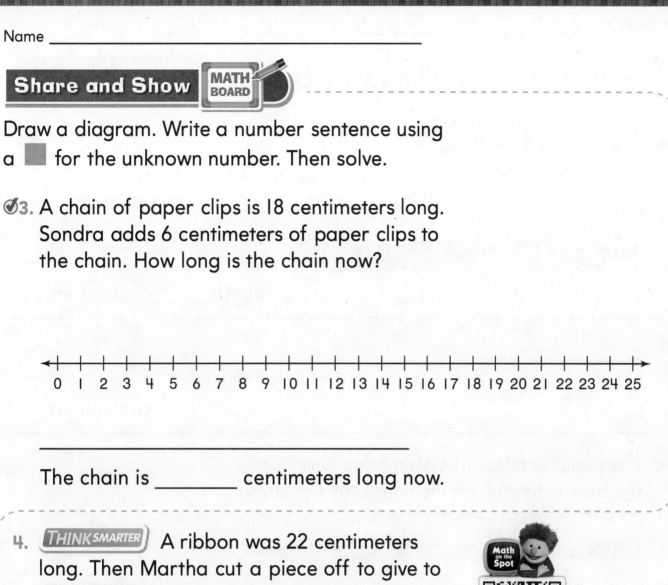

0 1 2 3 4 5 6 7 8 9 10 11 12 13 14 15 16 17 18 19 20 21 22 23 24 25

_____

The chain is _____ centimeters long now.

4. **THINK SMARTER** A ribbon was 22 centimeters long. Then Martha cut a piece off to give to Tao. Now the ribbon is 5 centimeters long. How many centimeters of ribbon did Martha give to Tao?

0 1 2 3 4 5 6 7 8 9 10 11 12 13 14 15 16 17 18 19 20 21 22 23 24 25

Martha gave _____ centimeters of ribbon to Tao.

TAKE HOME ACTIVITY • Have your child explain how he or she used a diagram to solve one problem in this lesson.

© Houghton Mifflin Harcourt Publishing Company

Name _____

✓ Mid-Chapter Checkpoint

Personal Math Trainer
Online Assessment
and Intervention

Concepts and Skills

Use a unit cube. Measure the length in centimeters. (2.MD.A.1)

1.

about _____ centimeters

2.

about _____ centimeters

3. The pencil is about 11 centimeters long. Circle
the best estimate for the length of the string. (2.MD.A.3)

7 centimeters

10 centimeters

16 centimeters

4. **THINK SMARTER** Use a centimeter ruler. What is the
length of this ribbon to the nearest centimeter? (2.MD.A.1)

_____ centimeters

Problem Solving • Add and Subtract Lengths

Common Core **COMMON CORE STANDARDS—2.MD.B.6, 2.MD.B.5** *Relate addition and subtraction to length.*

Draw a diagram. Write a number sentence using a ▢ for the unknown number. Then solve.

1. A straw is 20 centimeters long. Mr. Jones cuts 8 centimeters off the straw. How long is the straw now?

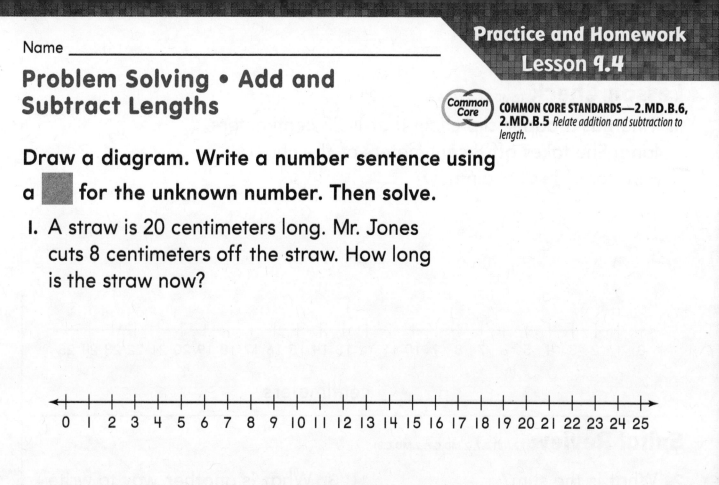

0 1 2 3 4 5 6 7 8 9 10 11 12 13 14 15 16 17 18 19 20 21 22 23 24 25

_____

The straw is _____ centimeters long now.

2. **WRITE Math** Draw and describe a diagram for a problem about the total length of two ribbons, 13 centimeters long and 5 centimeters long.

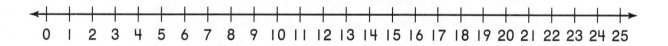

0 1 2 3 4 5 6 7 8 9 10 11 12 13 14 15 16 17 18 19 20 21 22 23 24 25

Lesson Check (2.MD.B.6, 2.MD.B.5)

1. Tina has a paper clip chain that is 25 centimeters long. She takes off 8 centimeters of the chain. How long is the chain now?

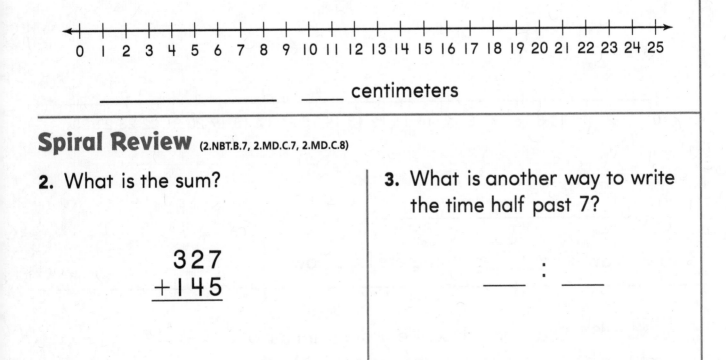

_____ ____ centimeters

Spiral Review (2.NBT.B.7, 2.MD.C.7, 2.MD.C.8)

2. What is the sum?

$$\begin{array}{r} 327 \\ +145 \\ \hline \end{array}$$

3. What is another way to write the time half past 7?

____ : ____

4. Molly has these coins in her pocket. How much money does she have in her pocket?

_____ or ____ cents

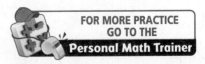

FOR MORE PRACTICE
GO TO THE
Personal Math Trainer

Name _____

Centimeters and Meters

Essential Question How is measuring in meters different from measuring in centimeters?

Common Core Measurement and Data—
2.MD.A.2
MATHEMATICAL PRACTICES
MP1, MP5, MP7

Listen and Draw

Draw or write to describe how you did each measurement.

1st measurement

2nd measurement

FOR THE TEACHER • Have each small group use a 1-meter piece of yarn to measure a distance marked on the floor with masking tape. Then have them measure the same distance using a sheet of paper folded in half lengthwise.

Math Talk
MATHEMATICAL PRACTICES 1

Describe how the lengths of the yarn and the sheet of paper are different.

Chapter 9

Model and Draw

1 **meter** is the same as 100 centimeters.

The real door is about 200 centimeters tall.
The real door is also about 2 meters tall.

Share and Show MATH BOARD

Measure to the nearest centimeter.
Then measure to the nearest meter.

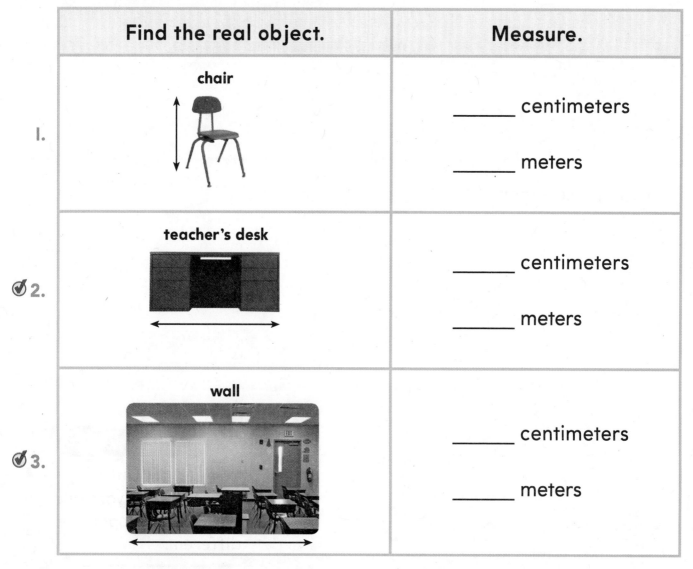

Find the real object.	Measure.
1. **chair**	_____ centimeters _____ meters
✓ 2. **teacher's desk**	_____ centimeters _____ meters
✓ 3. **wall**	_____ centimeters _____ meters

Name _____

On Your Own

Measure to the nearest centimeter.
Then measure to the nearest meter.

Find the real object.	Measure.
4. **chalkboard** 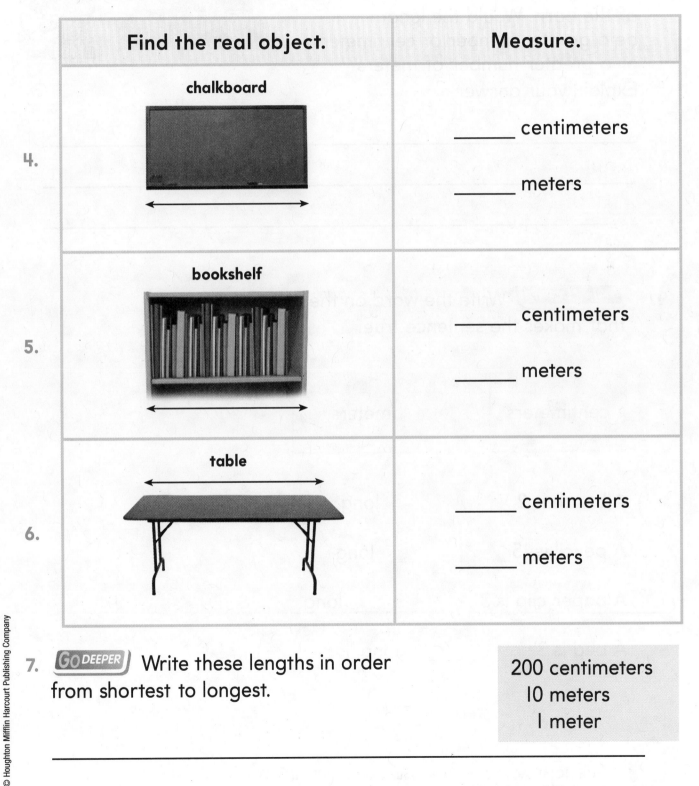	_____ centimeters _____ meters
5. **bookshelf**	_____ centimeters _____ meters
6. **table**	_____ centimeters _____ meters

7. **GO DEEPER** Write these lengths in order from shortest to longest.

> 200 centimeters
> 10 meters
> 1 meter

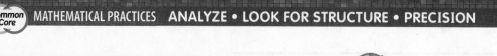

Problem Solving • Applications

WRITE Math

8. **THINK SMARTER** Mr. Ryan walked next to a barn. He wants to measure the length of the barn. Would the length be a greater number of centimeters or a greater number of meters? Explain your answer.

_____

_____

_____

9. **THINK SMARTER** Write the word on the tile that makes the sentence true.

| centimeters | meters |

A bench is 2 _____ long.

A pencil is 15 _____ long.

A paper clip is 3 _____ long.

A bed is 3 _____ long.

 TAKE HOME ACTIVITY • Have your child describe how centimeters and meters are different.

Centimeters and Meters

Common Core
COMMON CORE STANDARD—2.MD.A.2
Measure and estimate lengths in standard units.

**Measure to the nearest centimeter.
Then measure to the nearest meter.**

Find the real object.	Measure.
1. bookcase	_____ centimeters _____ meters
2. window	_____ centimeters _____ meters

Problem Solving · Real World

3. Sally will measure the length of a wall in both centimeters and meters. Will there be fewer centimeters or fewer meters? Explain.

_____

_____

_____

4. **WRITE Math** Would you measure the length of a bench in centimeters or in meters? Explain your choice.

_____

Lesson Check (2.MD.A.2)

I. Use a centimeter ruler. What is the length of the toothbrush to the nearest centimeter?

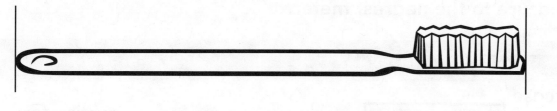

_____ centimeters

Spiral Review (2.NBT.B.7, 2.MD.A.2, 2.MD.C.8)

2. Draw and label a group of coins that has a total value of 65 cents.

3. Janet has a poster that is about 3 feet long. Write **inches** or **feet** in each blank to make the statement true.

3 _____is longer than

12 _____.

4. Last week, 483 children checked books out from the library. This week, only 162 children checked books out from the library. How many children checked out library books in the last two weeks?

$$483$$
$$+\ 162$$

5. Draw and label a group of coins that has a total value of $1.00.

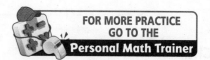

FOR MORE PRACTICE
GO TO THE
Personal Math Trainer

Name _____

Estimate Lengths in Meters

Essential Question How do you estimate the lengths of objects in meters?

Common Core Measurement and Data—
2.MD.A.3
MATHEMATICAL PRACTICES
MP6, MP7

Listen and Draw

Find an object that is about 10 centimeters long.
Draw and label it.

Is there a classroom object that is about
50 centimeters long? Draw and label it.

 FOR THE TEACHER • Provide a collection of objects for children to choose from. Above the table of displayed objects, draw and label a 10-centimeter line segment and a 50-centimeter line segment.

Math Talk MATHEMATICAL PRACTICES 6

Describe how the lengths of the two real objects compare.

Chapter 9

six hundred thirty-three **633**

Estimate. About how many meter sticks will match the width of a door?

A 1-meter measuring stick is about 100 centimeters long.

about _____ meters

Share and Show MATH BOARD

Find the real object.
Estimate its length in meters.

☑ 1. bookshelf

about _____ meters

☑ 2. bulletin board

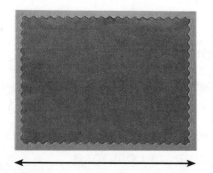

about _____ meters

Name _____

Find the real object.
Estimate its length in meters.

3. teacher's desk

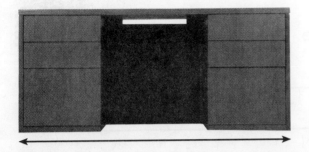

about _____ meters

4. wall

about _____ meters

5. window

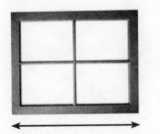

about _____ meters

6. chalkboard

about _____ meters

Problem Solving • Applications  WRITE Math

7. **THINK SMARTER** In meters, estimate the distance from your teacher's desk to the door of your classroom.

about _____ meters

Explain how you made your estimate.

_____

_____

_____

_____

8. **THINK SMARTER** Estimate the length of an adult's bicycle. Fill in the bubble next to all the sentences that are true.

- ○ The bicycle is about 2 meters long.
- ○ The bicycle is about 200 centimeters long.
- ○ The bicycle is less than I meter long.
- ○ The bicycle is about 2 centimeters long.
- ○ The bicycle is more than 200 meters long.

TAKE HOME ACTIVITY • With your child, estimate the lengths of some objects in meters.

Name _____

Estimate Lengths in Meters

COMMON CORE STANDARD—2.MD.A.3
Measure and estimate lengths in standard units.

Find the real object.
Estimate its length in meters.

1. poster

about _____ meters

2. chalkboard

about _____ meters

Problem Solving Real World

3. Barbara and Luke each placed 2 meter sticks
end-to-end along the length of a large table.
About how long is the table?

about _____ meters

4. WRITE Math Choose one object from above.
Describe how you estimated its length.

_____

_____

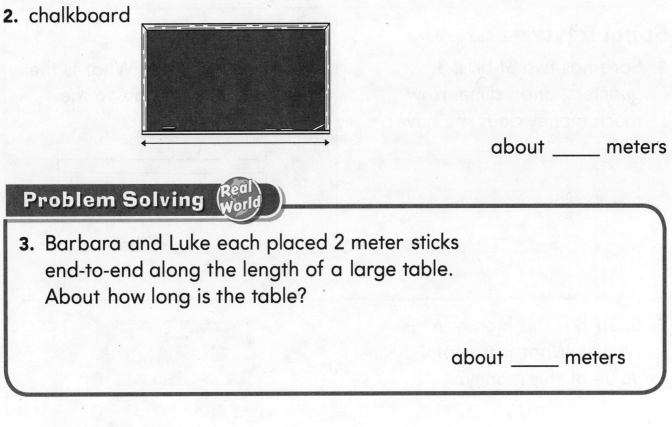

Lesson Check (2.MD.A.3)

1. What is the best estimate for the length of a real baseball bat?

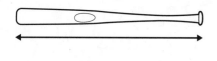

_____ meter

2. What is the best estimate for the length of a real couch?

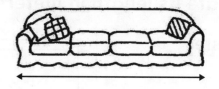

_____ meters

Spiral Review (2.MD.A.1, 2.MD.C.8)

3. Sara has two $1 bills, 3 quarters, and 1 dime. How much money does she have?

$ _____

4. Use an inch ruler. What is the length of this straw to the nearest inch?

_____ inches

5. Scott has this money in his pocket. What is the total value of this money?

$ _____

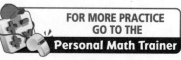

FOR MORE PRACTICE
GO TO THE
Personal Math Trainer

Name _____

Measure and Compare Lengths

Essential Question How do you find the difference between the lengths of two objects?

Common Core Measurement and Data—
2.MD.A.4
MATHEMATICAL PRACTICES
MP1, MP2, MP6

Listen and Draw *Real World*  Hands On

Measure and record each length.

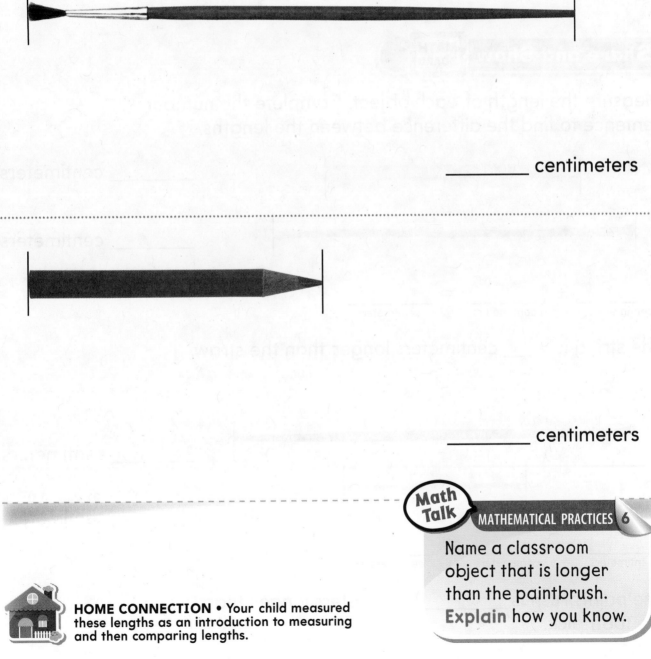

_____ centimeters

_____ centimeters

Math Talk MATHEMATICAL PRACTICES 6

Name a classroom object that is longer than the paintbrush. **Explain** how you know.

HOME CONNECTION • Your child measured these lengths as an introduction to measuring and then comparing lengths.

Chapter 9

six hundred thirty-nine **639**

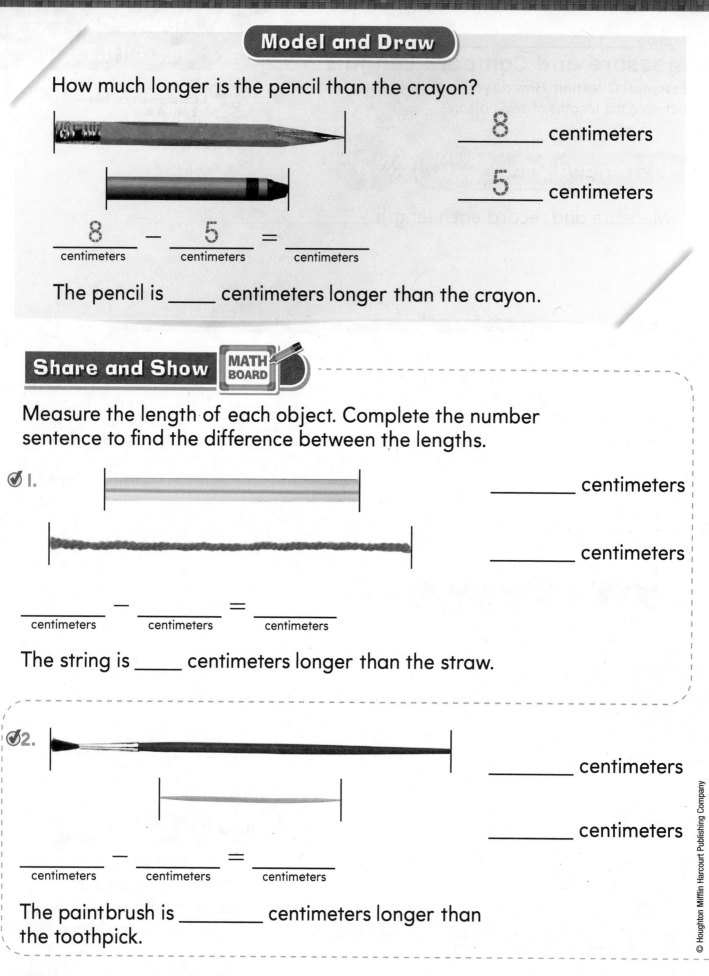

Model and Draw

How much longer is the pencil than the crayon?

_8_ centimeters

_5_ centimeters

$\dfrac{8}{\text{centimeters}} - \dfrac{5}{\text{centimeters}} = \dfrac{}{\text{centimeters}}$

The pencil is _____ centimeters longer than the crayon.

Share and Show MATH BOARD

Measure the length of each object. Complete the number sentence to find the difference between the lengths.

☑ 1.

_____ centimeters

_____ centimeters

$\dfrac{}{\text{centimeters}} - \dfrac{}{\text{centimeters}} = \dfrac{}{\text{centimeters}}$

The string is _____ centimeters longer than the straw.

☑ 2.

_____ centimeters

_____ centimeters

$\dfrac{}{\text{centimeters}} - \dfrac{}{\text{centimeters}} = \dfrac{}{\text{centimeters}}$

The paintbrush is _____ centimeters longer than the toothpick.

Name _____

Measure the length of each object. Complete the number sentence to find the difference between the lengths.

3.

CRAYON

_____ centimeters

_____ centimeters

_____ − _____ = _____
centimeters   centimeters   centimeters

The yarn is _____ centimeters longer than the crayon.

4.

_____ centimeters

_____ centimeters

_____ − _____ = _____
centimeters   centimeters   centimeters

The string is _____ centimeters longer than the paper clip.

5. **THINK SMARTER** Use a centimeter ruler. Measure the length of your desk and the length of a book.

desk: _____ centimeters

book: _____ centimeters

Which is shorter? _____

How much shorter is it? _____

Problem Solving • Applications   Real World   WRITE Math

MATHEMATICAL PRACTICE 1   Analyze Relationships

6. Mark has a rope that is 23 centimeters long. He cuts 15 centimeters off. What is the length of the rope now?

_____ centimeters

7. The yellow ribbon is 15 centimeters longer than the green ribbon. The green ribbon is 29 centimeters long. What is the length of the yellow ribbon?

_____ centimeters

8.   THINK SMARTER +

Personal Math Trainer

Measure the length of each object. Which object is longer? How much longer? Explain.

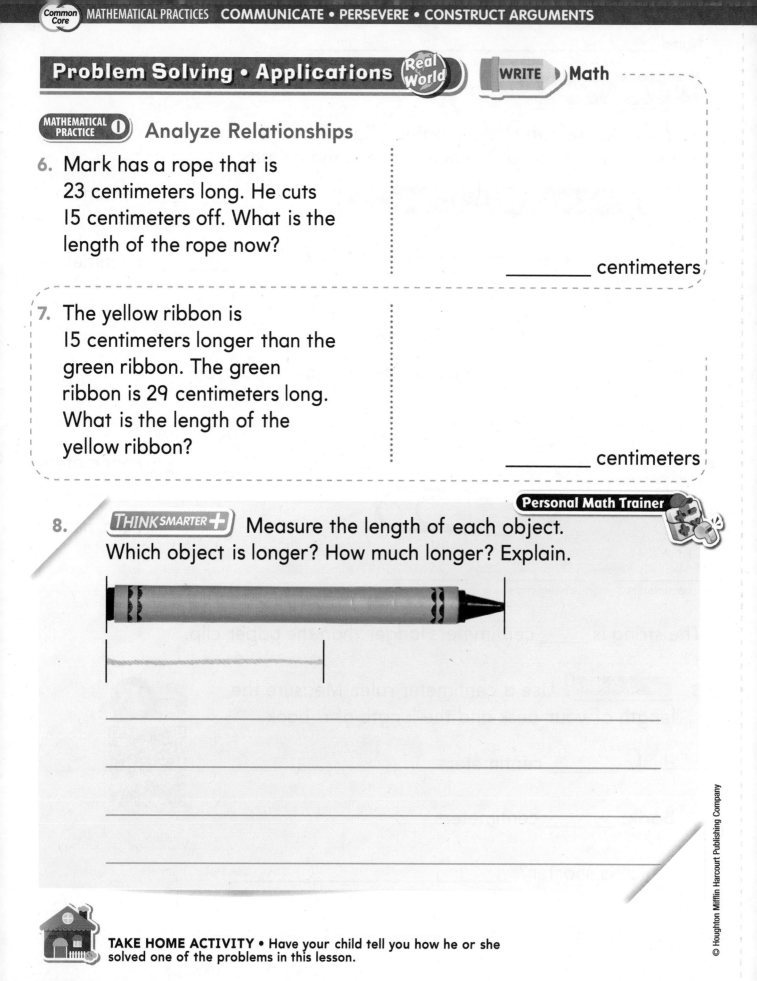

_____

_____

_____

_____

🏠 **TAKE HOME ACTIVITY** • Have your child tell you how he or she solved one of the problems in this lesson.

© Houghton Mifflin Harcourt Publishing Company

Measure and Compare Lengths

Practice and Homework
Lesson 9.7

Common Core   **COMMON CORE STANDARD—2.MD.A.4**
Measure and estimate lengths in standard units.

Measure the length of each object. Write a number sentence to find the difference between the lengths.

1.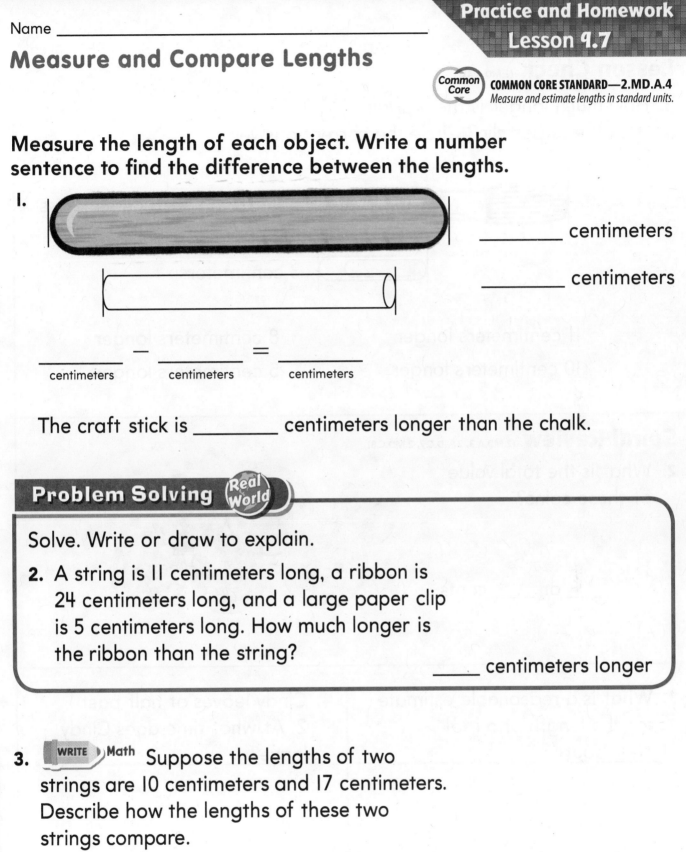

_____ centimeters

_____ centimeters

_____ − _____ = _____
centimeters   centimeters   centimeters

The craft stick is _____ centimeters longer than the chalk.

Problem Solving · Real World

Solve. Write or draw to explain.

2. A string is 11 centimeters long, a ribbon is 24 centimeters long, and a large paper clip is 5 centimeters long. How much longer is the ribbon than the string?

_____ centimeters longer

3. **WRITE** Math Suppose the lengths of two strings are 10 centimeters and 17 centimeters. Describe how the lengths of these two strings compare.

_____

_____

Lesson Check (2.MD.A.4)

1. How much longer is the marker
   than the paper clip? Circle the correct answer.

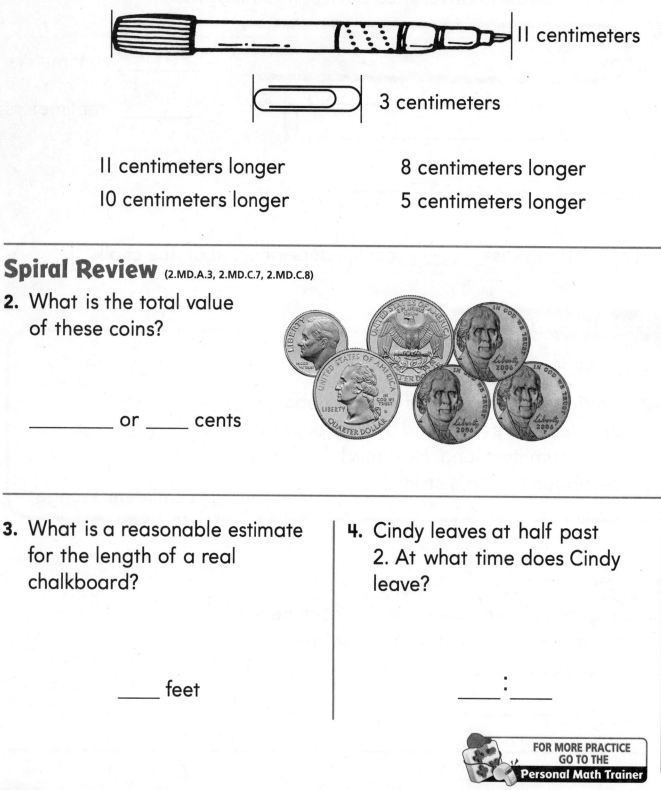

11 centimeters

3 centimeters

11 centimeters longer   8 centimeters longer

10 centimeters longer   5 centimeters longer

Spiral Review (2.MD.A.3, 2.MD.C.7, 2.MD.C.8)

2. What is the total value
   of these coins?

_____ or ____ cents

3. What is a reasonable estimate
   for the length of a real
   chalkboard?

   ____ feet

4. Cindy leaves at half past
   2. At what time does Cindy
   leave?

   ____ : ____

FOR MORE PRACTICE
GO TO THE
Personal Math Trainer

✓ Chapter 9 Review/Test

1. Michael uses unit cubes to measure the length of the yarn. Circle the number in the box that makes the sentence true.

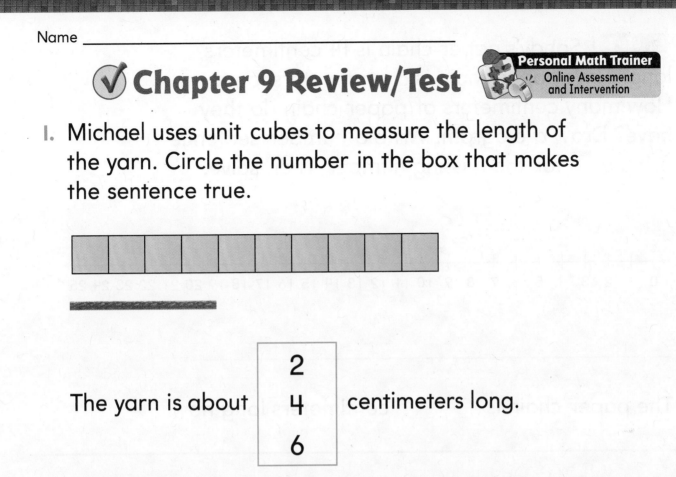

The yarn is about
2
4
6
centimeters long.

2. The paper clip is about 4 centimeters long. Robin says the string is about 7 centimeters long. Gale says the string is about 20 centimeters long.

Which girl has the better estimate? Explain.

_____

_____

Assessment Options
Chapter Test

3. **GO DEEPER** Sandy's paper chain is 14 centimeters long. Tim's paper chain is 6 centimeters long. How many centimeters of paper chain do they have? Draw a diagram. Write a number sentence using a ▪ for the missing number. Then solve.

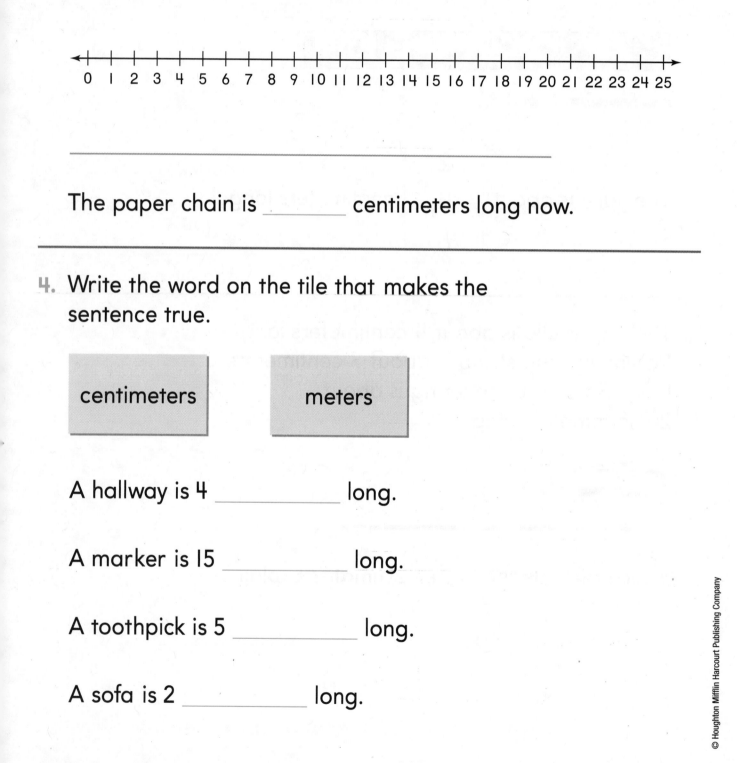

0 1 2 3 4 5 6 7 8 9 10 11 12 13 14 15 16 17 18 19 20 21 22 23 24 25

_____

The paper chain is _____ centimeters long now.

___

4. Write the word on the tile that makes the sentence true.

| centimeters | meters |

A hallway is 4 _____ long.

A marker is 15 _____ long.

A toothpick is 5 _____ long.

A sofa is 2 _____ long.

Name _____

5. Estimate the length of a real car. Fill in the bubble next to all the sentences that are true.

○ The car is more than 100 centimeters long.

○ The car is less than 1 meter long.

○ The car is less than 10 meters long.

○ The car is about 20 centimeters long.

○ The car is more than 150 meters long.

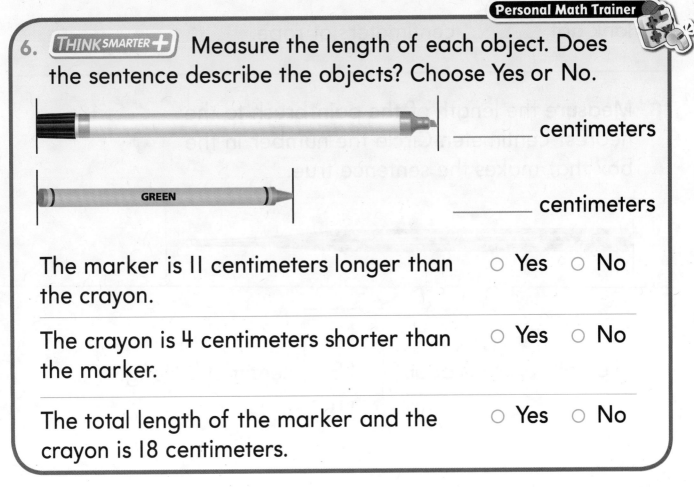

Personal Math Trainer

6. **THINK SMARTER +** Measure the length of each object. Does the sentence describe the objects? Choose Yes or No.

_____ centimeters

GREEN

_____ centimeters

The marker is 11 centimeters longer than the crayon.	○ Yes ○ No
The crayon is 4 centimeters shorter than the marker.	○ Yes ○ No
The total length of the marker and the crayon is 18 centimeters.	○ Yes ○ No

© Houghton Mifflin Harcourt Publishing Company • Image Credits: ©Robert Churchill/Getty Images

7. Ethan's rope is 25 centimeters long. Ethan cuts the rope and gives a piece to Hank. Ethan's rope is now 16 centimeters long. How many centimeters of rope did Hank get from Ethan?

Draw a diagram. Write a number sentence using a ■ for the unknown number. Then solve.

_____

Hank got _____ centimeters of rope.

_____

8. Measure the length of the paintbrush to the nearest centimeter. Circle the number in the box that makes the sentence true.

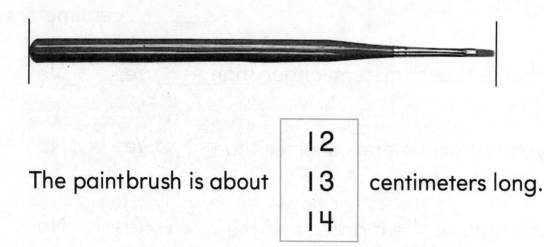

The paintbrush is about
| 12 |
| 13 |
| 14 |
centimeters long.

Data

Look at the different kinds of balloons.

What are some ways you can sort these balloons?

Name _____

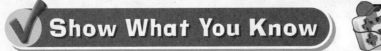
Read a Picture Graph

Use the picture graph. (1.MD.C.4)

Fruit We Like				
🍊 orange	🍊	🍊	🍊	🍊
🍐 pear	🍐	🍐		

1. How many children chose pear? _____ children

2. Circle the fruit that more children chose.

🍊 🍐

Read a Tally Chart

Complete the tally chart. (1.MD.C.4)

Color We Like		Total
green	|||	
red	⟍⟍⟍⟍		
blue	⟍⟍⟍⟍ |||	

3. How many children chose red?

_____ children

4. Which color did the fewest children choose?

_____

Addition and Subtraction Facts

Write the sum or difference. (1.OA.C.6)

5. $10 - 4 =$ _____

6. $4 + 5 =$ _____

7. $6 + 5 =$ _____

8. $9 - 3 =$ _____

9. $5 + 7 =$ _____

10. $11 - 3 =$ _____

This page checks understanding of important skills needed for success in Chapter 10.

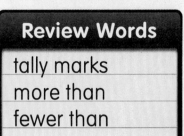
Vocabulary Builder

Visualize It

Draw **tally marks** to show each number.

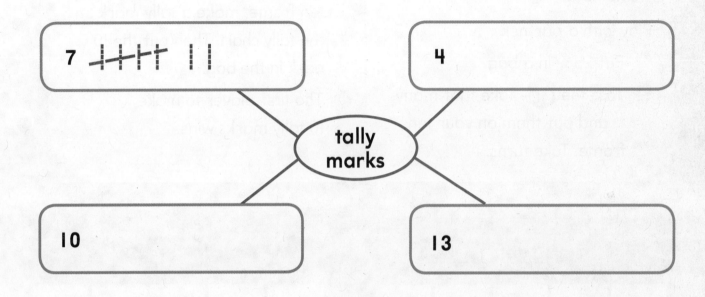

| 7 ~~IIII~~ II | 4 |

tally marks

| 10 | 13 |

Understand Vocabulary

Write a number to complete the sentence.

1. 10 apples is **more than** _____ apples.

2. 6 bananas is **fewer than** _____ bananas.

3. _____ grapes is **more than** 6 grapes.

4. _____ oranges is **fewer than** 5 oranges.

 • **Interactive Student Edition**
• **Multimedia eGlossary**

Game

Making Tens

Materials •  • 25 ▫
• small bag

Play with a partner.

① Put 25 ▫ in a bag.

② Toss the ⚅. Take that many ▫ and put them on your ten frame. Take turns.

③ When you have 10 ▫ on your ten frame, make a tally mark on the tally chart. Then put the 10 ▫ back in the bag.

④ The first player to make 10 tally marks wins.

Player 1	Player 2

Making Tens

Player	Tally
Player 1	
Player 2	

bar graph

gráfica de barras

4

compare

comparar

8

data

datos

12

digit

dígito

15

key

clave

36

picture graph

gráfica con dibujos

48

sum

suma o total

59

survey

encuesta

60

Use these symbols when you **compare**: >, <, =.

241 > 234

123 < 128

247 = 247

Children Playing Games

Outdoor Game: kickball, four square, tag, jump rope

Number of Children: 0 1 2 3 4 5 6 7 8 9

0, 1, 2, 3, 4, 5, 6, 7, 8, and 9 are **digits**.

Favorite Lunch	
Lunch	Tally
pizza	IIII
sandwich	⊬⊦ I
salad	III
pasta	⊬⊦

The information in this chart is called **data**.

Playground Toys

soccer ball	★ ★ ★
jump ropes	★
soft ball	★ ★

Key: Each ★ stands for 5 toys.

A **picture graph** uses pictures to show data.

Number of Soccer Games

March							
April							
May							
June							

Key: Each ⚽ stands for 1 game.

The **key** tells how many each picture stands for.

Favorite Lunch	
Lunch	Tally
pizza	IIII
sandwich	⊬⊦ I
salad	III
pasta	⊬⊦

A **survey** is a collection of data from answers to a question.

---

4 + 2 = 6

↑ sum

Picture It

Word Box
bar graph
compare
data
digit
key
picture graph
sum
survey

For 3 to 4 players

Materials

- timer
- sketch pad

How to Play

1. Choose a math word from the Word Box. Do not tell the other players.

2. Set the timer for 1 minute.

3. Draw pictures to give clues about the word. Draw only pictures and numbers.

4. The first player to guess the word gets 1 point. If that player can use the word in a sentence, he or she gets 1 more point. Then that player takes a turn.

5. The first player to score 5 points wins.

The Write Way

Reflect

Choose one idea. Write about it in the space below.

- Explain how you would take a survey and record the data.
- Tell when you would use a picture graph and a bar graph.
- Write two questions you have about the chapter we are working on.

Name _____

Collect Data

Essential Question How do you use a tally chart to record data from a survey?

Common Core **Measurement and Data—**
2.MD.D.10
MATHEMATICAL PRACTICES
MP3, MP4, MP6

Listen and Draw

Take turns choosing a cube from the bag.
Draw a tally mark in the chart for each cube.

Cube Colors	
Color	**Tally**
blue	
red	
green	

Math Talk
MATHEMATICAL PRACTICES **4**

Use Diagrams Explain how tally marks help you keep track of what has been chosen.

HOME CONNECTION • Your child made tally marks to record the color of cubes chosen from a bag. This activity prepares children for using and recording data in this chapter.

You can take a **survey** to collect **data**.
You can record the data with tally marks.

Greg asked his classmates which lunch
was their favorite.

Favorite Lunch

Lunch	Tally
pizza	IIII
sandwich	ⅣⅡ I
salad	III
pasta	ⅣⅡ

The tally marks in the tally chart show the children's answers. Each tally mark stands for one child's choice.

Share and Show MATH BOARD

1. Take a survey. Ask 10 classmates which pet is their favorite. Use tally marks to show their choices.

2. How many classmates chose dog?

   _____ classmates

3. Which pet did the fewest classmates choose?

   _____

Favorite Pet

Pet	Tally
cat	
dog	
fish	
bird	

4. Did more classmates choose cat or dog? _____

   How many more? _____ more classmates

Name _____

5. Take a survey. Ask 10 classmates which indoor game is their favorite. Use tally marks to show their choices.

Favorite Indoor Game	
Game	**Tally**
board	
card	
computer	
puzzle	

6. How many classmates chose board game?

_____ classmates

7. Which game did the most classmates choose?

_____

8. **GO DEEPER** Did more classmates choose a card game or a computer game?

_____

How many more?   _____ more classmates

9. Which game did the fewest classmates choose?

_____

10. **MATHEMATICAL PRACTICE ③** Apply How many classmates did not choose a board game or a puzzle? Explain how you know.

_____

_____

_____

_____

Problem Solving • Applications Real World

WRITE Math

11. **THINK SMARTER** Maeko asked her classmates to choose their favorite subject. She made this tally chart.

How many more classmates chose math than reading?

_____ more classmates

Write a question about the data in the chart. Then write the answer to your question.

Favorite Subject	
Subject	Tally
reading	卌 I
math	卌 IIII
science	卌 卌

_____

_____

_____

12. **THINK SMARTER** Fill in the bubble next to all the sentences that describe data in the tally chart.

○ 10 children voted for lunch.

○ 13 children voted for breakfast.

○ More children voted for dinner than for lunch.

○ A total of 35 children voted for their favorite meal.

Favorite Meal	
Meal	Tally
breakfast	卌 III
lunch	卌 卌
dinner	卌 卌 II

TAKE HOME ACTIVITY • With your child, take a survey about favorite games and make a tally chart to show the data.

Collect Data

Common
Core

COMMON CORE STANDARD—2.MD.D.10
Represent and interpret data.

1. Take a survey. Ask 10 classmates how they got to school. Use tally marks to show their choices.

How We Got to School	
Way	**Tally**
walk	
bus	
car	
bike	

_____

2. How many classmates rode in a bus to school?

_____ classmates

3. How many classmates rode in a car to school?

_____ classmates

4. In which way did the fewest classmates get to school?

_____

5. In which way did the most classmates get to school?

_____

6. **WRITE** ▸Math   Explain how you would take a survey to find your classmates' favorite shirt color.

_____

© Houghton Mifflin Harcourt Publishing Company

Lesson Check (2.MD.D.10)

1. Use the tally chart. Which color did the fewest children choose?

_____

Favorite Color	
Color	Tally
blue	|||
green	||||| ||||
red	||||| ||
yellow	|||||	

Spiral Review (2.NBT.B.5, 2.MD.B.6, 2.MD.C.7, 2.MD.C.8)

2. How many dimes have the same value as $1.00?

_____ dimes

3. Jared has two ropes. Each rope is 9 inches long. How many inches of rope does he have in all?

_____ inches

4. The clock shows the time Lee got to school. At what time did she get to school?

_____ : _____

5. Liza finished studying at half past 3. What time did Liza finish studying?

_____ : _____

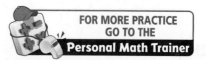

FOR MORE PRACTICE
GO TO THE
Personal Math Trainer

Read Picture Graphs

Essential Question How do you use a picture graph to show data?

Common Core **Measurement and Data—**
2.MD.D.10

MATHEMATICAL PRACTICES
MP1, MP2, MP4, MP6

Listen and Draw (Real World)

Use the tally chart to solve the problem.
Draw or write to show what you did.

Favorite Hobby	
Hobby	Tally
crafts	⊬⊬⊬ I
reading	IIII
music	⊬⊬⊬
sports	⊬⊬⊬ II

_____ more children

Math Talk MATHEMATICAL PRACTICES 2

Use Reasoning Can the chart be used to find how many girls chose music? Explain.

FOR THE TEACHER • Read the following problem. Mr. Martin's class made this tally chart. How many more children in his class chose sports than chose reading as their favorite hobby?

A **picture graph** uses pictures to show data.

Number of Soccer Games							
March	⚽	⚽	⚽	⚽			
April	⚽	⚽	⚽				
May	⚽	⚽	⚽	⚽	⚽		
June	⚽	⚽	⚽	⚽	⚽	⚽	⚽

Key: Each ⚽ stands for 1 game.

A **key** tells how many each picture stands for.

Share and Show MATH BOARD

Use the picture graph to answer the questions.

Favorite Snack								
pretzels	☺	☺	☺	☺	☺	☺	☺	☺
grapes	☺	☺	☺	☺	☺	☺	☺	
popcorn	☺	☺	☺					
apples	☺	☺	☺	☺	☺	☺		

Key: Each ☺ stands for 1 child.

☑ 1. Which snack was chosen by the fewest children? _____

☑ 2. How many more children chose pretzels
than apples?   _____ more children

Name _____

Use the picture graph to answer the questions.

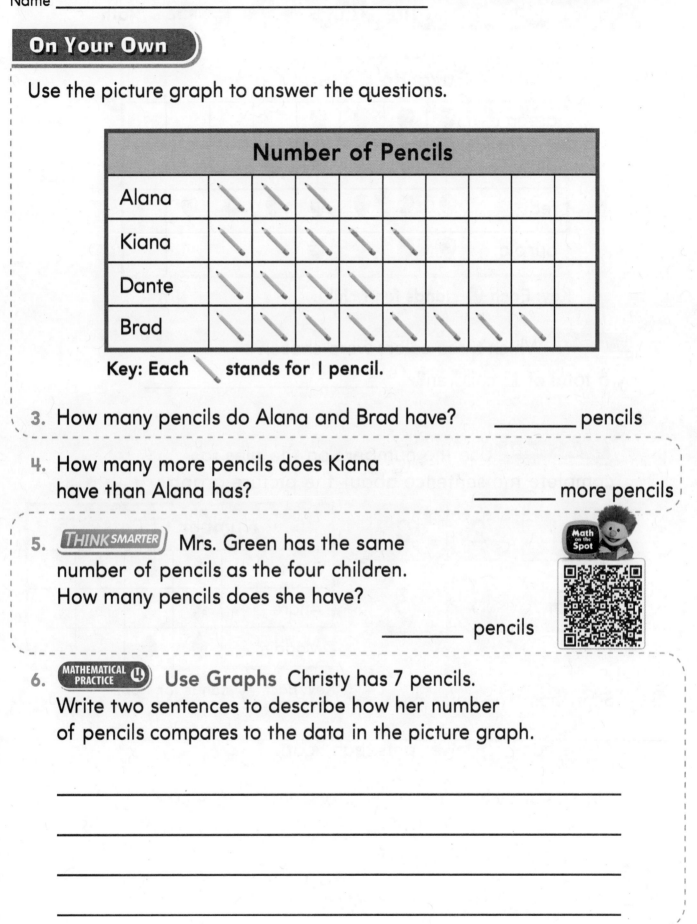

Number of Pencils

Alana	\	\	\						
Kiana	\	\	\	\	\				
Dante	\	\	\	\					
Brad	\	\	\	\	\	\	\	\	

Key: Each \ **stands for 1 pencil.**

3. How many pencils do Alana and Brad have?   _____ pencils

4. How many more pencils does Kiana have than Alana has?   _____ more pencils

5. **THINK SMARTER** Mrs. Green has the same number of pencils as the four children. How many pencils does she have?

_____ pencils

6. **MATHEMATICAL PRACTICE ④ Use Graphs** Christy has 7 pencils. Write two sentences to describe how her number of pencils compares to the data in the picture graph.

_____

_____

_____

_____

Problem Solving • Applications (Real World) WRITE Math

Favorite Balloon Color

green	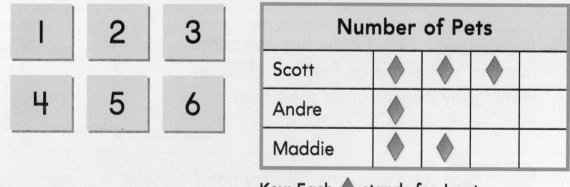						
blue							
red							
purple							

Key: Each 🎈 stands for 1 child.

7. **GO DEEPER** Which three colors were chosen by a total of 13 children? _____

8. **THINK SMARTER** Use the numbers on the tiles to complete the sentence about the picture graph.

1	2	3
4	5	6

Number of Pets

Scott	◆	◆	◆	
Andre	◆			
Maddie	◆	◆		

Key: Each ◆ stands for 1 pet.

Scott has ____ pets.

Andre has ____ fewer pets than Scott.

Maddie and Scott have ____ more pets than Andre.

 **TAKE HOME ACTIVITY** • Have your child explain how he or she solved one of the problems in this lesson.

Read Picture Graphs

Use the picture graph to answer the questions.

Common Core COMMON CORE STANDARD—2.MD.D.10
Represent and interpret data.

Number of Books Read

Ryan						

Key: Each 📕 stands for 1 book.

1. How many books in all did Henry and Anna read? _____ books

2. How many more books did Ryan read than Gwen? _____ more books

3. How many fewer books did Gwen read than Anna? _____ fewer books

Problem Solving Real World

Use the picture graph above. Write or draw to explain.

4. Carlos read 4 books. How many children
   read fewer books than Carlos?

   _____ children

5. **WRITE** Math Write a few sentences _____
   to describe the different parts of
   a picture graph. _____

   _____

Lesson Check (2.MD.D.10)

1. Use the picture graph. Who has the most fish?

_____

Our Fish					
Jane	🐟				
Will	🐟	🐟	🐟		
Gina	🐟	🐟	🐟	🐟	
Evan	🐟	🐟			

Key: Each 🐟 stands for 1 fish.

Spiral Review (2.MD.A.1, 2.MD.C.7, 2.MD.C.8)

2. What time is shown on this clock?

_____ : _____

3. Each unit cube is about 1 centimeter long. What is the length of the paper clip?

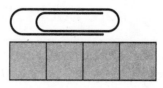

about _____ centimeters

4. What is the total value of this group of coins?

_____ ¢ or _____ cents

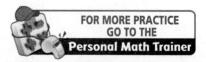
FOR MORE PRACTICE GO TO THE Personal Math Trainer

Name _____

Make Picture Graphs

Essential Question How do you make a picture graph to show data in a tally chart?

Common Core Measurement and Data—
2.MD.D.10
MATHEMATICAL PRACTICES
MP1, MP4, MP6

Listen and Draw Hands On

Take turns choosing a cube from the bag.
Draw a smiley face in the graph for each cube.

Cube Colors					
blue					
red					
green					
orange					

Key: Each ☺ stands for 1 cube.

Math Talk
MATHEMATICAL PRACTICES 6

Explain how you know that the number of smiley faces for blue matches the number of blue cubes.

HOME CONNECTION • Your child made a graph by recording smiley faces for the colors of cubes taken from a bag. This activity prepares children for working with picture graphs in this lesson.

Model and Draw

Each picture in the graph stands for 1 flower.
Draw pictures to show the data in the tally chart.

Number of Flowers Picked

Name	Tally
Jessie	III
Inez	IIII
Paulo	IIII

Number of Flowers Picked

Jessie	◯	◯	◯		
Inez					
Paulo					

Key: Each ◯ stands for 1 flower.

Share and Show MATH BOARD

1. Use the tally chart to complete the picture graph.
   Draw a ☺ for each child.

Favorite Sandwich

Sandwich	Tally
cheese	IIII
ham	II
tuna	IIII
turkey	III

Favorite Sandwich

cheese					
ham					
tuna					
turkey					

Key: Each ☺ stands for 1 child.

☑ 2. How many children chose tuna? _____ children

☑ 3. How many more children chose cheese than ham? _____ more children

© Houghton Mifflin Harcourt Publishing Company

Name _____

4. Use the tally chart to complete the picture graph.
Draw a ☺ for each child.

Favorite Fruit	
Fruit	**Tally**
apple	IIII
plum	II
banana	~~IIII~~
orange	III

Favorite Fruit				
apple				
plum				
banana				
orange				

Key: Each ☺ stands for 1 child.

5. How many children chose banana? _____ children

6. How many fewer children chose plum
than banana? _____ fewer children

7. [THINK SMARTER] How many children chose
a fruit that was not a plum?

_____ children

8. [GO DEEPER] Which three fruits were
chosen by a total of 10 children?

_____

🏠 **TAKE HOME ACTIVITY** • Ask your child to explain how to
read the picture graph on this page.

Name _____

✓ Mid-Chapter Checkpoint

Personal Math Trainer
Online Assessment
and Intervention

Concepts and Skills

Use the picture graph to answer the questions. (2.MD.D.10)

Favorite Season									
spring	☺	☺	☺	☺	☺	☺			
summer	☺	☺	☺	☺	☺	☺	☺	☺	
fall	☺	☺	☺	☺					
winter	☺	☺	☺	☺	☺	☺	☺		

Key: Each ☺ stands for 1 child.

1. Which season did the fewest children choose?

_____

2. How many more children chose spring than fall?

_____ more children

3. How many children chose a season that was not winter?

_____ children

4. **THINK SMARTER** How many children chose a favorite season?

_____ children

Draw tally marks to show this number.

_____

© Houghton Mifflin Harcourt Publishing Company

Make Picture Graphs

 COMMON CORE STANDARD—2.MD.D.10
Represent and interpret data.

1. Use the tally chart to complete the picture graph.
Draw a 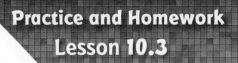 for each child.

Favorite Cookie	
Cookie	Tally
chocolate	|||
oatmeal	|
peanut butter	⊬⊬
shortbread	||||

Favorite Cookie					
chocolate					
oatmeal					
peanut butter					
shortbread					

Key: Each ☺ stands for 1 child.

2. How many children chose chocolate? _____ children

3. How many fewer children chose oatmeal than
peanut butter? _____ fewer children

4. Which cookie did the most children choose?

_____

5. How many children in all chose a favorite cookie? _____ children

6. Look at the picture graph above. Write about the
information shown in this graph.

_____

_____

Lesson Check (2.MD.D.10)

I. Use the picture graph. How many more rainy days were there in April than in May?

Number of Rainy Days					
March					
April					
May					

Key: Each ☂ stands for 1 day.

_____ more rainy days

Spiral Review (2.MD.A.1, 2.MD.C.8)

2. Rita has one $1 bill, 2 quarters, and 3 dimes. What is the total value of Rita's money?

$_____

3. Lucas put 4 quarters and 3 nickels into his coin bank. How much money did Lucas put into his coin bank?

$_____

---

4. Use a centimeter ruler. What is the length of this string to the nearest centimeter?

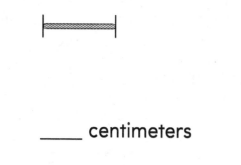

_____ centimeters

5. What is the total value of this group of coins?

_____ ¢ or _____ cents

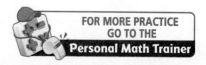
FOR MORE PRACTICE GO TO THE Personal Math Trainer

Name _____

Read Bar Graphs

Essential Question How is a bar graph used to show data?

Common Core **Measurement and Data—2.MD.D.10**

MATHEMATICAL PRACTICES
MP1, MP2, MP6

Listen and Draw

Use the picture graph to solve the problem.
Draw or write to show what you did.

Red Trucks Seen Last Week								
Morgan	■	■	■					
Terrell	■	■	■	■	■	■		
Jazmin	■	■	■	■	■	■	■	■
Carlos	■	■	■	■				

Key: Each ■ **stands for 1 red truck.**

_____ red trucks

Math Talk

MATHEMATICAL PRACTICES I

Describe Relationships
Describe how the data in the graph for Terrell and for Jazmin are different.

FOR THE TEACHER • Read this problem to children. Morgan made a picture graph to show the number of red trucks that she and her friends saw last week. How many red trucks did the four children see last week?

A **bar graph** uses bars to show data.
Look at where the bars end.
This tells how many.

There are
8 children playing
soccer.

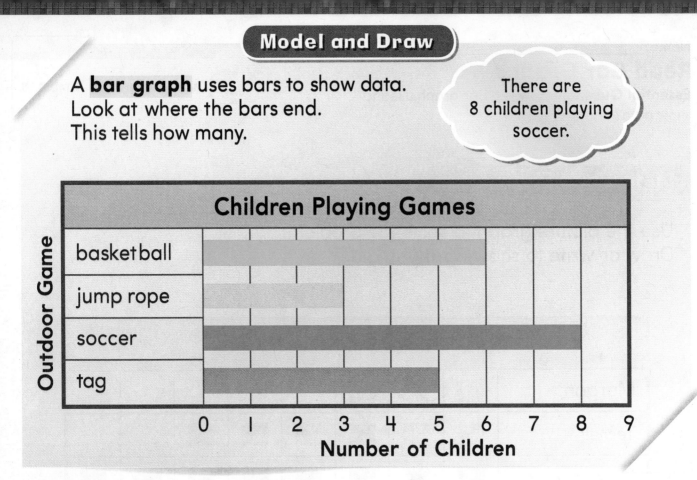

Children Playing Games

Outdoor Game: basketball, jump rope, soccer, tag

Number of Children: 0 1 2 3 4 5 6 7 8 9

Share and Show

Use the bar graph.

1. How many green marbles are in the bag?

   _____ green marbles

✓ 2. How many more blue marbles than purple marbles are in the bag?

   _____ more blue marbles

✓ 3. How many marbles are in the bag?

   _____ marbles

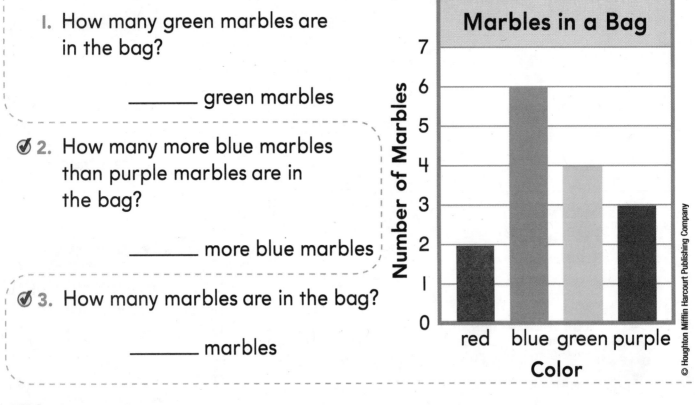

Marbles in a Bag

Number of Marbles: 7 6 5 4 3 2 1 0

Color: red blue green purple

© Houghton Mifflin Harcourt Publishing Company

Name _____

On Your Own

Use the bar graph.

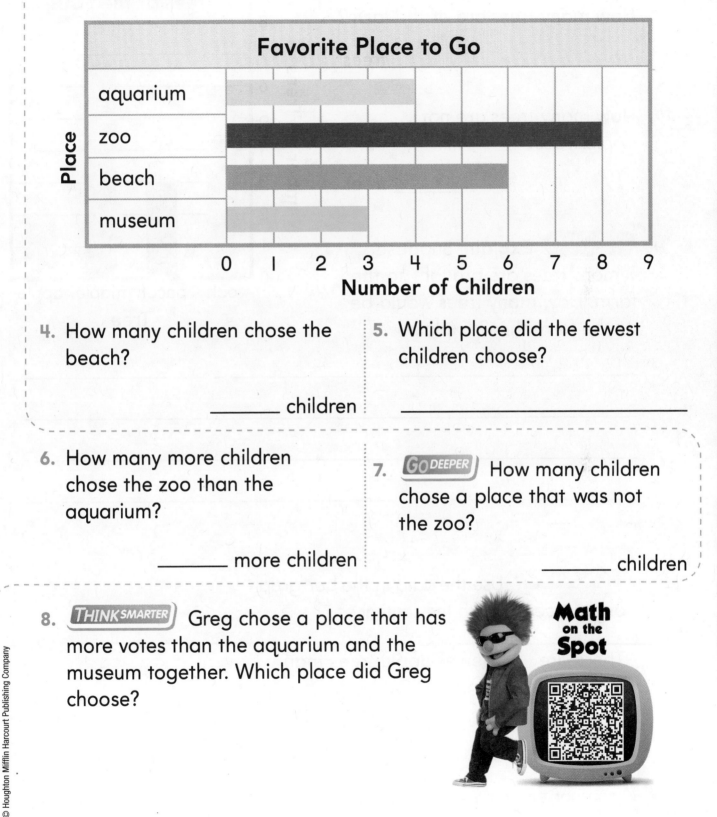

Favorite Place to Go

Place: aquarium, zoo, beach, museum

Number of Children
0 1 2 3 4 5 6 7 8 9

4. How many children chose the beach?

_____ children

5. Which place did the fewest children choose?

_____

6. How many more children chose the zoo than the aquarium?

_____ more children

7. **GO DEEPER** How many children chose a place that was not the zoo?

_____ children

8. **THINK SMARTER** Greg chose a place that has more votes than the aquarium and the museum together. Which place did Greg choose?

Math on the Spot

Problem Solving • Applications (Real World)   WRITE) Math

Use the bar graph.

9. How many trees are at the farm?

   _____ trees

10. How many trees are not
    apple trees?

    _____ trees

11. MATHEMATICAL PRACTICE 6 **Explain** Suppose
    7 more trees are brought to the
    farm. How many trees would be
    at the farm then? Explain.

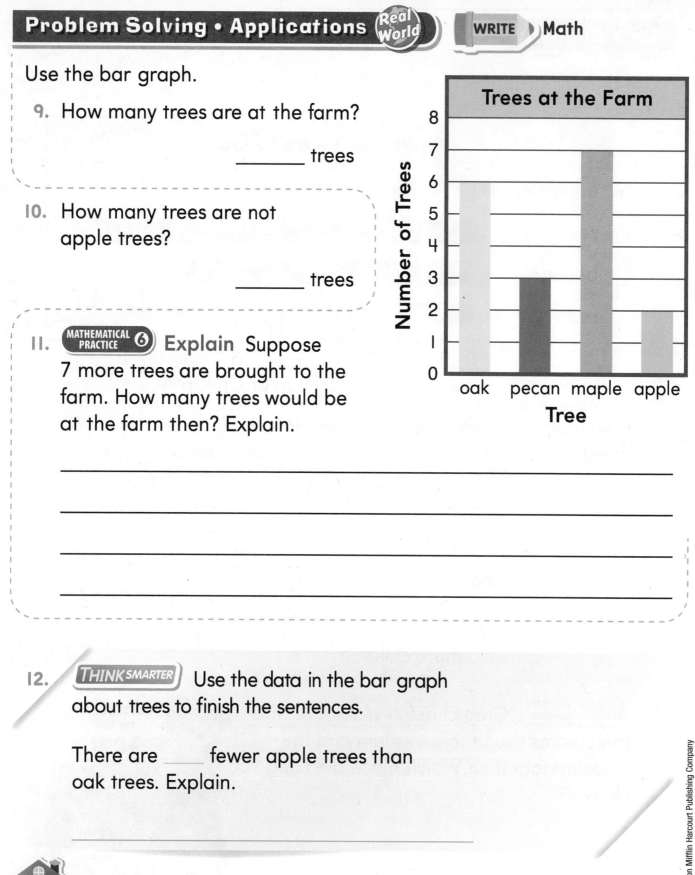

Trees at the Farm

Number of Trees — oak, pecan, maple, apple — Tree

_____

_____

_____

_____

12. THINK SMARTER Use the data in the bar graph
    about trees to finish the sentences.

    There are _____ fewer apple trees than
    oak trees. Explain.

    _____

🏠 **TAKE HOME ACTIVITY** • Ask your child to explain how
to read a bar graph.

Read Bar Graphs

Use the bar graph.

COMMON CORE STANDARD—2.MD.D.10
Represent and interpret data.

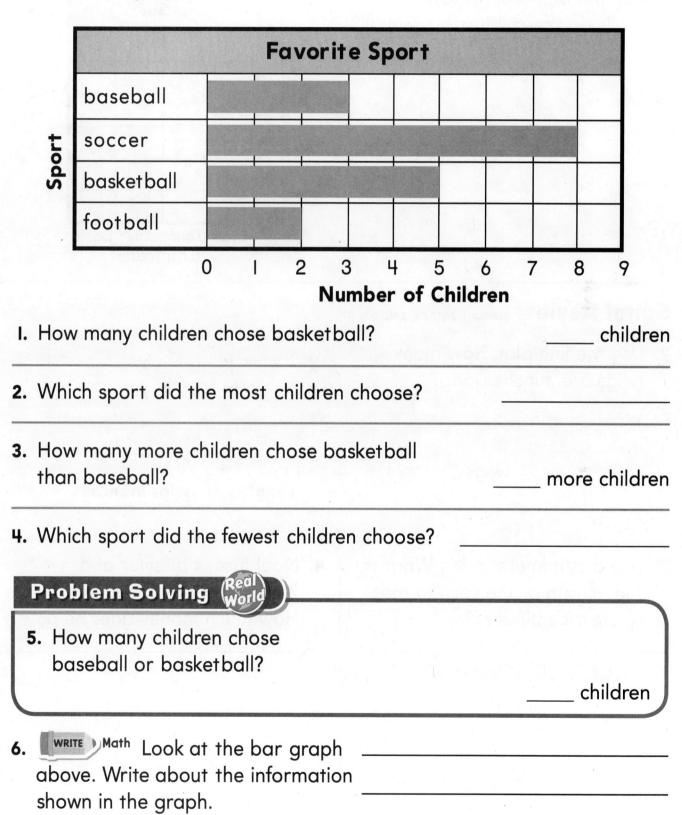

1. How many children chose basketball?   _____ children

_____

2. Which sport did the most children choose?   _____

_____

3. How many more children chose basketball
than baseball?   _____ more children

_____

4. Which sport did the fewest children choose?   _____

Problem Solving Real World

5. How many children chose
baseball or basketball?

_____ children

6. WRITE ▸ Math Look at the bar graph   _____
above. Write about the information
shown in the graph.   _____

_____

Lesson Check (2.MD.D.10)

1. Use the bar graph. How many shells do the children have in all?

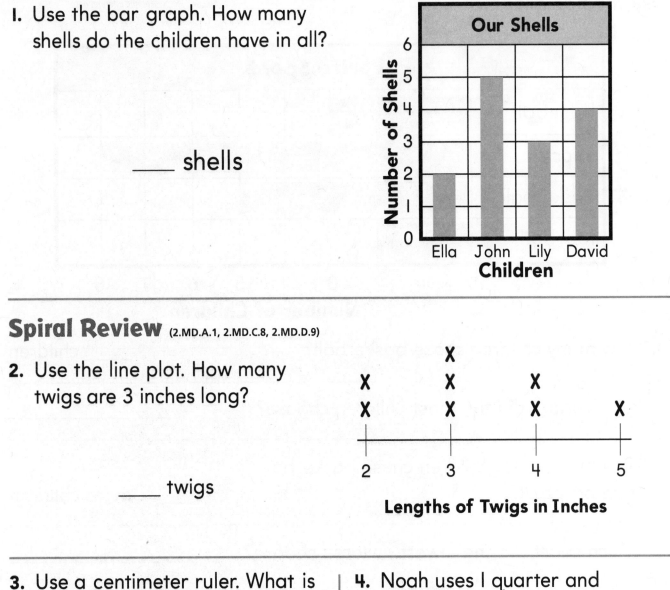

_____ shells

Spiral Review (2.MD.A.1, 2.MD.C.8, 2.MD.D.9)

2. Use the line plot. How many twigs are 3 inches long?

```
                  X
    X             X             X
    X             X             X             X
    +-------------+-------------+-------------+
    2             3             4             5
```

Lengths of Twigs in Inches

_____ twigs

---

3. Use a centimeter ruler. What is the length of the yarn to the nearest centimeter?

_____ centimeters

4. Noah uses 1 quarter and 2 nickels to pay for a pencil. How much money does he pay for the pencil?

_____ ¢ or _____ cents

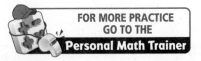

FOR MORE PRACTICE
GO TO THE
Personal Math Trainer

Name _____

Make Bar Graphs

Essential Question How do you make a bar graph to show data?

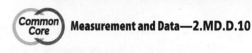

Common Core Measurement and Data—2.MD.D.10

MATHEMATICAL PRACTICES
MP3, MP4, MP6

Listen and Draw (Real World)

Use the bar graph to solve the problem.
Draw or write to show what you did.

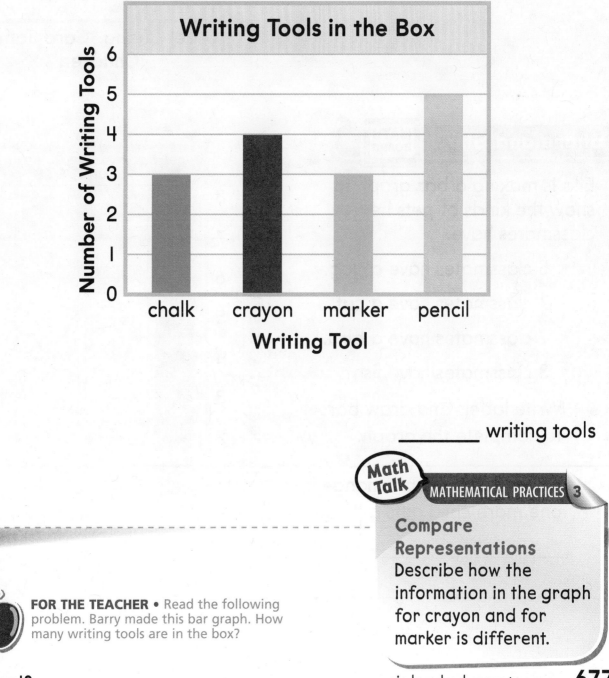

_____ writing tools

Math Talk

MATHEMATICAL PRACTICES **3**

Compare Representations Describe how the information in the graph for crayon and for marker is different.

FOR THE TEACHER • Read the following problem. Barry made this bar graph. How many writing tools are in the box?

© Houghton Mifflin Harcourt Publishing Company

Chapter 10

Model and Draw

Abel read 2 books, Jiang read 4 books, Cara read 1 book, and Jamila read 3 books.

Complete the bar graph to show this data.

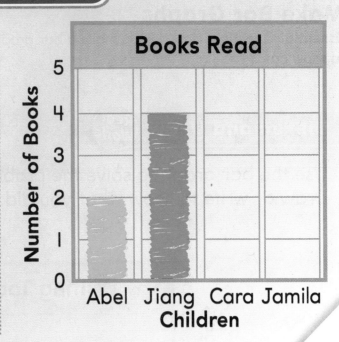

Share and Show

Ella is making a bar graph to show the kinds of pets her classmates have.

- 5 classmates have a dog.
- 7 classmates have a cat.
- 2 classmates have a bird.
- 3 classmates have fish.

☑ 1. Write labels and draw bars to complete the graph.

☑ 2. How will the graph change if one more child gets a bird?

_____

_____

_____

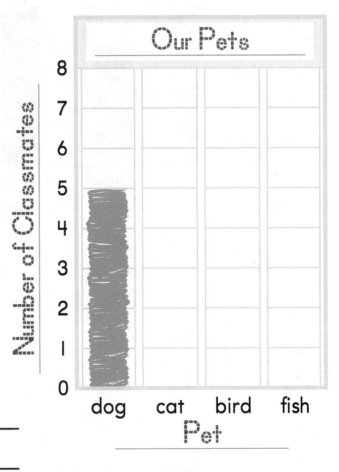

Name _____

Dexter asked his classmates which pizza topping is their favorite.

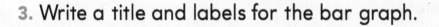

- 4 classmates chose peppers.
- 7 classmates chose meat.
- 5 classmates chose mushrooms.
- 2 classmates chose olives.

3. Write a title and labels for the bar graph.

4. Draw bars in the graph to show the data.

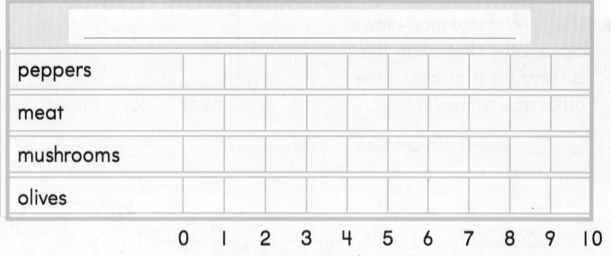

	0	1	2	3	4	5	6	7	8	9	10
peppers											
meat											
mushrooms											
olives											

5. Which topping did the most classmates choose? _____

6. **THINK SMARTER** Did more classmates choose peppers and olives than meat? Explain.

_____

_____

Problem Solving • Applications Real World   WRITE Math

Cody asked his classmates which zoo animal is their favorite.

- 6 classmates chose bear.
- 4 classmates chose lion.
- 7 classmates chose tiger.
- 3 classmates chose zebra.

7. Use the data to complete the bar graph. Write a title and labels. Draw bars.

8. GO DEEPER How many fewer classmates chose lion than classmates that chose the other zoo animals?

_____ fewer classmates

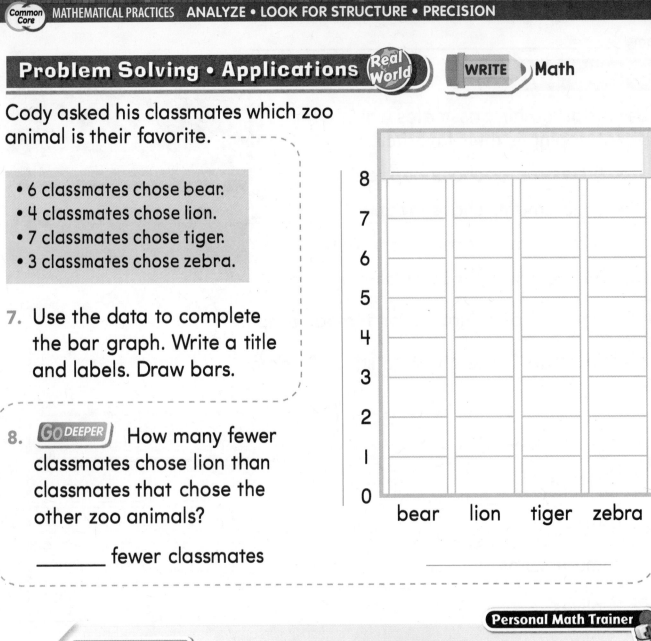

Personal Math Trainer

9. THINK SMARTER ➕ Look at the bar graph above.

Suppose 2 of Cody's classmates chose zebra instead of bear. Explain how the bar graph would change.

_____

_____

_____

 TAKE HOME ACTIVITY • Ask your child to describe how to make a bar graph to show data.

Name _____

Make Bar Graphs

Common Core **COMMON CORE STANDARD—2.MD.D.10**
Represent and interpret data.

Maria asked her friends how many hours they practice soccer each week.

- Jessie practices for 3 hours.
- Victor practices for 2 hours.
- Samantha practices for 5 hours.
- David practices for 6 hours.

1. Write a title and labels for the bar graph.

_____

2. Draw bars in the graph to show the data.

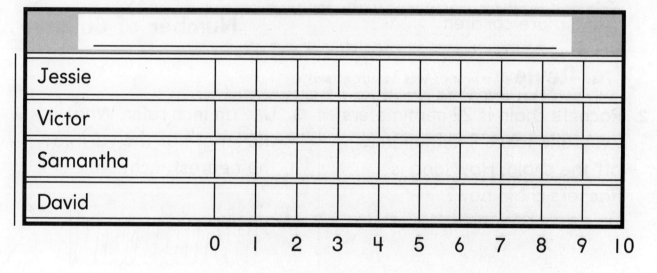

3. Which friend practices soccer for the most hours each week?

_____

Problem Solving (Real World)

4. Which friends practice soccer for fewer than 4 hours each week? _____

5. **WRITE** Math Look at the bar graph above. Describe how you shaded bars to show the data. _____

_____

Lesson Check (2.MD.D.10)

1. Use the bar graph. How many more children chose summer than spring?

Favorite Season

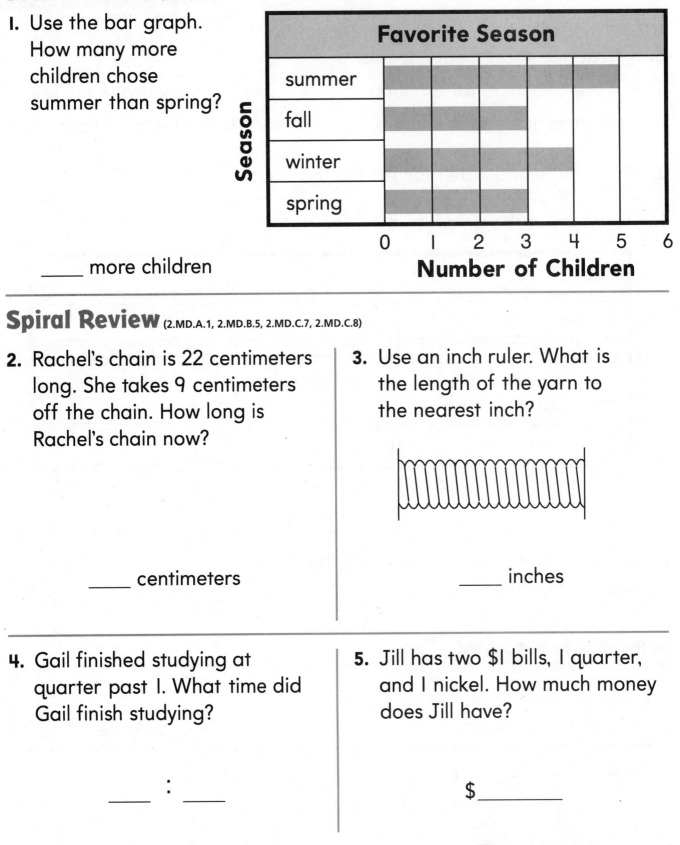

_____ more children

Spiral Review (2.MD.A.1, 2.MD.B.5, 2.MD.C.7, 2.MD.C.8)

2. Rachel's chain is 22 centimeters long. She takes 9 centimeters off the chain. How long is Rachel's chain now?

_____ centimeters

3. Use an inch ruler. What is the length of the yarn to the nearest inch?

_____ inches

4. Gail finished studying at quarter past 1. What time did Gail finish studying?

_____ : _____

5. Jill has two $1 bills, 1 quarter, and 1 nickel. How much money does Jill have?

$ _____

FOR MORE PRACTICE
GO TO THE
Personal Math Trainer

Name _____

Problem Solving • Display Data

Essential Question How does making a bar graph help when solving problems about data?

Common Core **Measurement and Data—2.MD.D.10**
MATHEMATICAL PRACTICES
MP1, MP3, MP4

Maria recorded the rainfall in her town for four months. How did the amount of rainfall change from September to December?

September	4 inches
October	3 inches
November	2 inches
December	1 inch

Unlock the Problem

What do I need to find?

how the amount of ___rainfall___ changed from September to December

What information do I need to use?

the amount of ___rainfall___ in each of the four months

Show how to solve the problem.

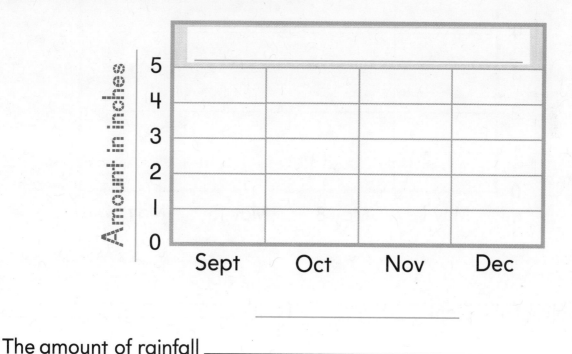

Amount in inches

5
4
3
2
1
0

Sept   Oct   Nov   Dec

The amount of rainfall _____

_____

HOME CONNECTION • Your child made a bar graph to show the data. Making a graph helps your child organize data to solve problems.

Try Another Problem

Make a bar graph to solve the problem.

- What do I need to find?
- What information do I need to use?

I. Matthew measured the height of his plant once a week for four weeks. Describe how the height of the plant changed from May 1 to May 22.

May 1	2 inches
May 8	3 inches
May 15	5 inches
May 22	7 inches

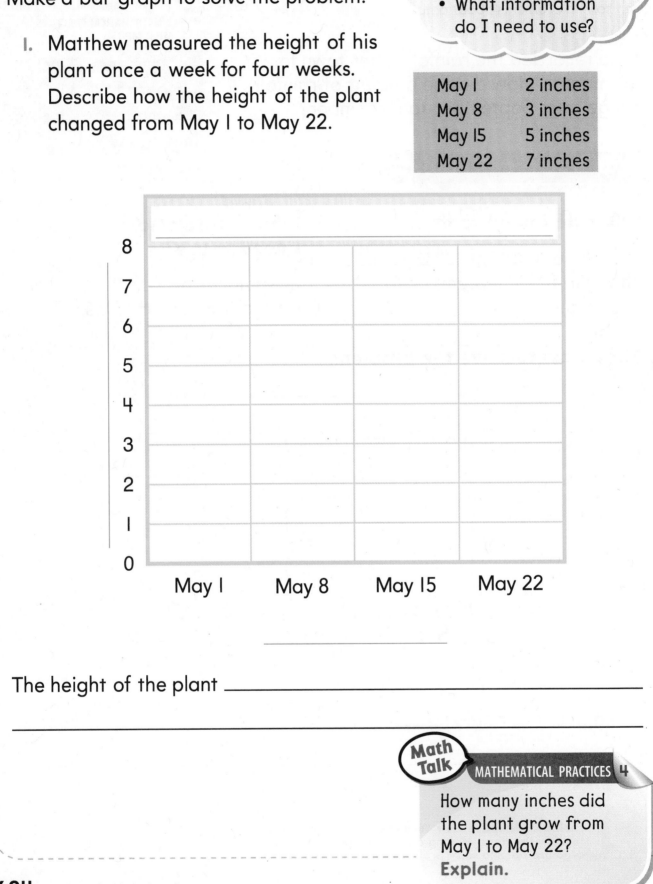

The height of the plant _____

_____

Math Talk MATHEMATICAL PRACTICES 4

How many inches did the plant grow from May 1 to May 22? **Explain.**

Name _____

Make a bar graph to solve the problem.

2. Bianca wrote the number of hours that she practiced playing guitar in June. Describe how the amount of practice time changed from Week 1 to Week 4.

Week 1	1 hour
Week 2	2 hours
Week 3	4 hours
Week 4	5 hours

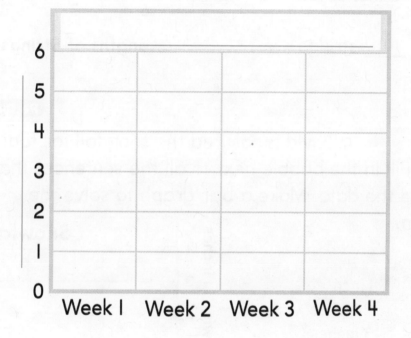

The amount of practice time _____

_____

3. **THINK SMARTER** If Bianca's practice time is 4 hours in Week 5, how does her practice time change from Week 1 to Week 5?

_____

_____

_____

Problem Solving · Applications

WRITE Math

4. How many strings are 9 inches long?

_____ strings

5. GO DEEPER How many strings are more than 6 inches long?

_____ strings

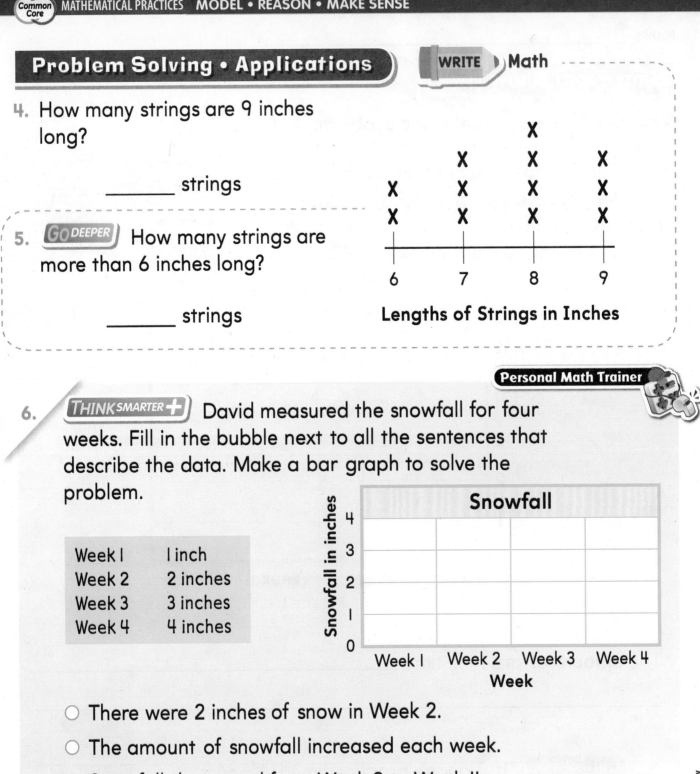

Lengths of Strings in Inches

Personal Math Trainer

6. THINK SMARTER + David measured the snowfall for four weeks. Fill in the bubble next to all the sentences that describe the data. Make a bar graph to solve the problem.

Week 1	1 inch
Week 2	2 inches
Week 3	3 inches
Week 4	4 inches

Snowfall

○ There were 2 inches of snow in Week 2.

○ The amount of snowfall increased each week.

○ Snowfall decreased from Week 3 to Week 4.

○ There were a total of 4 inches of snow in Week 2 and Week 3.

○ There were 3 more inches of snow in Week 4 than in Week 1.

TAKE HOME ACTIVITY · Have your child explain how he or she solved one of the problems in this lesson.

Problem Solving • Display Data

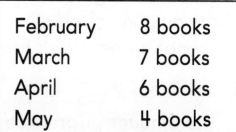

COMMON CORE STANDARD—2.MD.D.10
Represent and interpret data.

Make a bar graph to solve the problem.

1. The list shows the number of books that Abby read each month. Describe how the number of books she read changed from February to May.

February	8 books
March	7 books
April	6 books
May	4 books

	0	1	2	3	4	5	6	7	8	9	10
February											
March											
April											
May											

The number of books read _____

_____

_____

2. How many books in all did Abby read in February and March?   _____ books

3. In which months did Abby read fewer than 7 books?   _____

4. **WRITE** **Math** Explain how you decided where the bar for March should end. _____

_____

Lesson Check (2.MD.D.10)

1. Use the bar graph. Describe how the amount of practice time changed from Week 1 to Week 4.

The amount of practice time

_____

_____

_____

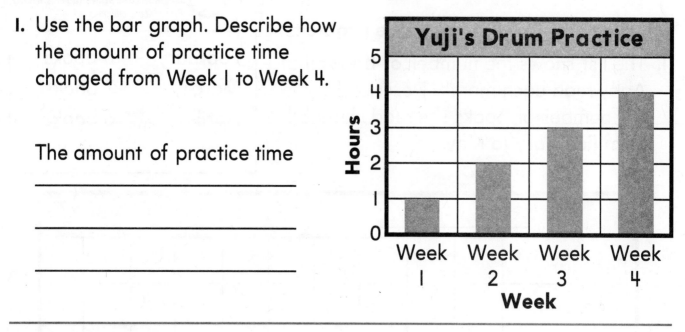

Spiral Review (2.MD.A.3, 2.MD.C.8)

2. The string is about 10 centimeters long.
Circle the best estimate for the length of the feather.

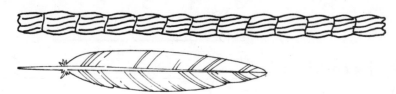

2 centimeters   3 centimeters   7 centimeters

3. What is the total value of this group of coins?

_____ ¢ or _____ cents

4. Rick has one $1 bill, 2 dimes, and 3 pennies. How much money does Rick have?

$_____

© Houghton Mifflin Harcourt Publishing Company

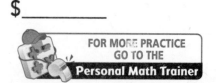

FOR MORE PRACTICE
GO TO THE
Personal Math Trainer

✓ Chapter 10 Review/Test

1. Hara asked her friends to choose their favorite yogurt flavor. Use the data to make a tally chart.

   peach - 3 friends
   berry - 5 friends
   lime - 2 friends
   vanilla - 7 friends

| Favorite Yogurt Flavor ||
Yogurt	Tally
peach	
berry	
lime	
vanilla	

2. Does the sentence describe the data in the tally chart above? Choose Yes or No.

7 friends chose berry and peach together	○ Yes	○ No
More friends chose peach than lime	○ Yes	○ No
More friends chose vanilla than any other flavor.	○ Yes	○ No

3. Hara asked 5 more friends to choose their favorite flavor. 3 friends chose berry and 2 friends chose lime. Do more friends like berry or vanilla now? Explain.

   _____

   _____

   _____

4. Teresa counted the leaves on her plant once a month for four months. Describe how the number of leaves on the plant changed from May I to August I. Make a bar graph to solve the problem.

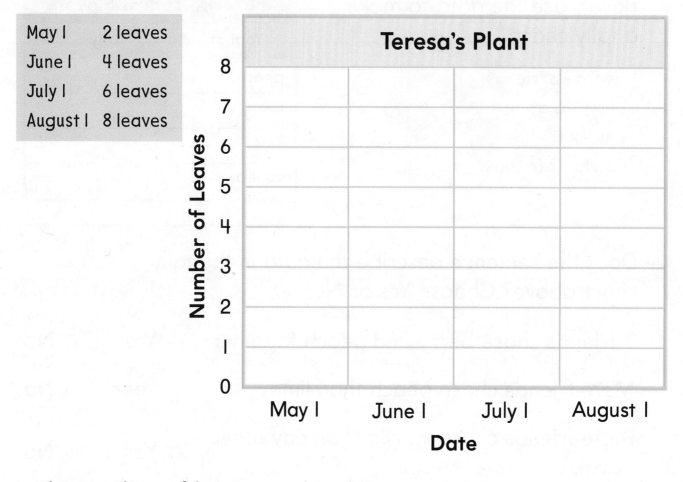

May I	2 leaves
June I	4 leaves
July I	6 leaves
August I	8 leaves

The number of leaves on the plant _____

_____

5. If Teresa counts 9 leaves on September I, how will the number of leaves change from May I to September I?

_____

_____

6. Use the tally chart to complete the picture graph. Draw a ☺ for each child.

Favorite Recess Game	
tag	I
hopscotch	IIHI
kickball	III
jacks	II

Favorite Recess Game				
tag				
hopscotch				
kickball				
jacks				

Key: Each ☺ stands for 1 child.

7. How many children chose hopscotch?

_____ children

8. How many fewer children chose tag than kickball?

_____ fewer children

9. GO DEEPER Which two games were chosen by a total of 4 children?

_____

10. Mr. Sanchez asked the children in his class to name their favorite type of book. Use the data to complete the bar graph.

8 children chose fiction
4 children chose science
6 children chose history
9 children chose poetry

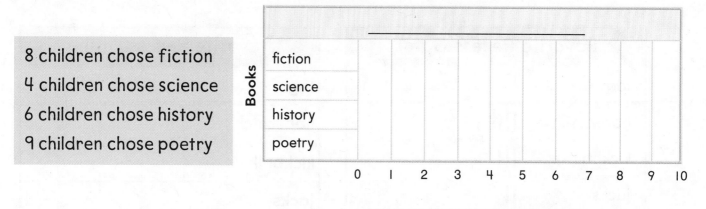

11. THINK SMARTER + Fill in the bubble next to all the sentences that describe the data in the bar graph above.

- ○ 8 children chose fiction.
- ○ Fewer children chose fiction than history.
- ○ 3 more children chose history than science.
- ○ More children chose poetry than any other kind of book.

12. Did more children choose science and history books together than poetry books? Explain.

_____

_____

13. How many children chose a book that is not fiction?

_____ children

© Houghton Mifflin Harcourt Publishing Company

A Farmer's Job

by Tami Morton

Common Core **CRITICAL AREA** Describing and analyzing shapes

A farmer's job is never done. Farmers are busy during all of the seasons of the year. They grow fruits and vegetables for people to eat.
What shapes do you see?

_____

Social Studies

Why is a farmer's work important?

In the spring, farmers get the fields ready.

They plow the fields and fertilize the soil.

They plant their seeds.

What shapes do you see?

Social Studies

How is a farmer's work today different from long ago?

In the summer, farmers take care of their crops. They make sure that the plants have enough water when it does not rain. What shapes do you see?

_____

Social Studies

Why does a farmer need to know about changes in the weather?

In the fall, farmers harvest many fruits and vegetables. They sell most of these fruits and vegetables to other people. What shapes do you see?

_____

Social Studies

Why does a farmer grow more fruits and vegetables than his or her family can eat?

697

In the winter, farmers clear the fields
and get ready for the next season.

They plan what they are going to plant.

They check their machines.

A farmer's job is never done.

What shapes do you see?

_____

Social Studies

Why are the seasons
important to a farmer?

Write About the Story

Look at the pictures of the farm objects. Draw a picture and write your own story about the objects. Tell about the shapes that the objects look like.

Vocabulary Review

cylinder	cube
cone	circle
sphere	triangle
square	rectangle
rectangular prism	

WRITE Math

_____

_____

_____

_____

_____

What shape do you see?

Draw a line to match the shape with the name.

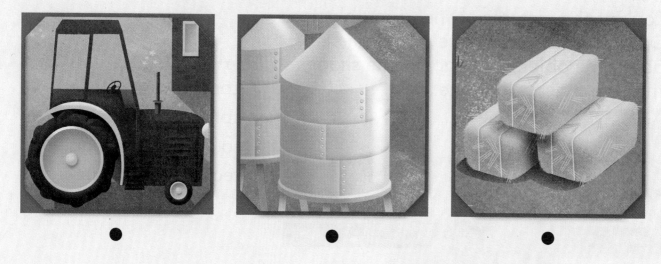

•   •   •

•   •   •

cylinder   rectangular prism   circle

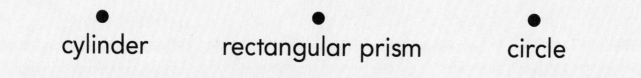

Circle each shape that has a curved surface.

cylinder   rectangular prism

cube   cone

sphere

   Write a riddle about a shape. Ask a classmate to read the riddle and name the shape.

Geometry and Fraction Concepts

Curious about Math

Hot air rises. A balloon filled with hot air will float up into the sky.

Some balloons look as though they have two-dimensional shapes on them. Name some two-dimensional shapes. Then draw some examples of them.

Name_____

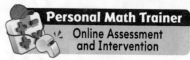
Personal Math Trainer
Online Assessment
and Intervention

Equal Parts

Circle the shape that has two equal parts. (1.G.A.3)

1.

2.

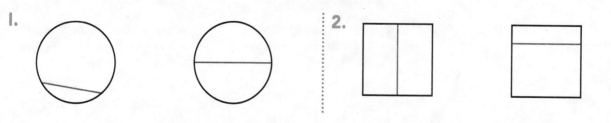

Identify Three-Dimensional Shapes

3. Circle each  . (1.G.A.1)

---

4. Circle each  . (1.G.A.1)

Identify Shapes

Circle all the shapes that match the shape name. (1.G.A.1)

5. triangle

6. rectangle

This page checks understanding of important skills needed
for success in Chapter 11.

Name _____

Review Words
equal parts
shape
rectangle
triangle
square

Vocabulary Builder

Visualize It
Draw pictures to complete the graphic organizer.

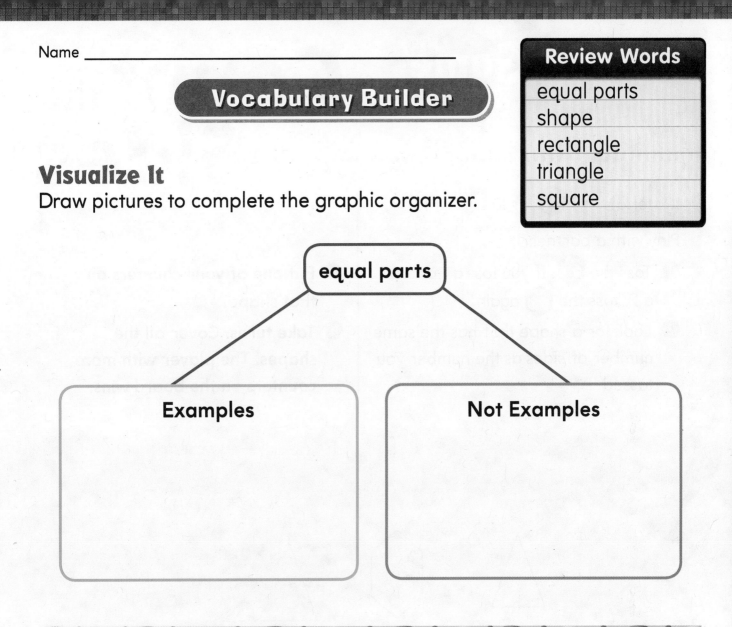

equal parts

Examples

Not Examples

Understand Vocabulary
Draw a **shape** to match the shape name.

rectangle	triangle	square

Game

Count the Sides

Materials • 1 🎲 • 10 ⬤ • 10 ⬤

Play with a partner.

1 Toss the 🎲. If you toss a 1 or a 2, toss the 🎲 again.

2 Look for a shape that has the same number of sides as the number you tossed.

3 Put one of your counters on that shape.

4 Take turns. Cover all the shapes. The player with more counters on the board wins.

Chapter 11 Vocabulary

angle
ángulo
3

cone
cono
9

cube
cubo
10

cylinder
cilindro
11

edge
arista
20

face
cara
23

fourth of
cuarto de
25

fourths
cuartos
26

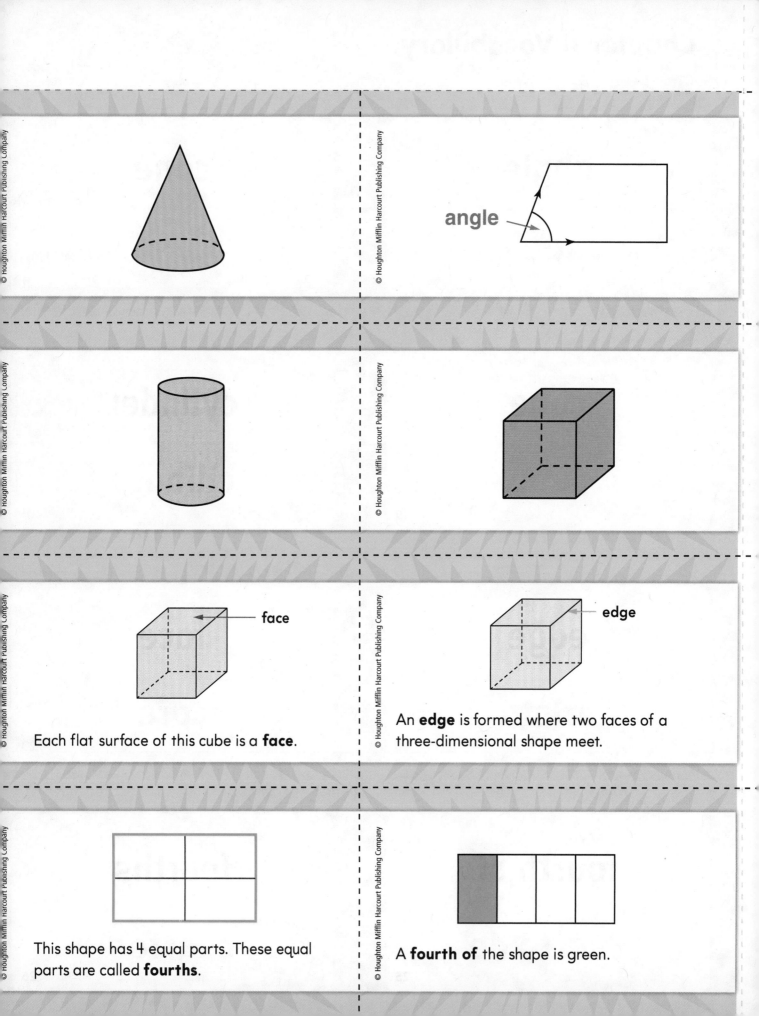

angle

Each flat surface of this cube is a **face**.

An **edge** is formed where two faces of a three-dimensional shape meet.

This shape has 4 equal parts. These equal parts are called **fourths**.

A **fourth of** the shape is green.

half of

mitad de

27

halves

mitades

28

hexagon

hexágono

29

pentagon

pentágono

47

quadrilateral

cuadrilátero

51

quarter of

cuarta parte de

53

rectangular prism

prisma rectangular

55

side

lado

57

This shape has 2 equal parts. These equal parts are called **halves**.

A **half of** the shape is green.

A two-dimensional shape with 5 sides is a **pentagon**.

A two-dimensional shape with 6 sides is a **hexagon**.

A **quarter of** the shape is green.

A two-dimensional shape with 4 sides is a **quadrilateral**.

← side

Triangles have 3 sides.

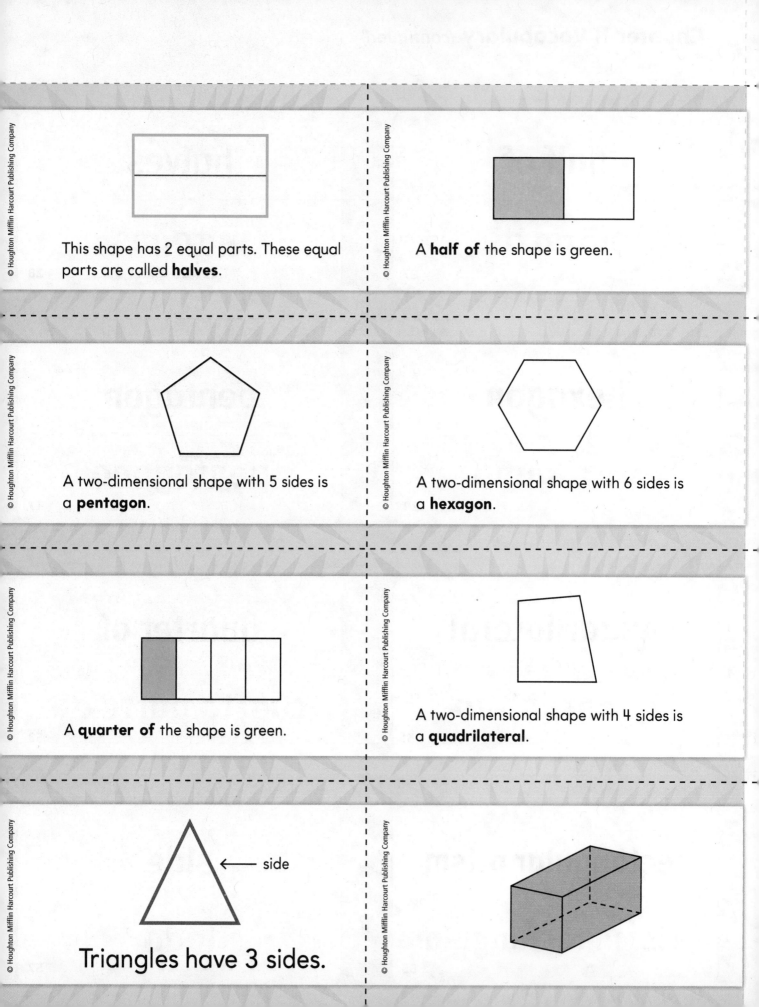

sphere esfera 58	**third of** tercio de 62
thirds tercios 63	**vertex/vertices** vértice/vértices 65

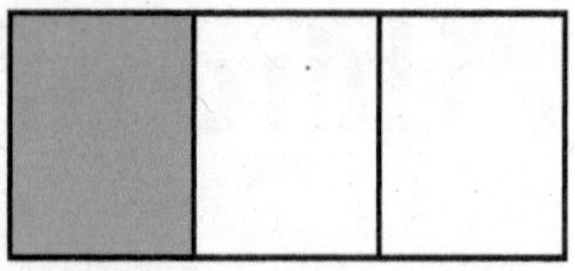

A **third of** the shape is green.

vertex

vertex

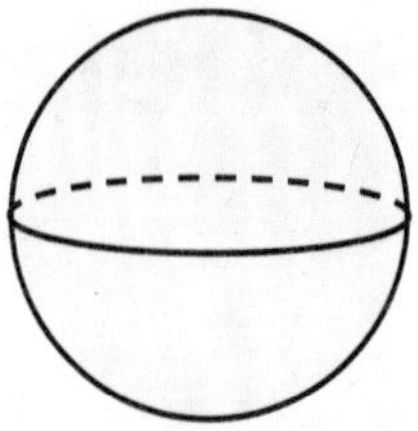

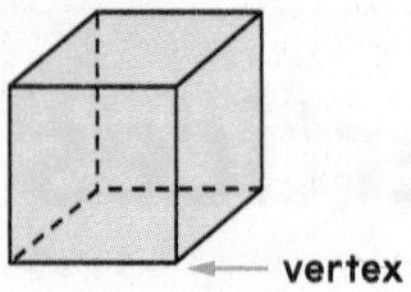

A corner point of a three-dimensional shape is a vertex.

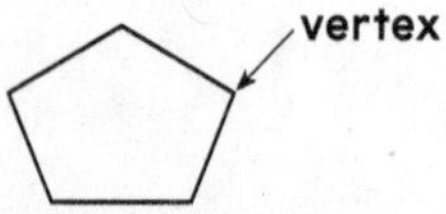

This shape has 5 vertices.

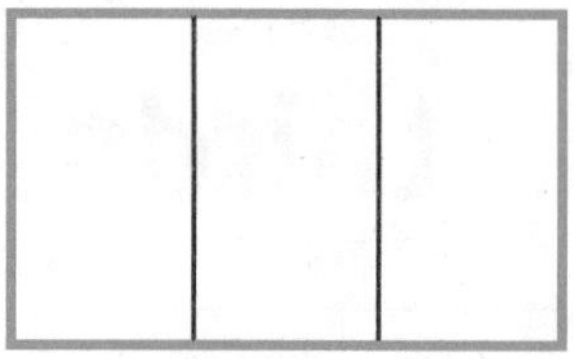

This shape has 3 equal parts. These equal parts are called **thirds**.

Going to a Balloon Race

For 2 players

Materials
- 1 ▣
- 1 ▣
- 1 🎲
- Clue Cards

How to Play

1. Put your ▣ on START.
2. Toss the 🎲, and move that many spaces.
3. If you land on these spaces:

   Blue Space Follow the directions.

   Red Space Take a Clue Card from the pile.

   If you answer the question correctly, keep the card.

   If not, return the card to the bottom of the pile.
4. Collect at least 5 Clue Cards. Move around
   the track as many times as you need to.
5. When you have 5 Clue Cards, follow the closest
   center path to reach FINISH.
6. The first player to reach FINISH wins.

Word Box
- angle
- cone
- cube
- cylinder
- edge
- face
- fourths
- halves
- hexagon
- pentagon
- quadrilateral
- rectangular prism
- side
- thirds
- vertex

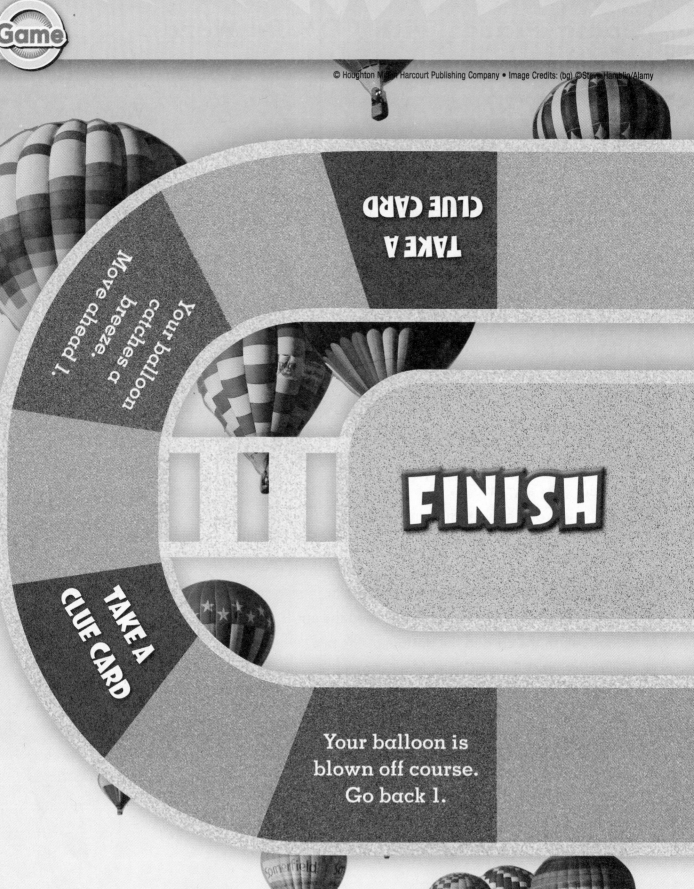

Game

© Houghton Mifflin Harcourt Publishing Company • Image Credits: (bg) ©Steve Hamblin/Alamy

TAKE A
CLUE CARD

Your balloon
catches a
breeze.
Move ahead 1.

TAKE A
CLUE CARD

FINISH

Your balloon is
blown off course.
Go back 1.

Game

TAKE A CLUE CARD

Your balloon is getting too close to the ground. Go back 1.

FINISH

Your balloon has a good launch. Move ahead 1.

TAKE A CLUE CARD

START ▶

The Write Way

Reflect

Choose one idea. Write about it in the space below.

- Draw and write about all of the words. Use a separate piece of paper for your drawings.

    face   edge   vertex

- Choose one of these shapes. Write three things you know about it.

    quadrilateral   pentagon   hexagon

- Explain how you know the difference between halves, thirds, and fourths. Draw pictures on a separate piece of paper if you need to.

Name _____

Three-Dimensional Shapes

Essential Question What objects match three-dimensional shapes?

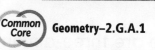
Geometry—2.G.A.1

MATHEMATICAL PRACTICES
MP3, MP6

Draw a picture of an object with the same shape shown.

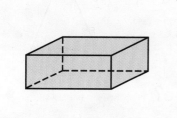

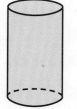

Math Talk

MATHEMATICAL PRACTICES 3

Apply Describe how the shapes are alike. Describe how they are different.

FOR THE TEACHER • Have children look at the first shape and name some real objects that have this shape, such as a cereal box. Have each child draw a picture of a real-life object that has the same shape. Repeat for the second shape.

Chapter 11

Model and Draw

These are three-dimensional shapes.

cube   **rectangular prism**

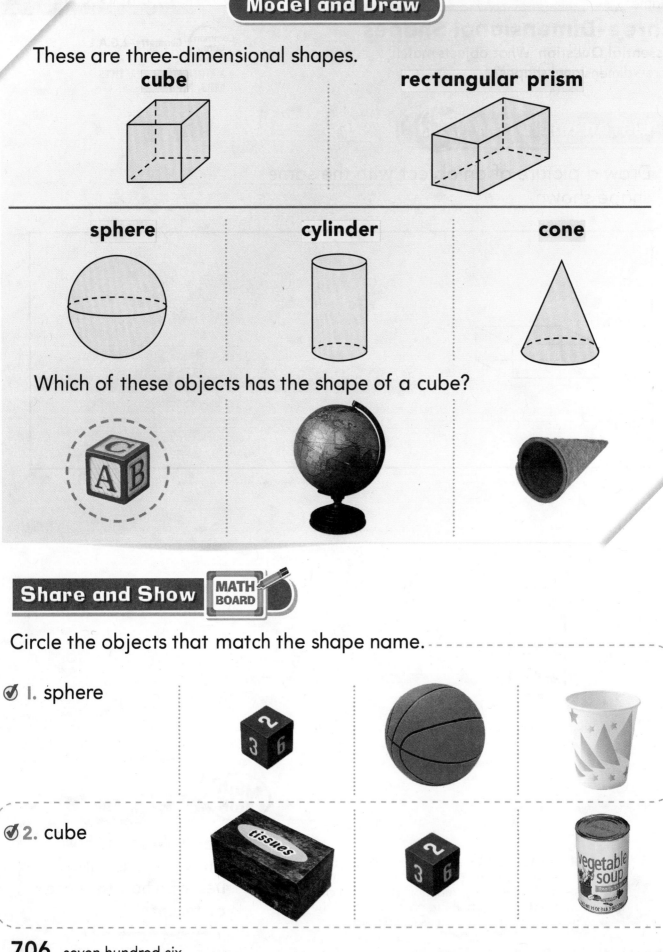

sphere   **cylinder**   **cone**

Which of these objects has the shape of a cube?

Share and Show   MATH BOARD

Circle the objects that match the shape name.

✓ 1. sphere

✓ 2. cube

seven hundred six

Name _____

On Your Own

Circle the objects that match the shape name.

3. cylinder

4. rectangular prism

5. cone

6. GO DEEPER Julio used cardboard
squares as the flat surfaces of a cube.
How many squares did he use?

_____ squares

7. THINK SMARTER Circle the shapes that have a curved surface.
Draw an X on the shapes that do not have a curved surface.

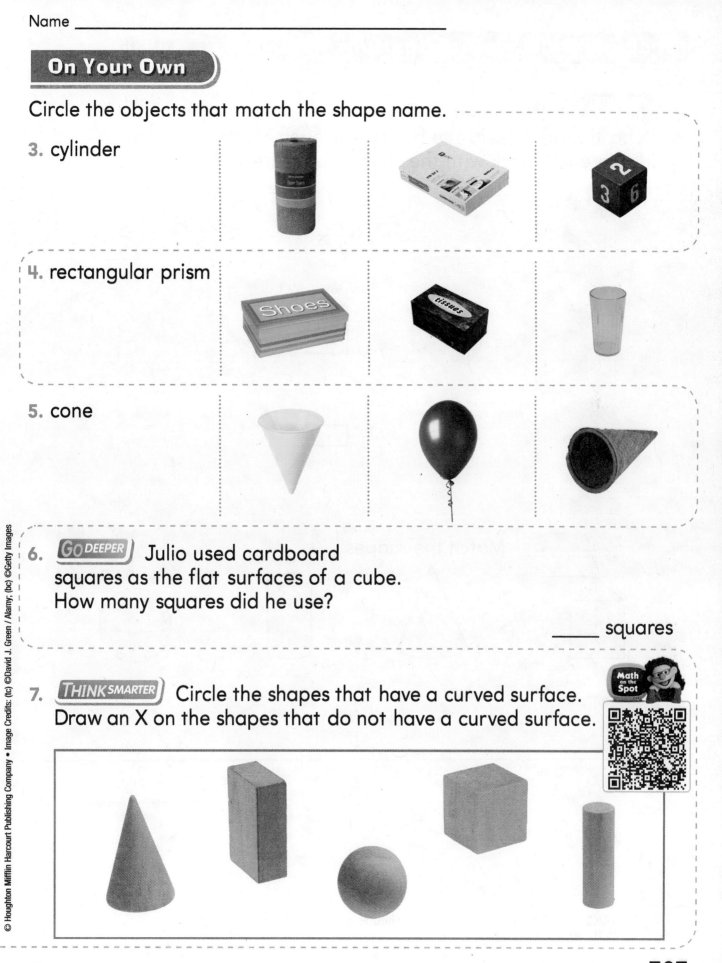

© Houghton Mifflin Harcourt Publishing Company • Image Credits: (tc) ©David J. Green / Alamy; (bc) ©Getty Images

Chapter 11 • Lesson 1

seven hundred seven **707**

Problem Solving • Applications

 WRITE Math

8. **MATHEMATICAL PRACTICE 6** Make Connections

Reba traced around the bottom of each block.
Match each block with the shape Reba drew.

9. THINK SMARTER Match the shapes.

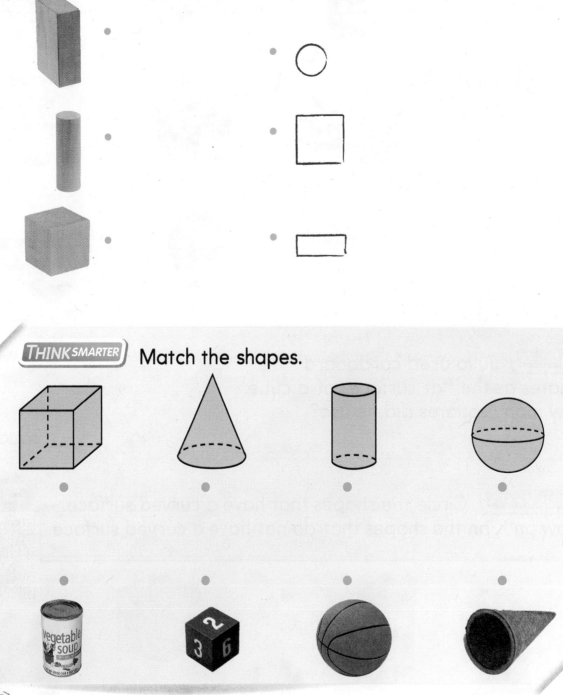

 TAKE HOME ACTIVITY • Ask your child to name an object that has the shape of a cube.

© Houghton Mifflin Harcourt Publishing Company

Three-Dimensional Shapes

Common Core **COMMON CORE STANDARD—2.G.A.1**
Reason with shapes and their attributes.

Circle the objects that match the shape name.

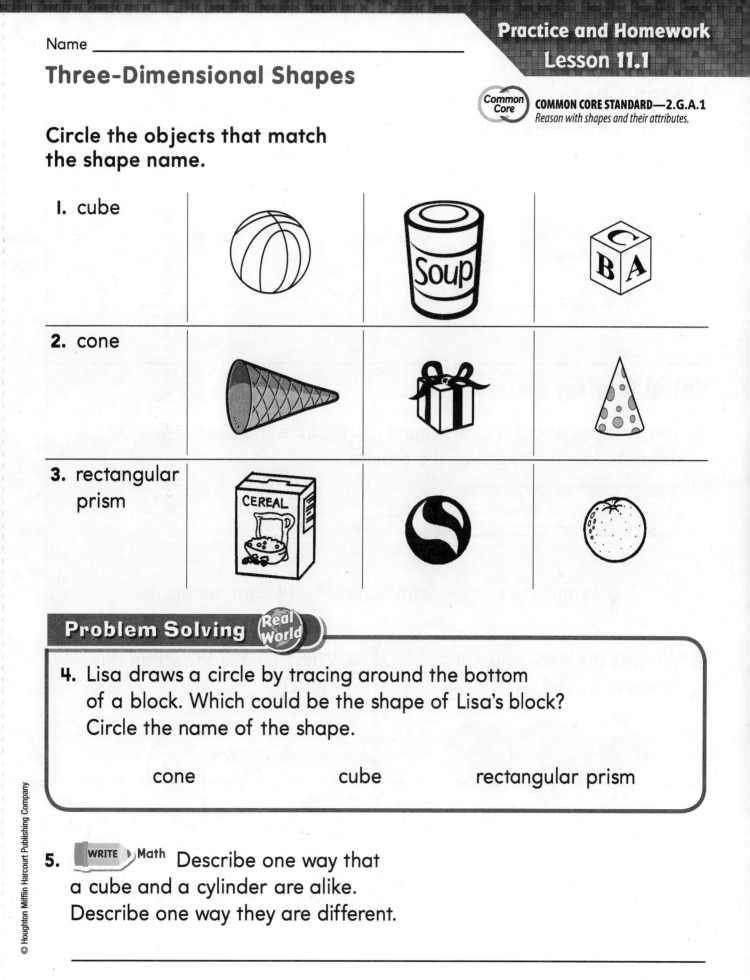

1. cube

2. cone

3. rectangular prism

Problem Solving Real World

4. Lisa draws a circle by tracing around the bottom of a block. Which could be the shape of Lisa's block? Circle the name of the shape.

    cone   cube   rectangular prism

5. WRITE Math Describe one way that a cube and a cylinder are alike. Describe one way they are different.

_____

Lesson Check (2.G.A.1)

1. What is the name of this shape?

_____

2. What is the name of this shape?

_____

Spiral Review (2.MD.A.3, 2.MD.C.7, 2.MD.C.8)

3. The string is about 6 centimeters long. Circle the best estimate for the length of the crayon.

3 centimeters   9 centimeters   14 centimeters

4. What is the total value of this group of coins?

_____

5. What time is shown on this clock?

_____ : _____

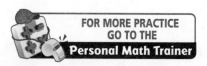

FOR MORE PRACTICE
GO TO THE
Personal Math Trainer

Name _____

Attributes of Three-Dimensional Shapes

Essential Question How would you describe the faces of a rectangular prism and the faces of a cube?

Common Core Geometry—2.G.A.1
MATHEMATICAL PRACTICES
MP1, MP5, MP6

Listen and Draw

Circle the cones. Draw an X on the sphere.

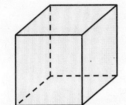
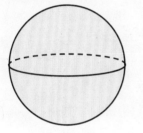

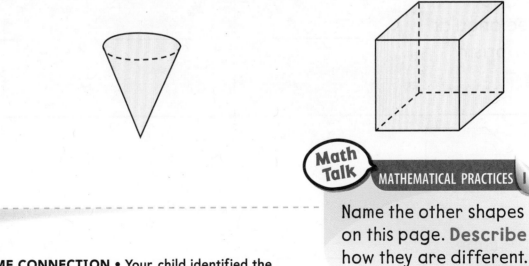

Math Talk MATHEMATICAL PRACTICES ❶

Name the other shapes on this page. **Describe** how they are different.

HOME CONNECTION • Your child identified the shapes on this page to review some of the different kinds of three-dimensional shapes.

Chapter 11

The **faces** of a cube are squares.

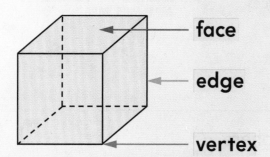

face

edge

vertex

The **vertices** are the corner points of the cube.

Share and Show

Write how many for each.

	faces	edges	vertices

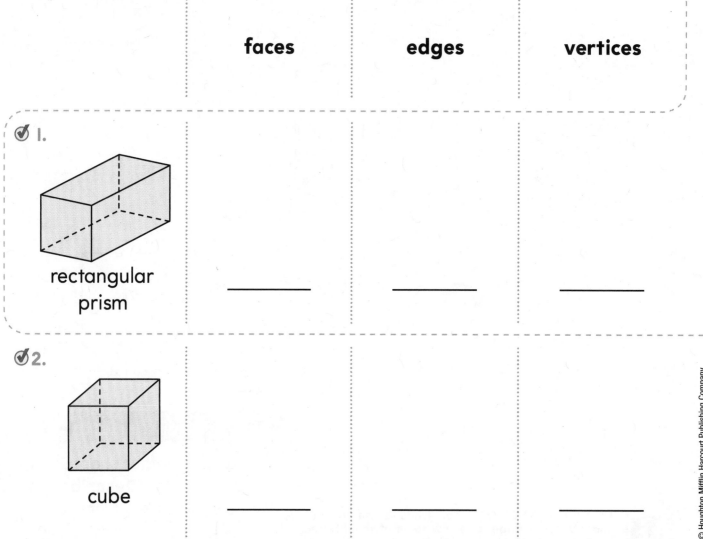

✔ 1.

rectangular prism

_____   _____   _____

✔ 2.

cube

_____   _____   _____

Name _____

3. **GO DEEPER** Use dot paper.
Follow these steps to draw a cube.

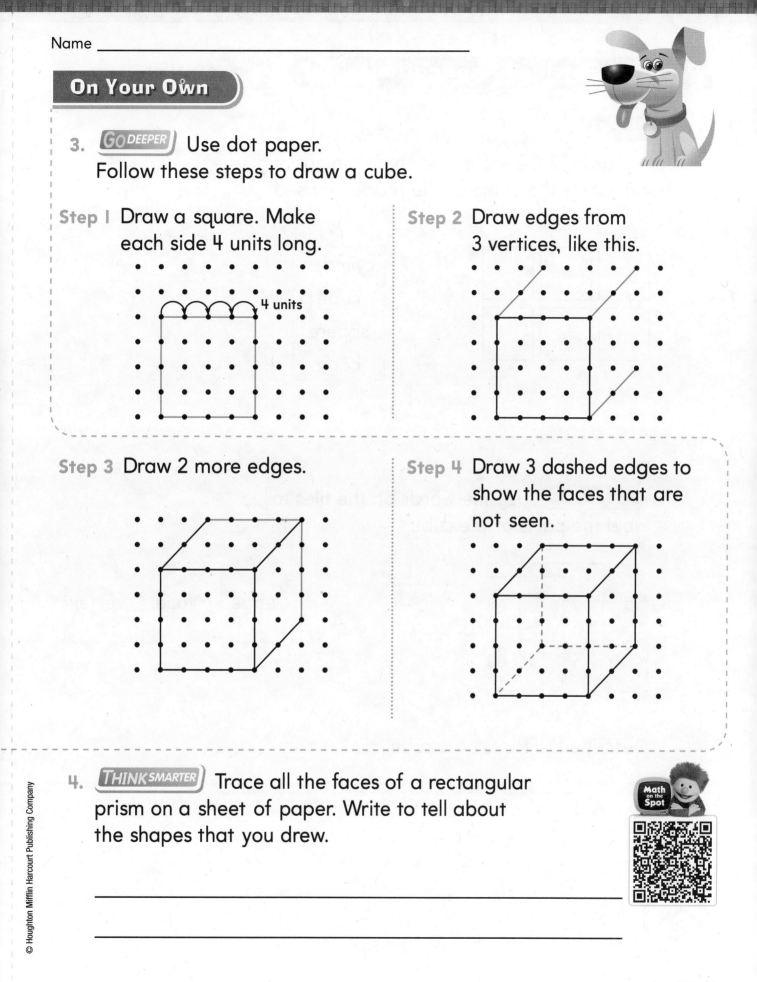

Step 1 Draw a square. Make each side 4 units long.

4 units

Step 2 Draw edges from 3 vertices, like this.

Step 3 Draw 2 more edges.

Step 4 Draw 3 dashed edges to show the faces that are not seen.

4. **THINK SMARTER** Trace all the faces of a rectangular prism on a sheet of paper. Write to tell about the shapes that you drew.

_____

_____

Problem Solving • Applications  WRITE Math

5. **MATHEMATICAL PRACTICE** ⑥ **Make Connections** Marcus traced around the faces of a three-dimensional shape. Circle the name of the shape he used.

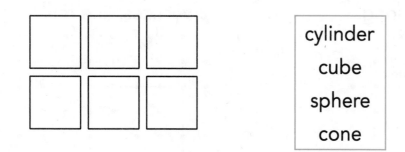

cylinder

cube

sphere

cone

6. **THINK SMARTER** Use the words on the tiles to label the parts of the cube.

edge   face   vertex

_____

_____

_____

Describe the faces of a cube.

_____

_____

TAKE HOME ACTIVITY • Have your child tell you about the faces on a cereal box or another kind of box.

Attributes of Three-Dimensional Shapes

Circle the set of shapes that are the faces of the three-dimensional shape.

Common Core
COMMON CORE STANDARD—2.G.A.1
Reason with shapes and their attributes.

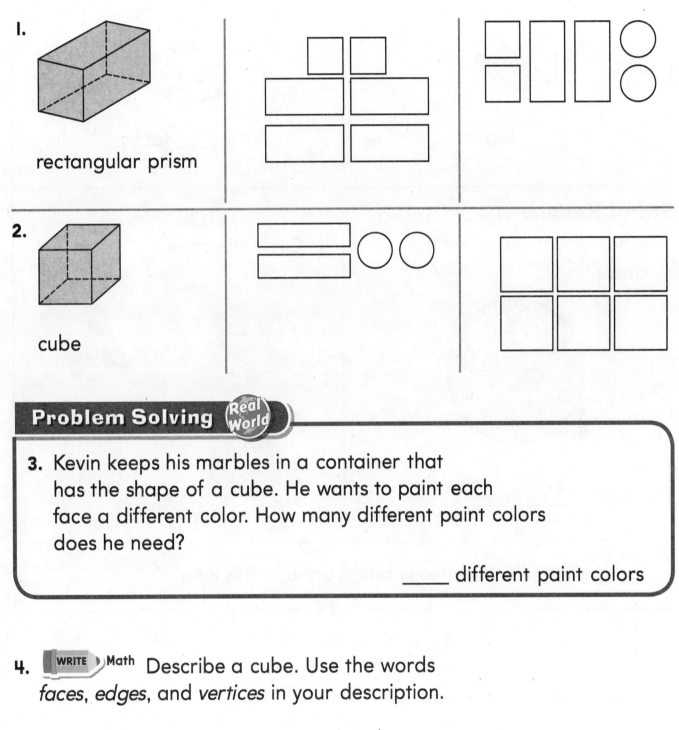

1. rectangular prism

2. cube

Problem Solving • Real World

3. Kevin keeps his marbles in a container that has the shape of a cube. He wants to paint each face a different color. How many different paint colors does he need?

_____ different paint colors

4. **WRITE** Math Describe a cube. Use the words *faces*, *edges*, and *vertices* in your description.

_____

_____

Lesson Check (2.G.A.1)

1. How many faces does a cube have?

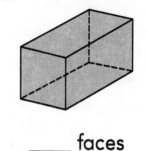

_____ faces

2. How many faces does a rectangular prism have?

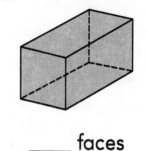

_____ faces

Spiral Review (2.MD.C.7, 2.MD.D.9, 2.G.A.1)

3. What time is shown on this clock?

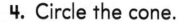

_____ : _____

4. Circle the cone.

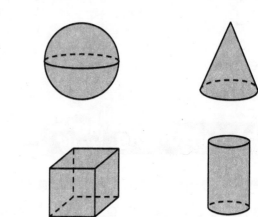

5. Use the line plot. How many books are 8 inches long?

_____ books

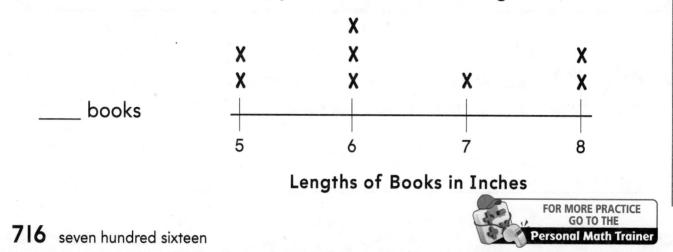

Lengths of Books in Inches

FOR MORE PRACTICE
GO TO THE
Personal Math Trainer

Name _____

Build Three-Dimensional Shapes

Essential Question How can you build a rectangular prism?

Common Core Geometry—2.G.A.1

MATHEMATICAL PRACTICES
MP1, MP3, MP4, MP7

Listen and Draw Real World

Circle the shapes with curved surfaces. Draw an X on the shapes with flat surfaces.

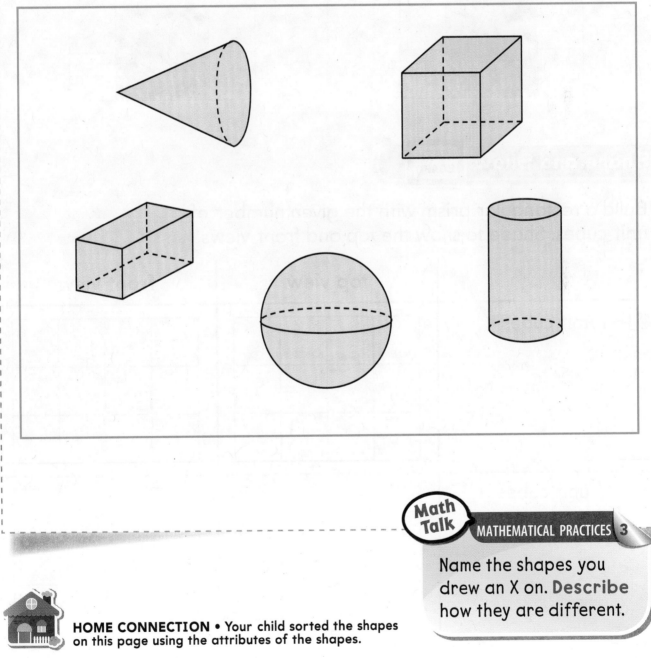

Math Talk MATHEMATICAL PRACTICES 3

Name the shapes you drew an X on. **Describe** how they are different.

HOME CONNECTION • Your child sorted the shapes on this page using the attributes of the shapes.

Model and Draw

Build this rectangular prism
using 12 unit cubes.

The shading shows the top and front views.

top view

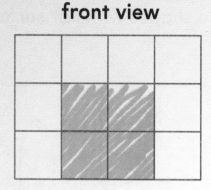

front view

Share and Show MATH BOARD

Build a rectangular prism with the given number of
unit cubes. Shade to show the top and front views.

	top view	front view
✓1. 9 unit cubes		
✓2. 16 unit cubes		

Name _____

Build a rectangular prism with the given number of unit cubes. Shade to show the top and front views.

	top view	**front view**
3. 24 unit cubes		

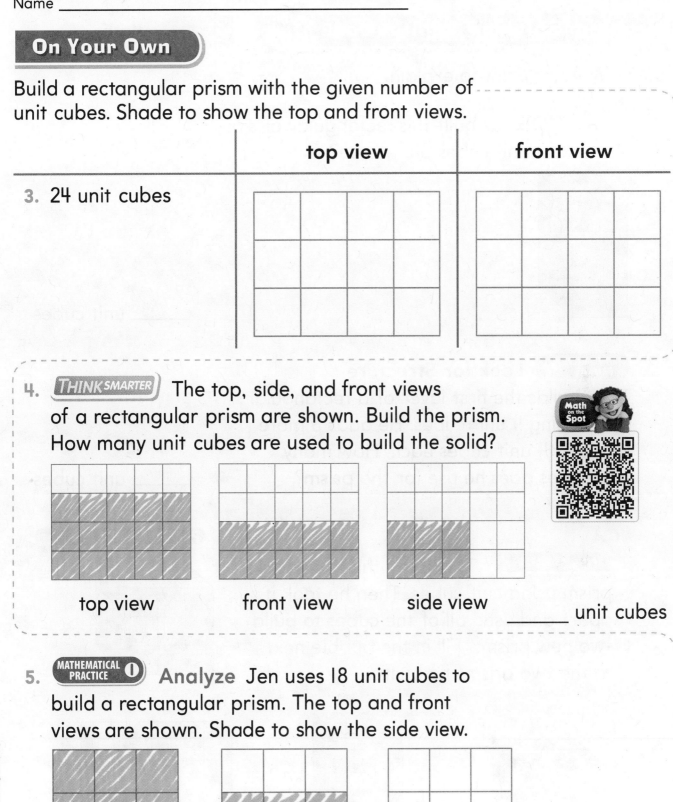

4. **THINK SMARTER** The top, side, and front views of a rectangular prism are shown. Build the prism. How many unit cubes are used to build the solid?

top view   front view   side view

_____ unit cubes

5. **MATHEMATICAL PRACTICE ①** **Analyze** Jen uses 18 unit cubes to build a rectangular prism. The top and front views are shown. Shade to show the side view.

top view   front view   side view

Problem Solving • Applications (Real World)  WRITE Math

Solve. Write or draw to explain.

6. **GO DEEPER** Tomas built this rectangular prism. How many unit cubes did he use?

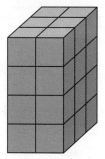

_____ unit cubes

7. **MATHEMATICAL PRACTICE 7** Look for Structure

Theo builds the first layer of a rectangular prism using 4 unit cubes. He adds 3 more layers of 4 unit cubes each. How many unit cubes does he use for the prism?

_____ unit cubes

Personal Math Trainer

8. **THINK SMARTER +** Tyler built this rectangular prism using unit cubes. Then he took it apart and used all of the cubes to build two new prisms. Fill in the bubble next to the two prisms he built.

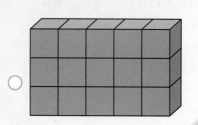

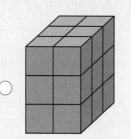

○   ○   ○

 TAKE HOME ACTIVITY • Ask your child to show how he or she solved a problem in the lesson.

Build Three-Dimensional Shapes

Common Core
COMMON CORE STANDARD—2.G.A.1
Reason with shapes and their attributes.

Build a rectangular prism with the given number of unit cubes. Shade to show the top and front views.

	top view	front view
I. 12 unit cubes		

Problem Solving Real World

Solve. Write or draw to explain.

2. Rosie built this rectangular prism. How many unit cubes did she use?

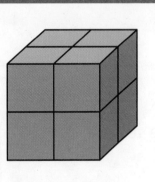

_____ unit cubes

3. **WRITE** Math Build a rectangular prism using cubes. Then, draw in your journal the top, side, and bottom views of your prism.

Lesson Check (2.G.A.1)

1. Milt builds the first layer of a rectangular prism using 3 unit cubes. He adds 2 more layers of 3 unit cubes each. How many unit cubes are used for the prism?

_____ unit cubes

2. Thea builds the first layer of a rectangular prism using 4 unit cubes. Raj adds 4 more layers of 4 unit cubes each. How many unit cubes are used for the prism?

_____ unit cubes

Spiral Review (2.NBT.5, 2.MD.C.7, 2.MD.D.10)

3. Patti's dance class starts at quarter past 4. At what time does her dance class start?

_____ : _____

4. Nicole has 56 beads. Charles has 34 beads. How many more beads does Nicole have than Charles?

_____ more beads

Use the bar graph.

5. Which fruit got the fewest votes?

_____

6. How many more votes did grape get than apple?

_____ more votes

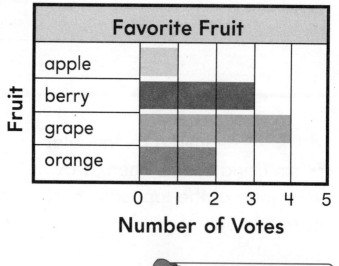

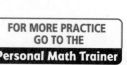

FOR MORE PRACTICE
GO TO THE
Personal Math Trainer

Name _____

Two-Dimensional Shapes

Essential Question What shapes can you name just by knowing the number of sides and vertices?

Common Core Geometry—2.G.A.1

MATHEMATICAL PRACTICES
MP4, MP7

Listen and Draw Hands On

Use a ruler. Draw a shape with 3 straight sides.
Then draw a shape with 4 straight sides.

 FOR THE TEACHER • Have children use rulers as straight edges for drawing the sides of shapes. Have children draw a two-dimensional shape with 3 sides and then a two-dimensional shape with 4 sides.

Math Talk

MATHEMATICAL PRACTICES 7

Describe how your shapes are different from the shapes a classmate drew.

Chapter 11

seven hundred twenty-three **723**

You can count **sides** and **vertices** to name two-dimensional shapes. Look at how many sides and vertices each shape has.

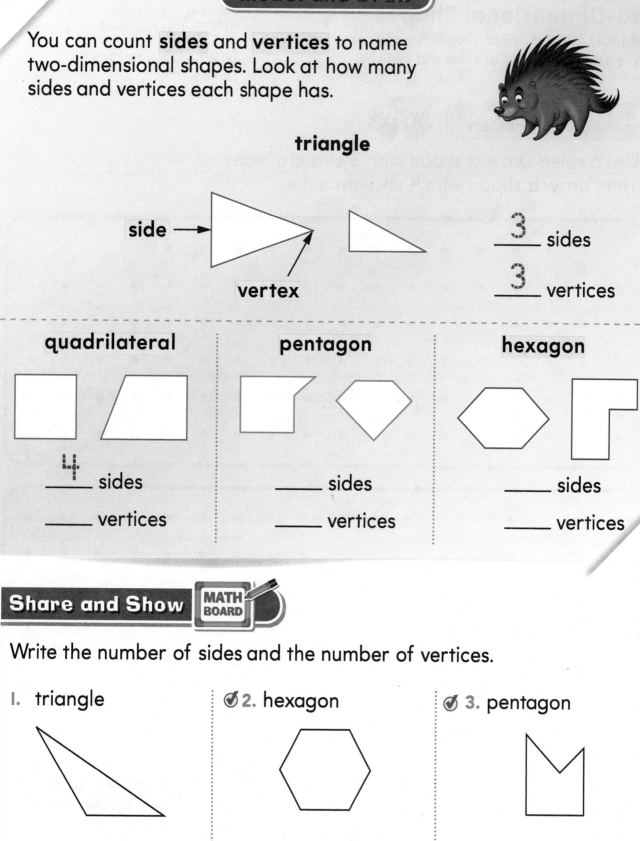

triangle

side ⟶

vertex

_3_ sides

_3_ vertices

quadrilateral

_4_ sides

____ vertices

pentagon

____ sides

____ vertices

hexagon

____ sides

____ vertices

Share and Show MATH BOARD

Write the number of sides and the number of vertices.

1. triangle

____ sides

____ vertices

✓ 2. hexagon

____ sides

____ vertices

✓ 3. pentagon

____ sides

____ vertices

Name _____

On Your Own

Write the number of sides and the number of vertices. Then write the name of the shape.

pentagon
triangle
hexagon
quadrilateral

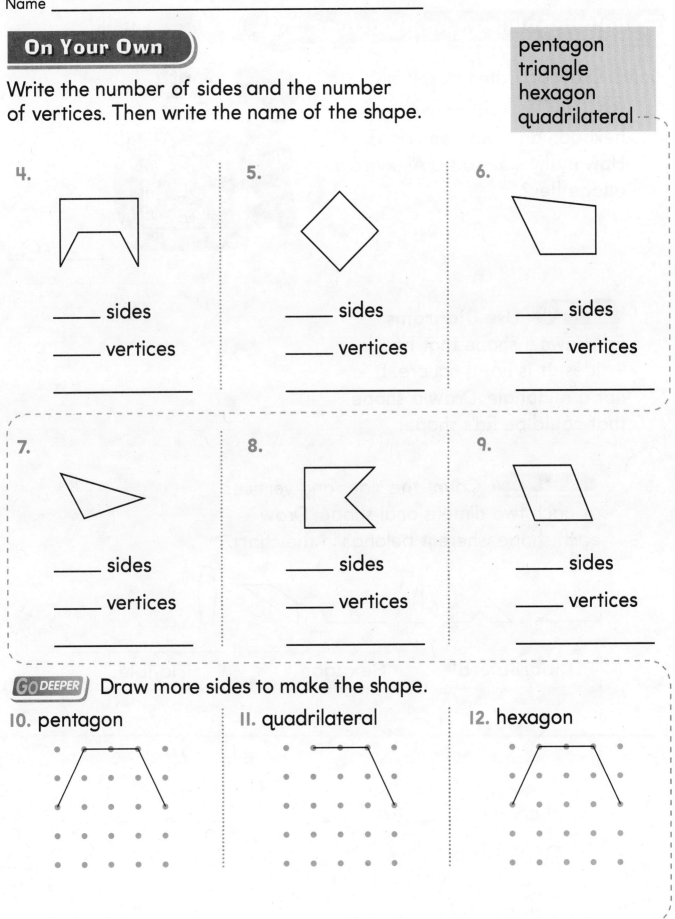

4.

_____ sides

_____ vertices

_____

5.

_____ sides

_____ vertices

_____

6.

_____ sides

_____ vertices

_____

7.

_____ sides

_____ vertices

_____

8.

_____ sides

_____ vertices

_____

9.

_____ sides

_____ vertices

_____

GO DEEPER Draw more sides to make the shape.

10. pentagon

11. quadrilateral

12. hexagon

Problem Solving • Applications (Real World)   WRITE Math

Solve. Draw or write to explain.

13. THINK SMARTER Alex draws a hexagon and two pentagons. How many sides does Alex draw altogether?

Math on the Spot

_____ sides

14. MATHEMATICAL PRACTICE ④ **Use Diagrams**
Ed draws a shape that has 4 sides. It is not a square. It is not a rectangle. Draw a shape that could be Ed's shape.

15. THINK SMARTER Count the sides and vertices of each two-dimensional shape. Draw each shape where it belongs in the chart.

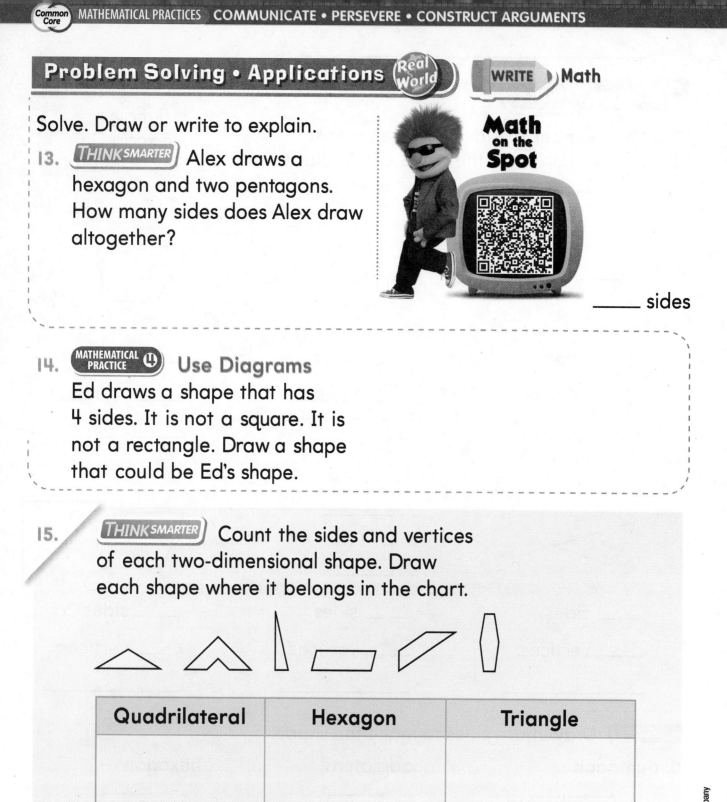

Quadrilateral	Hexagon	Triangle

 TAKE HOME ACTIVITY • Ask your child to draw a shape that is a quadrilateral.

Two-Dimensional Shapes

Common Core

COMMON CORE STANDARD—2.G.A.1
Reason with shapes and their attributes.

Write the number of sides and the number of vertices. Then write the name of the shape.

pentagon   triangle

hexagon   quadrilateral

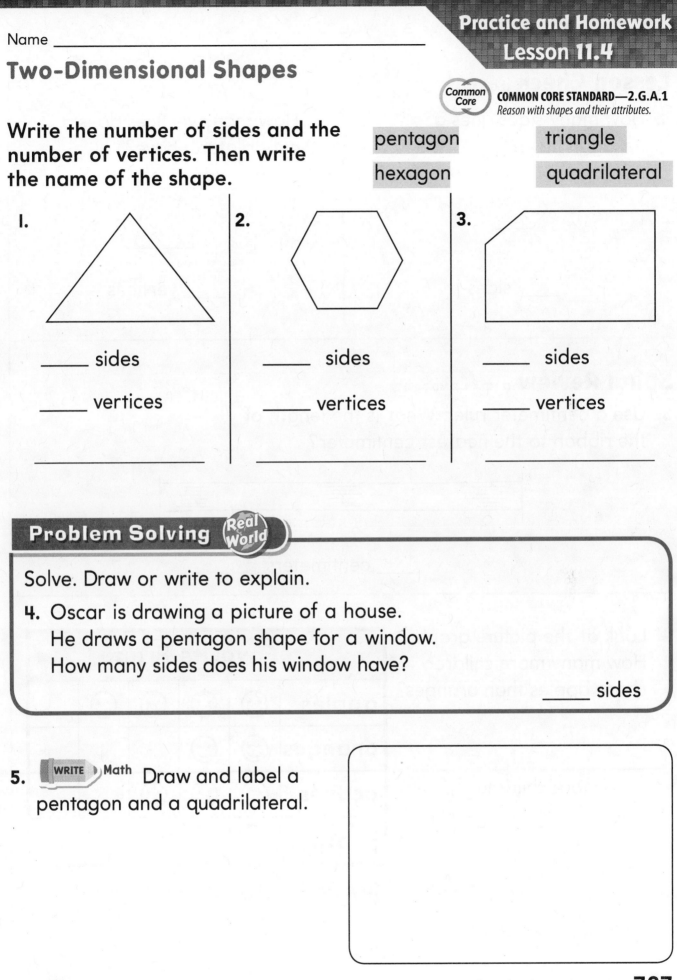

1.

_____ sides

_____ vertices

_____

2.

_____ sides

_____ vertices

_____

3.

_____ sides

_____ vertices

_____

Problem Solving Real World

Solve. Draw or write to explain.

4. Oscar is drawing a picture of a house.
   He draws a pentagon shape for a window.
   How many sides does his window have?

   _____ sides

5. WRITE Math Draw and label a pentagon and a quadrilateral.

Lesson Check (2.G.A.1)

1. How many sides does a hexagon have?

_____ sides

2. How many vertices does a quadrilateral have?

_____ vertices

Spiral Review (2.MD.A.1, 2.MD.D.10)

3. Use a centimeter ruler. What is the length of the ribbon to the nearest centimeter?

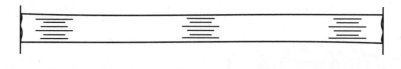

_____ centimeters

4. Look at the picture graph. How many more children chose apples than oranges?

_____ more children

Favorite Fruit				
apples	☺	☺	☺	☺
oranges	☺	☺		
grapes	☺	☺	☺	
peaches	☺	☺		

Key: Each ☺ stands for 1 child.

FOR MORE PRACTICE
GO TO THE
Personal Math Trainer

Name _____

Angles in Two-Dimensional Shapes

Essential Question How do you find and count angles in two-dimensional shapes?

Common Core Geometry—2.G.A.1
MATHEMATICAL PRACTICES
MP1, MP4, MP7

Listen and Draw

Use a ruler. Draw two different triangles. Then draw two different rectangles.

FOR THE TEACHER • Have children use pencils and rulers (or other straight edges) to draw the shapes. Have them draw two different triangles in the green box and two different rectangles in the purple box.

Math Talk

MATHEMATICAL PRACTICES

Describe a triangle and a rectangle. Tell about their sides and vertices.

When two sides of a shape meet, they form an **angle**.

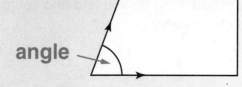

angle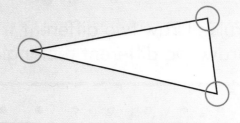

This shape has 3 angles.

Share and Show

Circle the angles in each shape. Write how many.

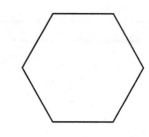

1.

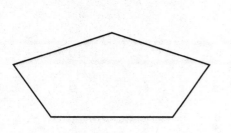

_____ angles

2.

_____ angles

3.

_____ angles

4.

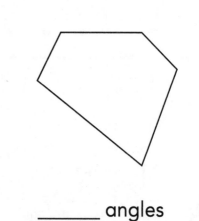

_____ angles

730 seven hundred thirty

Name _____

Circle the angles in each shape. Write how many.

5.

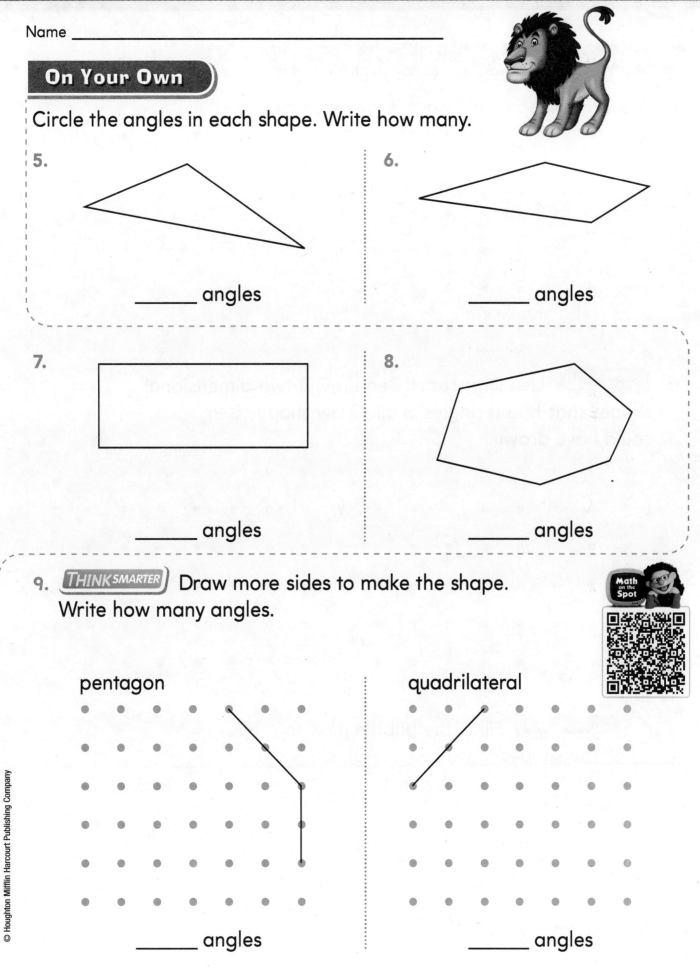

_____ angles

6.

_____ angles

7.

_____ angles

8.

_____ angles

9. THINK SMARTER Draw more sides to make the shape.
Write how many angles.

pentagon

_____ angles

quadrilateral

_____ angles

Problem Solving • Applications (Real World) WRITE ▸ Math

10. Draw two shapes that have 7 angles in all.

11. **MATHEMATICAL PRACTICE ④** Use Diagrams Ben drew 3 two-dimensional shapes that had 11 angles in all. Draw shapes Ben could have drawn.

12. **THINK SMARTER** Fill in the bubble next to all the shapes that have 5 angles.

○ ○ ○ ○

TAKE HOME ACTIVITY • Ask your child to draw a shape with 4 sides and 4 angles.

Angles in Two-Dimensional Shapes

Common Core **COMMON CORE STANDARD—2.G.A.1**
Reason with shapes and their attributes.

**Circle the angles in each shape.
Write how many.**

1.

_____ angles

2.

_____ angles

Problem Solving Real World

3. Logan drew 2 two-dimensional shapes that had
8 angles in all. Draw shapes Logan could have drawn.

4. **WRITE** Math Draw a two-dimensional
shape with 4 angles. Circle the
angles. Write the name of the
two-dimensional shape you drew.

_____

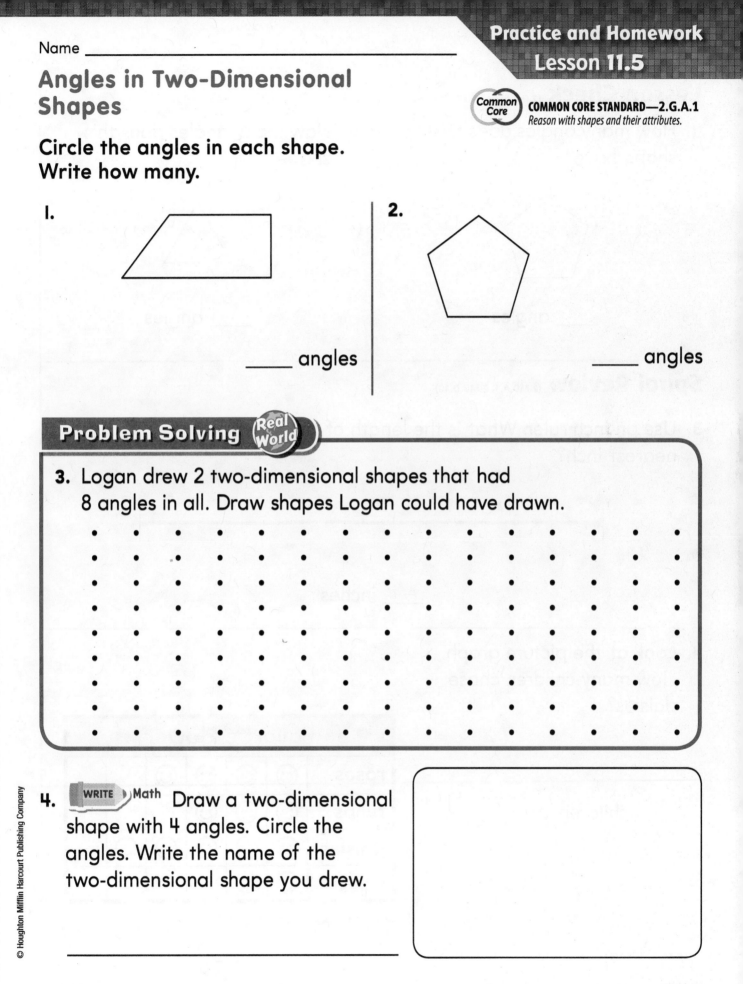

Lesson Check (2.G.A.1)

1. How many angles does this shape have?

____ angles

2. How many angles does this shape have?

____ angles

Spiral Review (2.MD.A.1, 2.MD.D.10)

3. Use an inch ruler. What is the length of the string to the nearest inch?

____ inches

4. Look at the picture graph. How many children chose daisies?

____ children

Favorite Flower					
roses	☺	☺	☺	☺	
tulips	☺	☺	☺		
daisies	☺	☺	☺	☺	☺
lillies	☺	☺			

Key: Each ☺ stands for 1 child.

FOR MORE PRACTICE
GO TO THE
Personal Math Trainer

Name _____

Sort Two-Dimensional Shapes

Essential Question How do you use the number of sides and angles to sort two-dimensional shapes?

Common Core Geometry—2.G.A.1
MATHEMATICAL PRACTICES
MP4, MP6

Listen and Draw Hands On

Make the shape with pattern blocks. Draw and color the blocks you used.

Use one block.

Use two blocks.

Use three blocks.

FOR THE TEACHER • Tell children that the shape shown three times on the page is a trapezoid. Have children use pattern blocks to make the trapezoid three times: with one pattern block, with two pattern blocks, and then with three pattern blocks.

Math Talk

MATHEMATICAL PRACTICES 6

Describe how you could sort the blocks you used.

Which shapes match the rule?

Shapes with more than 3 sides	Shapes with fewer than 5 angles

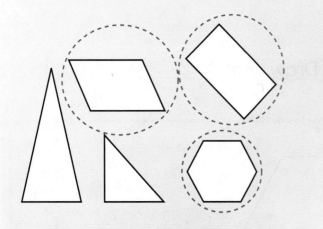

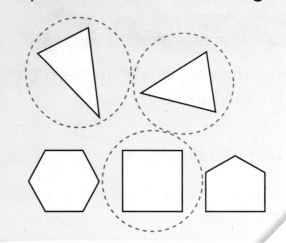

Share and Show  MATH BOARD

Circle the shapes that match the rule.

1. Shapes with 5 sides

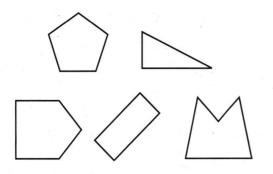

2. Shapes with more than 3 angles

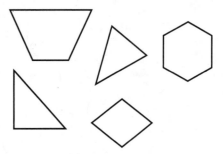

✓3. Shapes with fewer than 4 angles

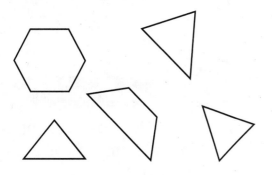

✓4. Shapes with fewer than 5 sides

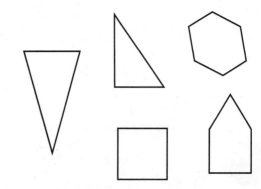

Name _____

Circle the shapes that match the rule.

5. Shapes with 4 sides

6. Shapes with more than 4 angles

7. Shapes with fewer than 4 angles

8. Shapes with fewer than 5 sides

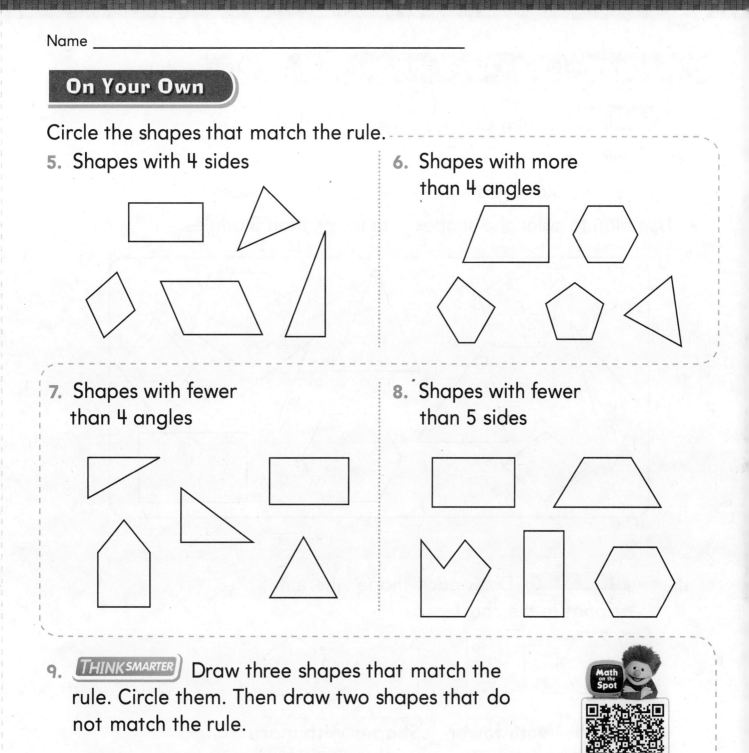

9. **THINK SMARTER** Draw three shapes that match the rule. Circle them. Then draw two shapes that do not match the rule.

Shapes with fewer than 5 angles

Problem Solving • Applications (Real World)   WRITE Math

10. MATHEMATICAL PRACTICE 6   **Make Connections**

Sort the shapes.

* Use red to color the shapes with more than 4 sides.

* Use blue to color the shapes with fewer than 5 angles.

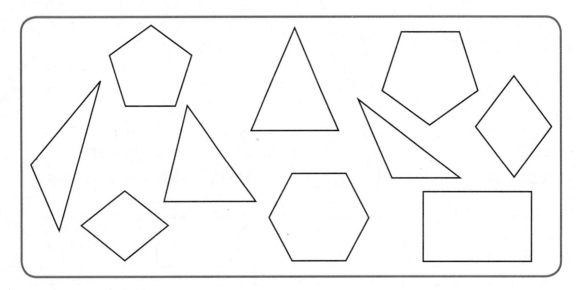

11. THINK SMARTER   Draw each shape where it belongs in the chart.

Shapes with fewer than 5 sides	Shapes with more than 4 sides

TAKE HOME ACTIVITY • Ask your child to draw some shapes that each have 4 angles.

Sort Two-Dimensional Shapes

Common Core **COMMON CORE STANDARD—2.G.A.1**
Reason with shapes and their attributes.

Circle the shapes that match the rule.

1. Shapes with fewer than 5 sides

2. Shapes with more than 4 sides

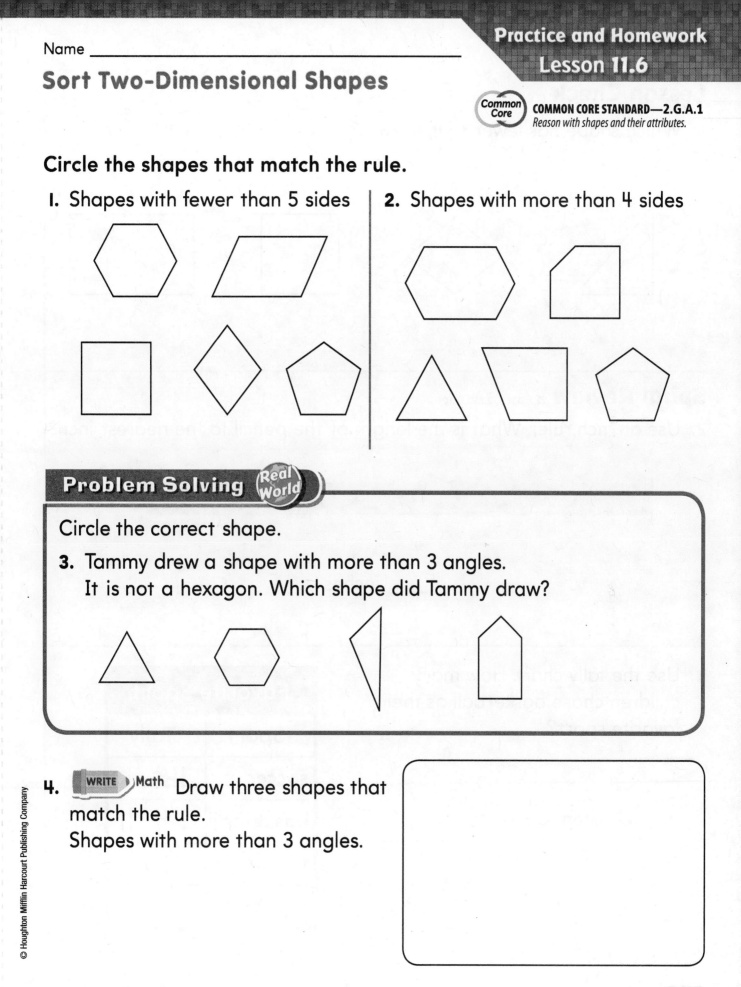

Problem Solving (Real World)

Circle the correct shape.

3. Tammy drew a shape with more than 3 angles.
It is not a hexagon. Which shape did Tammy draw?

4. WRITE Math Draw three shapes that
match the rule.
Shapes with more than 3 angles.

Lesson Check (2.G.A.1)

1. Which shape has fewer than 4 sides?

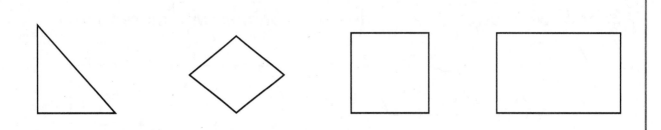

Spiral Review (2.MD.A.1, 2.MD.D.10)

2. Use an inch ruler. What is the length of the pencil to the nearest inch?

_____ inches

---

3. Use the tally chart. How many children chose basketball as their favorite sport?

_____ children

Favorite Sport	
Sport	Tally
soccer	ⱶⱵⱵⱵ
basketball	ⱶⱵⱵⱵ ||
football	||||
baseball	||||

FOR MORE PRACTICE
GO TO THE
Personal Math Trainer

Partition Rectangles

Essential Question How do you find the total number of same-size squares that will cover a rectangle?

Common Core **Geometry—2.G.A.2**
Also 2.OA.C.4
MATHEMATICAL PRACTICES
MP3, MP5, MP8

Listen and Draw

Put several color tiles together. Trace around the shape to draw a two-dimensional shape.

HOME CONNECTION • After putting together tiles, your child traced around them to draw a two-dimensional shape. This activity is an introduction to partitioning a rectangle into several same-size squares.

Math Talk MATHEMATICAL PRACTICES ③

Is there a different shape that can be made with the same number of tiles? **Explain.**

Trace around color tiles. How many square tiles cover this rectangle?

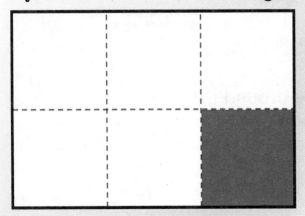

Number of rows: _2_

Number of columns: _3_

Total: _____ square tiles

Share and Show

Use color tiles to cover the rectangle.
Trace around the square tiles. Write how many.

1.

Number of rows: _____

Number of columns: _____

Total: _____ square tiles

2.

Number of rows: _____

Number of columns: _____

Total: _____ square tiles

Name _____

Use color tiles to cover the rectangle.
Trace around the square tiles. Write how many.

3.

Number of rows: _____

Number of columns: _____

Total: _____ square tiles

4.

Number of rows: _____

Number of columns: _____

Total: _____ square tiles

5. **THINK SMARTER** Mary started to
cover this rectangle with ones blocks.
Explain how you would estimate
the number of ones blocks that
would cover the whole rectangle.

_____

_____

_____

TAKE HOME ACTIVITY • Have your child describe what
he or she did in this lesson.

Name _____

✓ Mid-Chapter Checkpoint

Personal Math Trainer
Online Assessment
and Intervention

Concepts and Skills

Circle the objects that match the shape name. (2.G.A.1)

1. cylinder				

2. cube				

Write the number of sides and the number of vertices. (2.G.A.1)

3. quadrilateral

____ sides

____ vertices

4. pentagon

____ sides

____ vertices

5. hexagon

____ sides

____ vertices

6. **THINK SMARTER** How many angles does this shape have? (2.G.A.1)

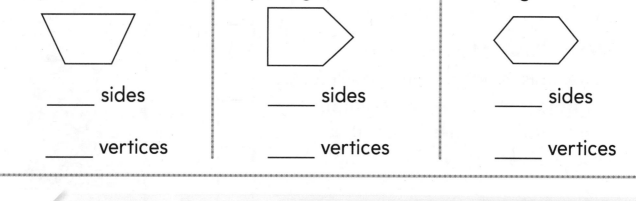

____ angles

© Houghton Mifflin Harcourt Publishing Company • Image Credits: (tcr) ©David J. Green / Alamy; (bcl) ©Getty Images/PhotoDisc

Name _____

Partition Rectangles

Use color tiles to cover the rectangle.
Trace around the square tiles.
Write how many.

Common Core **COMMON CORE STANDARD—2.G.A.2**
Reason with shapes and their attributes.

1.

Number of rows: _____

Number of columns: _____

Total: _____ square tiles

2.

Number of rows: _____

Number of columns: _____

Total: _____ square tiles

Problem Solving *Real World*

Solve. Write or draw to explain.

3. Nina wants to put color tiles on a square. 3 color tiles fit across the top of the square. How many rows and columns of tiles will Nina need? How many square tiles will she use in all?

Number of rows: _____

Number of columns: _____

Total: _____ square tiles

4. WRITE Math Look at Exercise 1 above. Is there a different rectangle that you could cover with 6 color tiles? Explain.

_____

Lesson Check (2.G.A.2)

I. Gina uses color tiles to cover the rectangle. How many square tiles does she use?

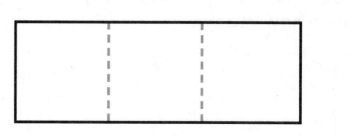

_____ square tiles

Spiral Review (2.MD.D.10, 2.G.A.1)

2. How many faces does a cube have?

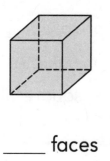

_____ faces

3. How many angles does this shape have?

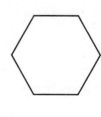

_____ angles

4. Use the tally chart. How many more children chose art than reading?

_____ more children

Favorite Subject	
Subject	Tally
reading	IIII III
math	IIII IIII
science	IIII
art	IIII IIII

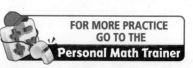

FOR MORE PRACTICE
GO TO THE
Personal Math Trainer

Name _____

Equal Parts

Essential Question What are halves, thirds, and fourths of a whole?

Common Core   Geometry—2.G.A.3

MATHEMATICAL PRACTICES
MP3, MP6, MP8

Listen and Draw

Put pattern blocks together to match the shape of the hexagon. Trace the shape you made.

FOR THE TEACHER • Have children place a yellow hexagon pattern block on the workspace and make the same shape by using any combination of pattern blocks. Discuss how they know if the outline of the blocks they used is the same shape as the yellow hexagon.

MATHEMATICAL PRACTICES 3

Compare models
Describe how the shapes you used are different from the shapes a classmate used.

Model and Draw

The green rectangle is the whole.
It can be divided into equal parts.

There are 2 halves.
Each part is a half.

There are 3 thirds.
Each part is a third.

There are 4 fourths.
Each part is a fourth.

Share and Show MATH BOARD

Write how many equal parts there are in the whole.
Write **halves**, **thirds**, or **fourths** to name the equal parts.

1.

_____ equal parts

_____

2.

_____ equal parts

_____

3.

_____ equal parts

_____

4.

_____ equal parts

_____

☑ 5.

_____ equal parts

_____

☑ 6.

_____ equal parts

_____

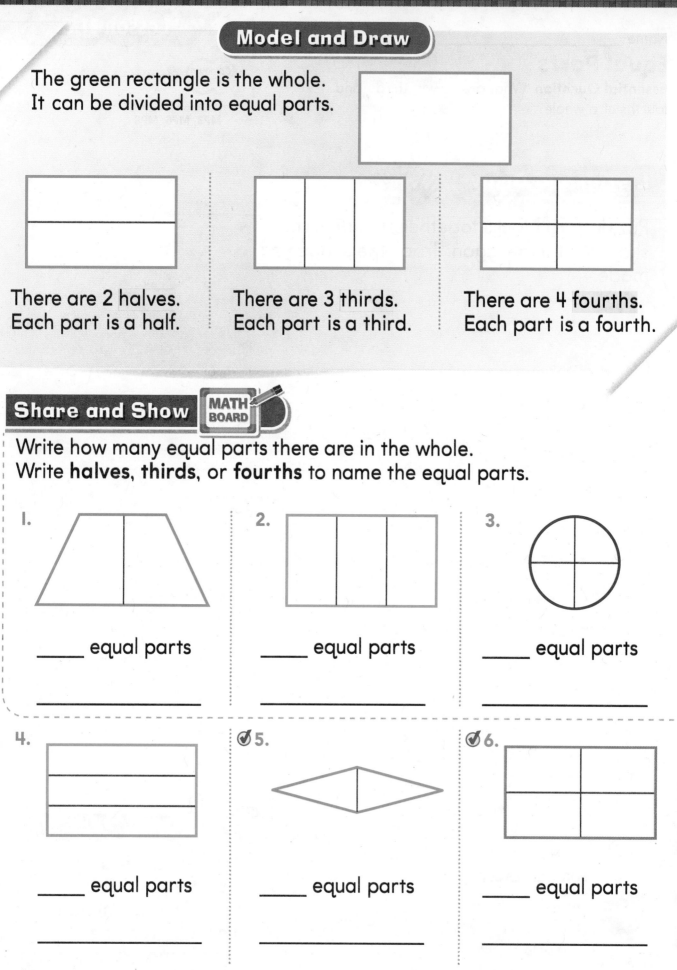

Name _____

Write how many equal parts there are in the whole.
Write **halves**, **thirds**, or **fourths** to name the equal parts.

7.

____ equal parts

_____

8.

____ equal parts

_____

9.

____ equal parts

_____

10.

____ equal parts

_____

11.

____ equal parts

_____

12.

____ equal parts

_____

13. **THINK SMARTER** Draw to show halves.
Explain how you know that the
parts are halves.

_____

_____

_____

Problem Solving • Applications

 WRITE Math

14. **MATHEMATICAL PRACTICE 6** Make Connections Sort the shapes.

- Draw an X on shapes that do **not** show equal parts.
- Use red to color the shapes that show thirds.
- Use blue to color the shapes that show fourths.

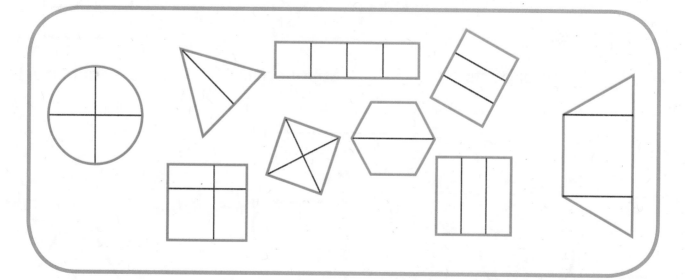

Personal Math Trainer

15. **THINK SMARTER +** Draw lines to show fourths three different ways.

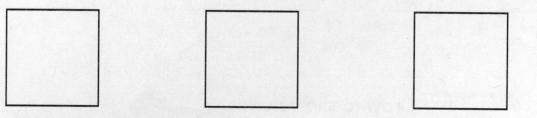

Explain how you know that the parts are fourths.

_____

_____

 TAKE HOME ACTIVITY • Ask your child to fold one sheet of paper into halves and another sheet of paper into fourths.

Equal Parts

Common Core
COMMON CORE STANDARD—2.G.A.3
Reason with shapes and their attributes.

**Write how many equal parts there are in the whole.
Write halves, thirds, or fourths to name the equal parts.**

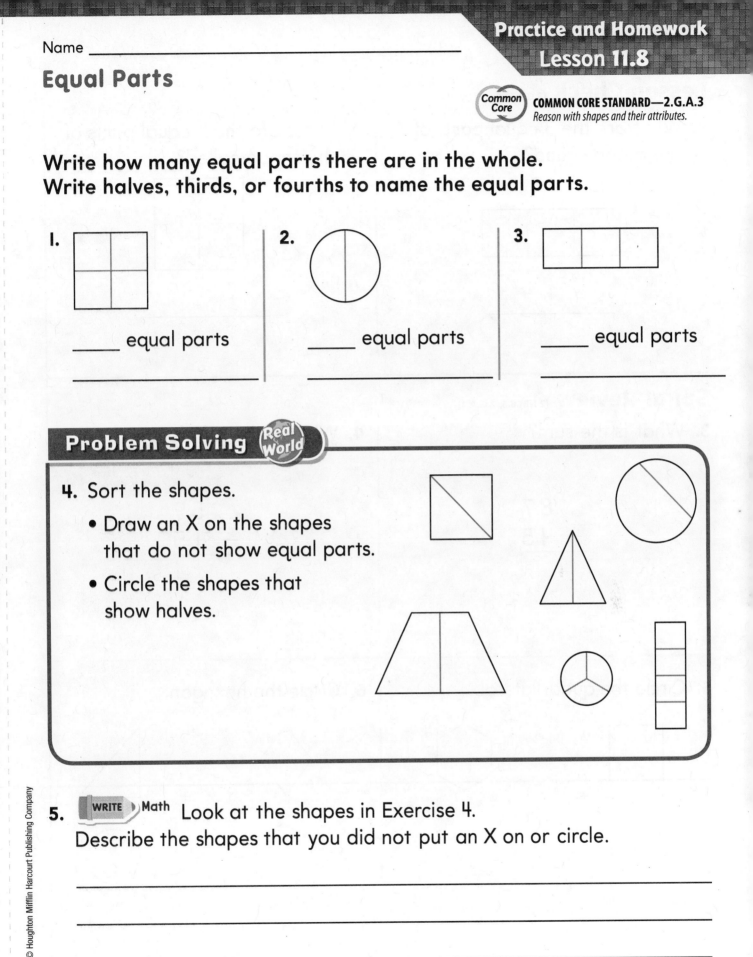

1.

____ equal parts

_____

2.

____ equal parts

_____

3.

____ equal parts

_____

Problem Solving Real World

4. Sort the shapes.

• Draw an X on the shapes
that do not show equal parts.

• Circle the shapes that
show halves.

5. WRITE Math Look at the shapes in Exercise 4.
Describe the shapes that you did not put an X on or circle.

_____

_____

_____

Lesson Check (2.G.A.3)

1. What are the 3 equal parts of the shape called?

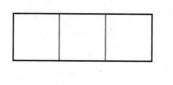

_____

2. What are the 4 equal parts of the shape called?

_____

Spiral Review (2.NBT.B.5, 2.G.A.1)

3. What is the sum?

$$87 + 45$$

4. What is the difference?

$$59 - 15$$

5. Circle the quadrilateral.

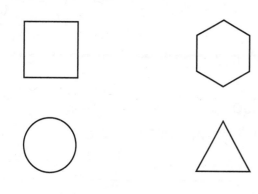

6. Circle the hexagon.

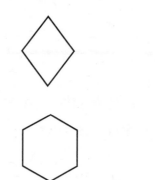

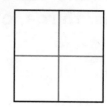

Name _____

Show Equal Parts of a Whole

Essential Question How do you know if
a shape shows halves, thirds, or fourths?

Common Core Geometry—2.G.A.3

MATHEMATICAL PRACTICES
MP5, MP6

Listen and Draw

Circle the shapes that show equal parts.

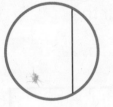

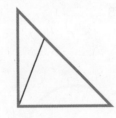

HOME CONNECTION • Your child completed
this sorting activity with shapes to review the
concept of equal parts.

Math Talk

MATHEMATICAL PRACTICES 6

Does the triangle
show halves? **Explain.**

Chapter 11

seven hundred fifty-three **753**

You can draw to show equal parts of a whole.

halves 2 equal parts	thirds 3 equal parts	fourths 4 equal parts

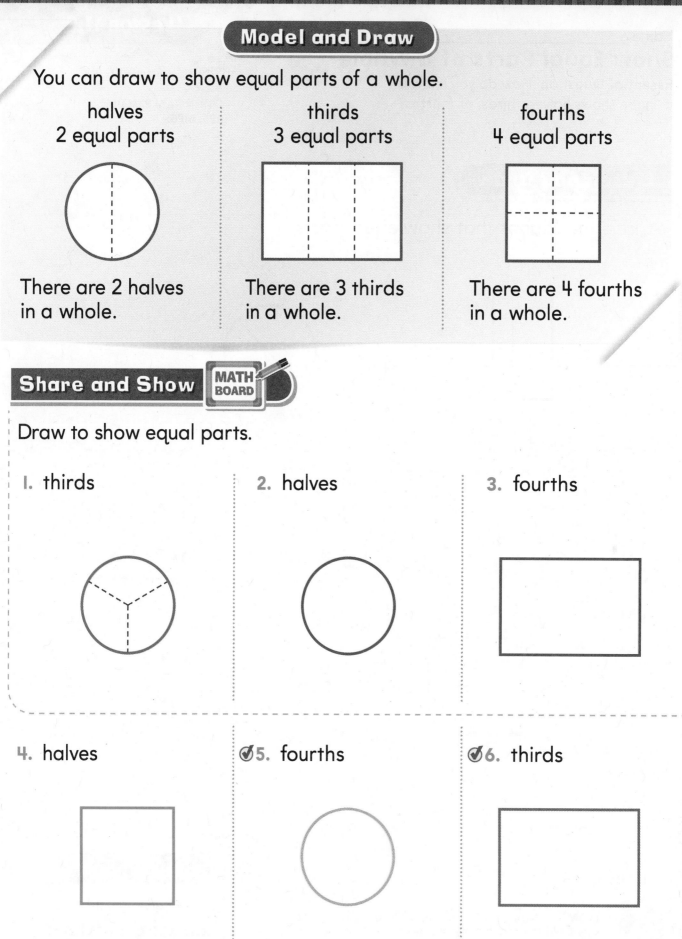

There are 2 halves in a whole.

There are 3 thirds in a whole.

There are 4 fourths in a whole.

Share and Show MATH BOARD

Draw to show equal parts.

1. thirds

2. halves

3. fourths

4. halves

☑5. fourths

☑6. thirds

Name _____

Draw to show equal parts.

7. halves

8. fourths

9. thirds

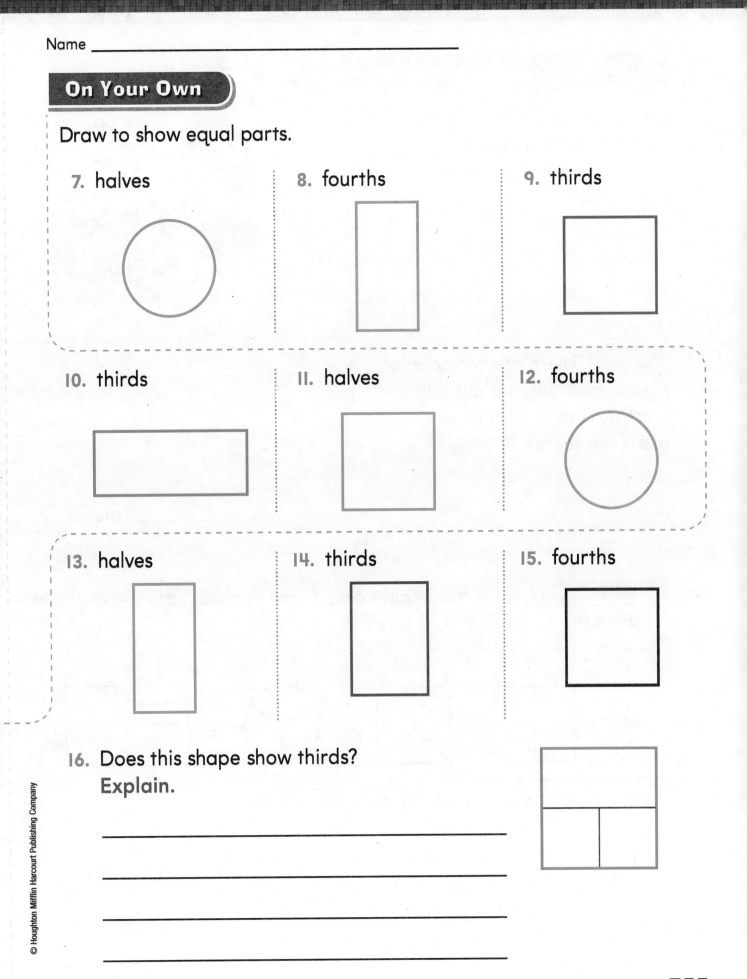

10. thirds

11. halves

12. fourths

13. halves

14. thirds

15. fourths

16. Does this shape show thirds?
Explain.

_____

_____

_____

_____

Problem Solving • Applications Real World WRITE Math

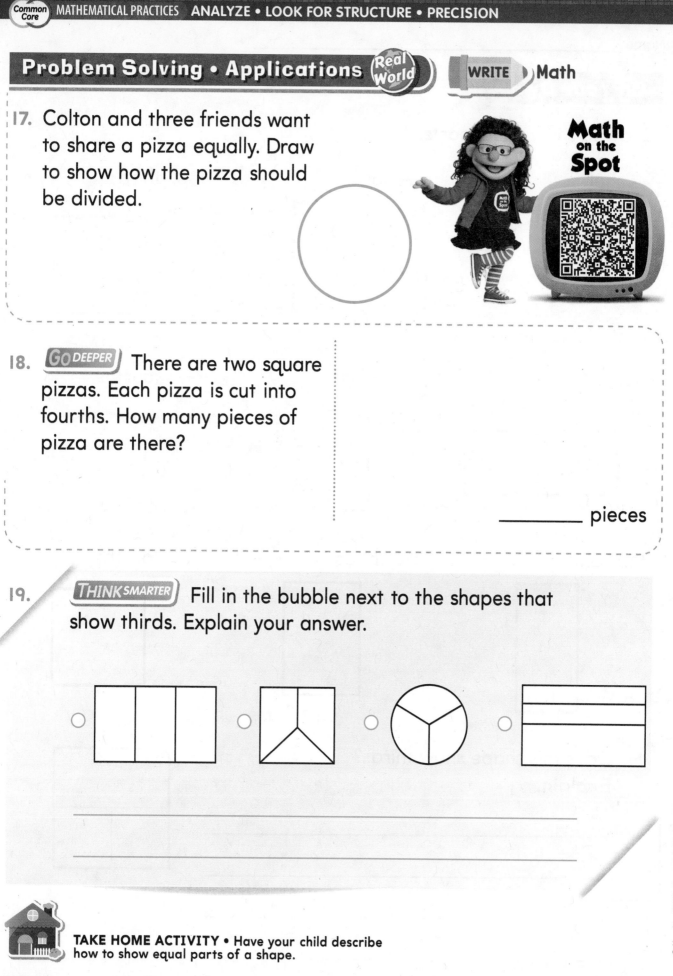

17. Colton and three friends want to share a pizza equally. Draw to show how the pizza should be divided.

Math on the Spot

18. GO DEEPER There are two square pizzas. Each pizza is cut into fourths. How many pieces of pizza are there?

_____ pieces

19. THINK SMARTER Fill in the bubble next to the shapes that show thirds. Explain your answer.

TAKE HOME ACTIVITY • Have your child describe how to show equal parts of a shape.

Show Equal Parts of a Whole

COMMON CORE STANDARD—2.G.A.3
Reason with shapes and their attributes.

Draw to show equal parts.

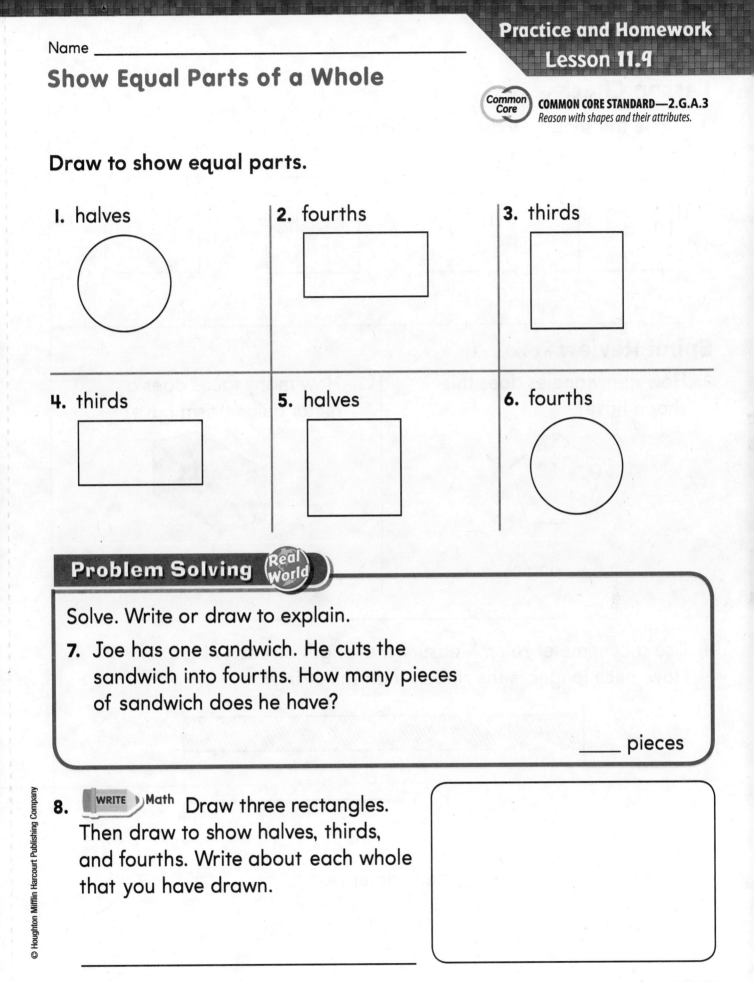

1. halves

2. fourths

3. thirds

4. thirds

5. halves

6. fourths

Problem Solving Real World

Solve. Write or draw to explain.

7. Joe has one sandwich. He cuts the
   sandwich into fourths. How many pieces
   of sandwich does he have?

   _____ pieces

8. **WRITE** Math Draw three rectangles.
   Then draw to show halves, thirds,
   and fourths. Write about each whole
   that you have drawn.

© Houghton Mifflin Harcourt Publishing Company

Lesson Check (2.G.A.3)

I. Circle the shape divided into fourths.

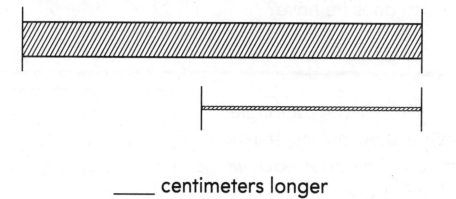

Spiral Review (2.MD.A.4, 2.G.A.1)

2. How many angles does this shape have?

_____ angles

3. How many faces does a rectangular prism have?

_____ faces

---

4. Use a centimeter ruler. Measure the length of each object. How much longer is the ribbon than the string?

_____ centimeters longer

FOR MORE PRACTICE
GO TO THE
Personal Math Trainer

Describe Equal Parts

Essential Question How do you find a half of, a third of, or a fourth of a whole?

Common Core Geometry—2.G.A.3

MATHEMATICAL PRACTICES
MP3, MP4, MP6

Listen and Draw

Find shapes that show fourths and color them green.
Find shapes that show halves and color them red.

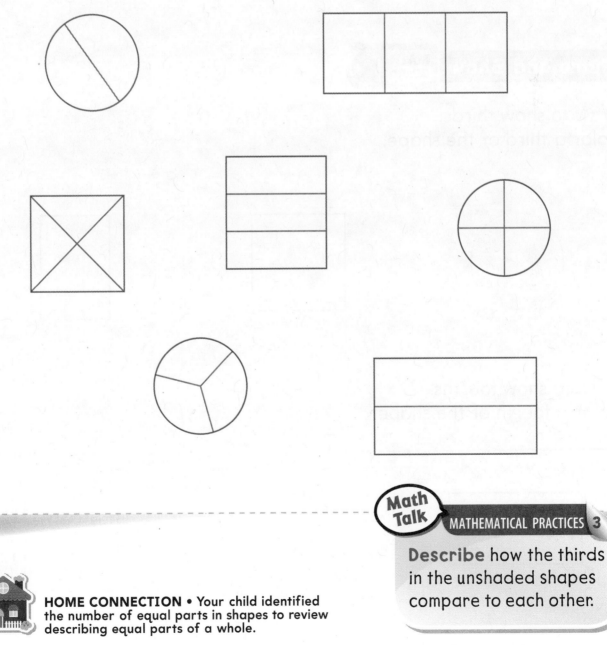

Math Talk

MATHEMATICAL PRACTICES 3

Describe how the thirds in the unshaded shapes compare to each other.

HOME CONNECTION • Your child identified the number of equal parts in shapes to review describing equal parts of a whole.

These are some ways to show and describe an equal part of a whole.

I of 4 equal parts is called a **quarter of** that shape.

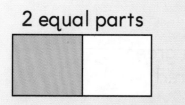

2 equal parts

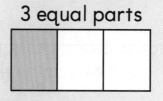

3 equal parts

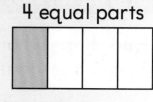

4 equal parts

A **half of** the shape is green.

A **third of** the shape is green.

A **fourth of** the shape is green.

Share and Show

Draw to show thirds.
Color a third of the shape.

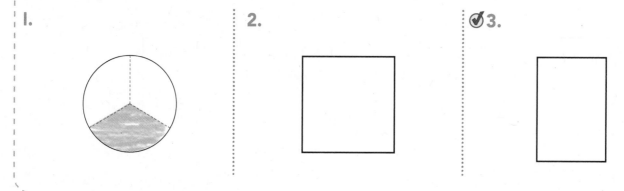

1.

2.

☑ 3.

Draw to show fourths.
Color a fourth of the shape.

4.

5.

☑ 6.

Name _____

Draw to show halves.
Color a half of the shape.

7.

8.

9.

Draw to show thirds.
Color a third of the shape.

10.

11.

12.

Draw to show fourths.
Color a fourth of the shape.

13.

14.

15.

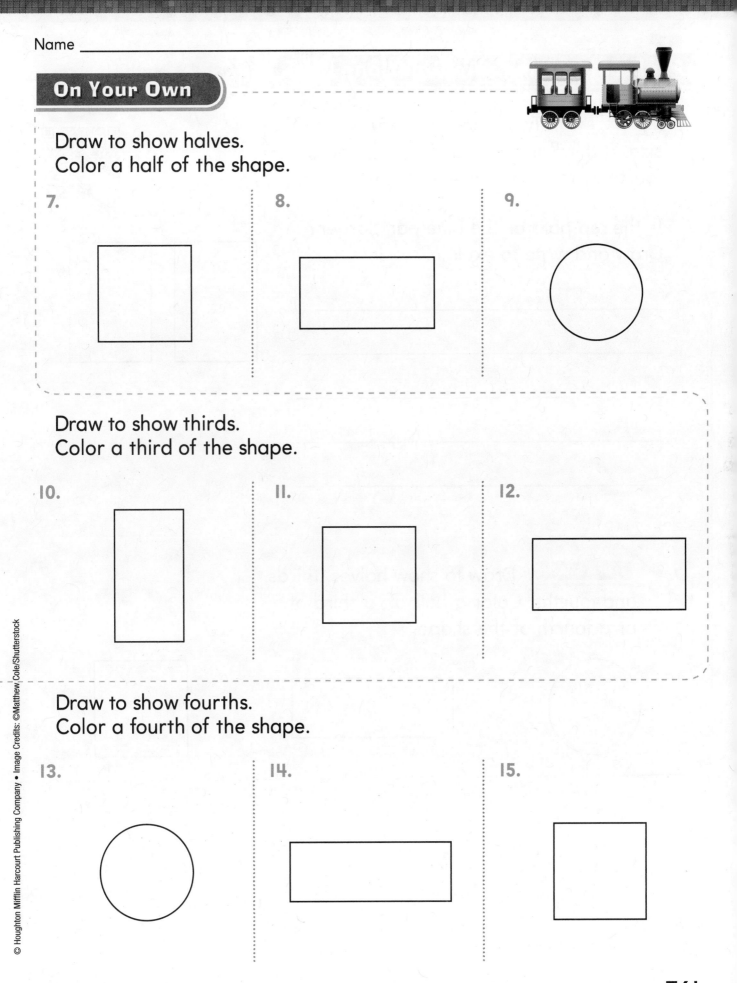

Problem Solving • Applications

WRITE Math

16. **THINK SMARTER** Two posters are the same size. A third of one poster is red, and a fourth of the other poster is blue.

Is the red part or the blue part larger? Draw and write to explain.

_____

_____

_____

_____

17. **THINK SMARTER** Draw to show halves, thirds, and fourths. Color a half of, a third of, or a fourth of the shape.

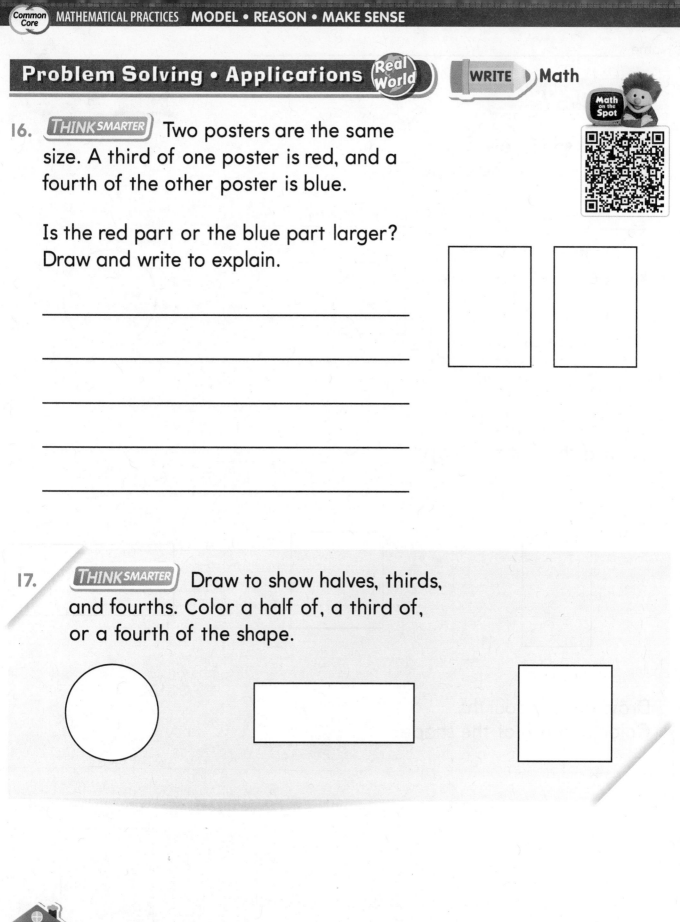

TAKE HOME ACTIVITY • Draw a square. Have your child draw to show thirds and color a third of the square.

Describe Equal Parts

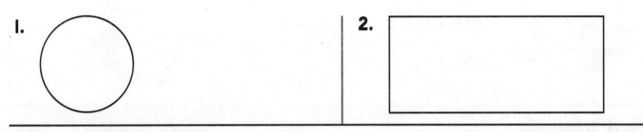

Common Core **COMMON CORE STANDARD—2.G.A.3**
Reason with shapes and their attributes.

Draw to show halves.
Color a half of the shape.

1.

2.

Draw to show thirds.
Color a third of the shape.

3.

4.

Problem Solving Real World

5. Circle all the shapes that have a third of the shape shaded.

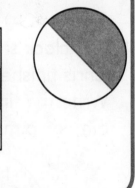

6. 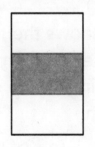**WRITE** Math Draw pictures to show a third of a whole and a fourth of a whole. Label each picture.

Chapter 11

Lesson Check (2.G.A.3)

1. Circle the shape that has a half of the shape shaded.

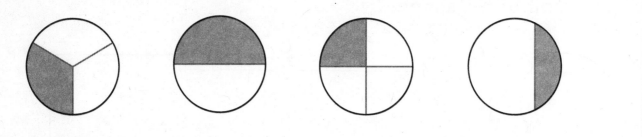

Spiral Review (2.MD.A.1, 2.MD.C.7, 2.G.A.1)

2. What is the name of this shape?

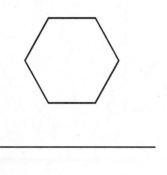

_____

3. Use a centimeter ruler. What is the length of the string to the nearest centimeter?

_____ centimeters

4. The clock shows the time Chris finished his homework. Write the time. Then circle a.m. or p.m.

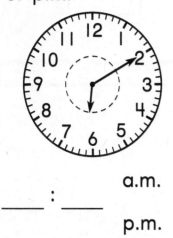

____ : ____

a.m.

p.m.

5. What time is shown on this clock?

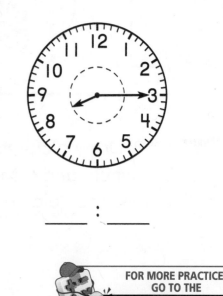

____ : ____

FOR MORE PRACTICE
GO TO THE
Personal Math Trainer

Problem Solving • Equal Shares

Essential Question How can drawing a diagram help when solving problems about equal shares?

Common Core Geometry—2.G.A.3

MATHEMATICAL PRACTICES
MP1, MP4, MP6

There are two sandwiches that are the same size. Each sandwich is divided into fourths, but the sandwiches are cut differently. How might the two sandwiches be cut?

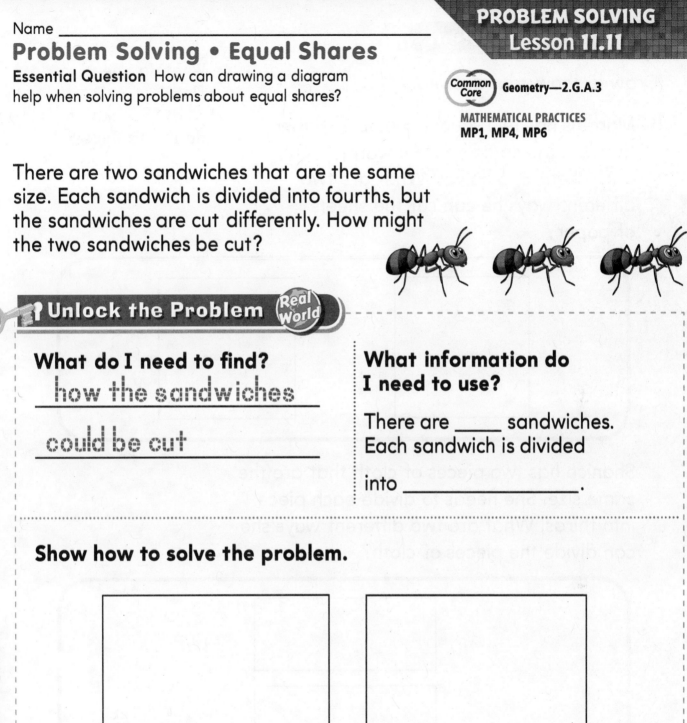

Unlock the Problem Real World

What do I need to find?

how the sandwiches

could be cut

What information do I need to use?

There are _____ sandwiches. Each sandwich is divided

into _____.

Show how to solve the problem.

© Houghton Mifflin Harcourt Publishing Company • Image Credits: ©Spasiblo/Shutterstock

HOME CONNECTION • Your child drew a diagram to represent and solve a problem about dividing a whole in different ways to show equal shares.

Draw to show your answer.

1. Marquis has two square sheets of paper that are the same size. He wants to cut each sheet into halves. What are two different ways he can cut the sheets of paper?

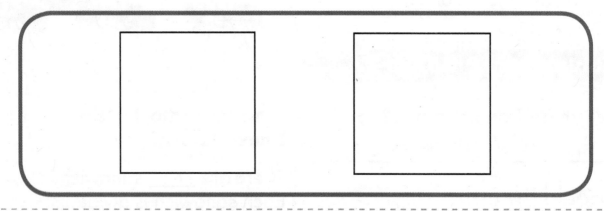

2. Shanice has two pieces of cloth that are the same size. She needs to divide each piece into thirds. What are two different ways she can divide the pieces of cloth?

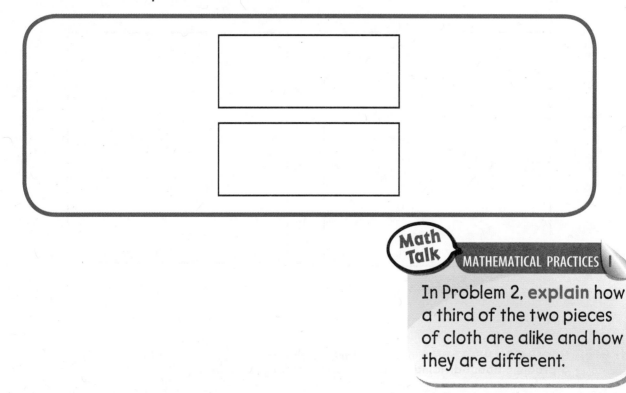

Math Talk

MATHEMATICAL PRACTICES 1

In Problem 2, **explain** how a third of the two pieces of cloth are alike and how they are different.

Name _____

Share and Show MATH BOARD

Draw to show your answer.

☑3. Brandon has two pieces of toast that are the same size. What are two different ways he can divide the pieces of toast into halves?

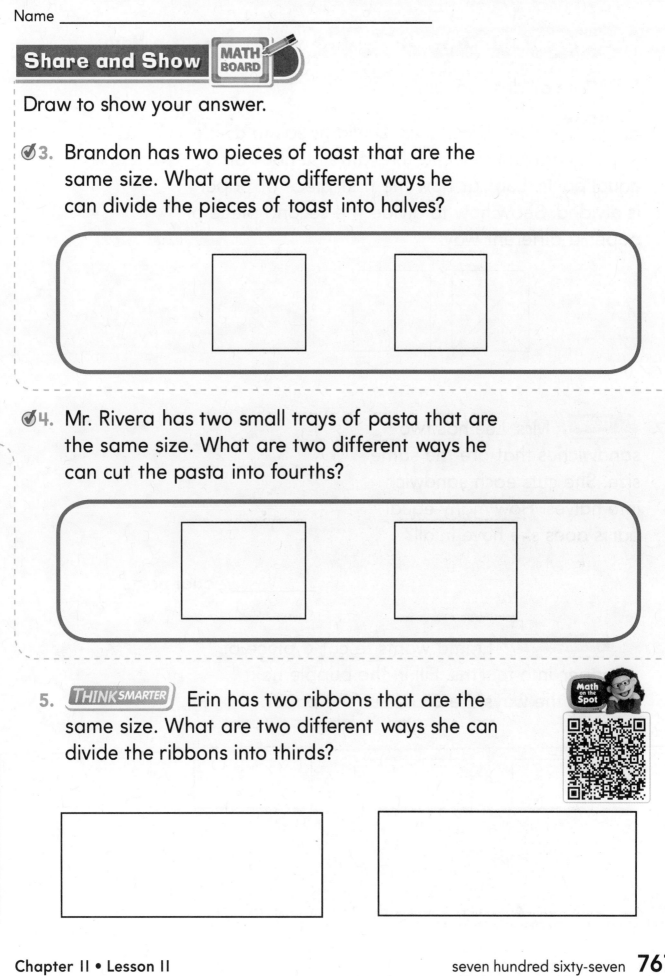

☑4. Mr. Rivera has two small trays of pasta that are the same size. What are two different ways he can cut the pasta into fourths?

5. THINK SMARTER Erin has two ribbons that are the same size. What are two different ways she can divide the ribbons into thirds?

Math on the Spot

Problem Solving • Applications  WRITE Math

Solve. Write or draw to explain.

6. **MATHEMATICAL PRACTICE ④** **Use Diagrams** David needs to divide two pieces of paper into the same number of equal parts. Look at how the first piece of paper is divided. Show how to divide the second piece of paper a different way.

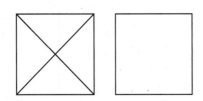

7. **GO DEEPER** Mrs. Lee has two sandwiches that are the same size. She cuts each sandwich into halves. How many equal parts does she have in all?

_____ equal parts

8. **THINK SMARTER** Emma wants to cut a piece of paper into fourths. Fill in the bubble next to all the ways she could cut the paper.

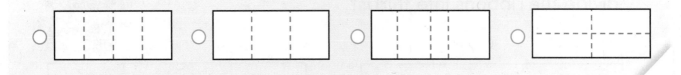

 TAKE HOME ACTIVITY • Ask your child to draw two rectangles and show two different ways to divide them into fourths.

Name _____

Problem Solving • Equal Shares

 COMMON CORE STANDARD—2.G.A.3
Reason with shapes and their attributes.

Draw to show your answer.

1. Max has square pizzas that are the same size. What are two different ways he can divide the pizzas into fourths?

2. Lia has two pieces of paper that are the same size. What are two different ways she can divide the pieces of paper into halves?

3. 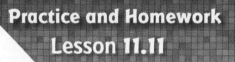 **WRITE** Math Draw and write to explain how you can divide a rectangle into thirds in two different ways.

_____

Lesson Check (2.G.A.3)

1. Bree cut a piece of cardboard into thirds like this.

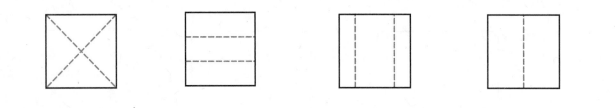

Circle the other shape that is divided into thirds.

Spiral Review (2.MD.C.7, 2.MD.A.3, 2.G.A.1)

2. Circle the shape with three equal parts.

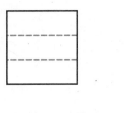

3. How many angles does this shape have?

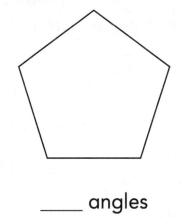

_____ angles

4. What is the best estimate for the length of a baseball bat?

_____ feet

5. Which is another way to write 10 minutes after 9?

_____ : _____

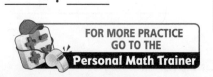

FOR MORE PRACTICE
GO TO THE
Personal Math Trainer

Name _____

1. Match the shapes.

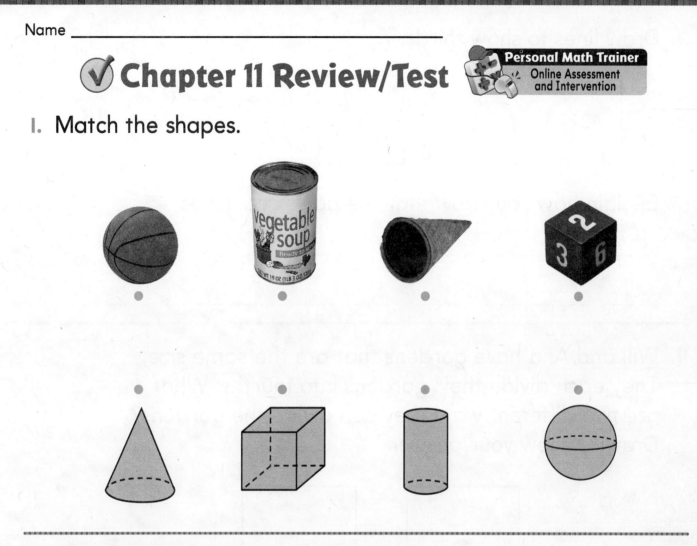

....

2. Do the sentences describe a cube?
   Choose Yes or No.

A cube has 4 faces.	○ Yes	○ No
A cube has 8 vertices.	○ Yes	○ No
A cube has 14 edges.	○ Yes	○ No
Each face of a cube is a square.	○ Yes	○ No

Rewrite each sentence that is not true to
make it a true sentence.

_____

_____

3. Draw lines to show thirds.

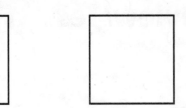

Explain how you know that the parts are thirds.

_____

_____

4. Will and Ana have gardens that are the same size. They each divide their gardens into fourths. What are two different ways they can divide the gardens? Draw to show your answer.

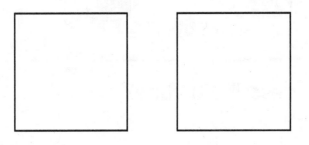

5. Draw to show halves, thirds, and fourths. Color a half of, a third of, and a fourth of the shape.

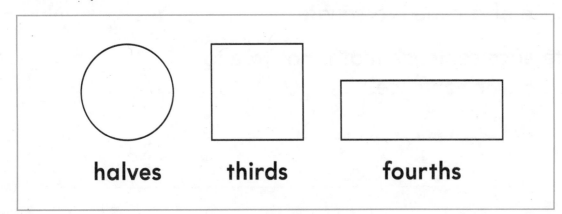

| halves | thirds | fourths |

6. Max wants to cover the rectangle with color tiles. Explain how you would estimate the number of square tiles he would need to cover the rectangle.

_____

_____

7. THINKSMARTER ✚ Jenna built this rectangular prism. Circle the number of unit cubes Jenna used.

Personal Math Trainer

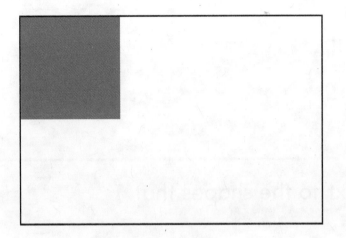

8. Rachel makes a pentagon and a quadrilateral with toothpicks. She uses one toothpick for each side of a shape. How many toothpicks does Rachel need?

_____ toothpicks

9. Kevin drew 2 two-dimensional shapes that had 9 angles in all. Draw the shapes Kevin could have drawn.

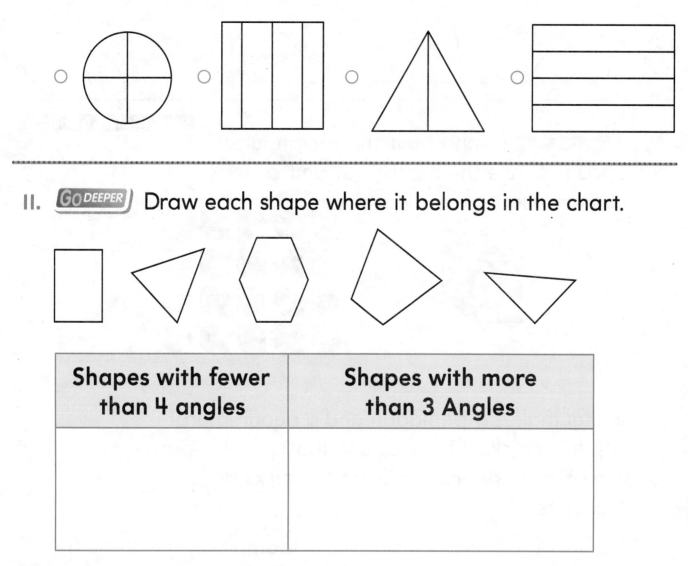

10. Fill in the bubble next to the shapes that show fourths.

11. GO DEEPER Draw each shape where it belongs in the chart.

Shapes with fewer than 4 angles	Shapes with more than 3 Angles

Picture Glossary

addend sumando

$$5 + 8 = 13$$
addends

a.m. a.m.

Times after midnight and before noon are written with **a.m.**

11:00 a.m. is in the morning.

angle ángulo

angle

bar graph gráfica de barras

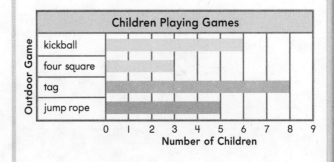

cent sign símbolo de centavo

53¢
cent sign

centimeter centímetro

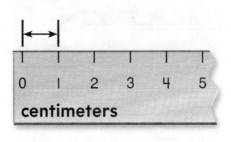

centimeters

column columna

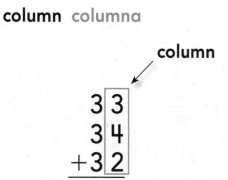

column

compare comparar

Use these symbols when you **compare**: >, <, =.

$$241 > 234$$

$$123 < 128$$

$$247 = 247$$

compare comparar

Compare the lengths of the pencil and the crayon.

The pencil is longer than the crayon.

The crayon is shorter than the pencil.

cone cono

cube cubo

cylinder cilindro

data datos

Favorite Lunch	
Lunch	**Tally**
pizza	IIII
sandwich	HHT I
salad	III
pasta	HHT

The information in this chart is called **data**.

decimal point punto decimal

$1.00
↑
decimal point

---

difference diferencia

9 − 2 = 7
↑
difference

---

digit dígito

0, 1, 2, 3, 4, 5, 6, 7, 8, and 9 are **digits**.

---

dime moneda de 10¢

A **dime** has a value of 10 cents.

dollar dólar

One **dollar** is worth 100 cents.

---

dollar sign símbolo de dólar

$1.00
↑
dollar sign

---

doubles dobles

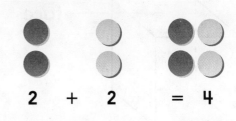

2 + 2 = 4

---

edge arista

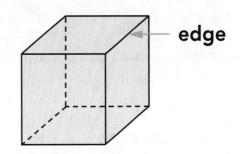

edge

An **edge** is formed where two faces of a three-dimensional shape meet.

estimate estimación

An **estimate** is an amount that tells about how many.

even par

2, 4, 6, 8, 10, . . .

even numbers

face cara

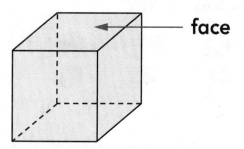

face

Each flat surface of this cube is a **face**.

foot pie

I **foot** is the same length as 12 inches.

fourth of cuarto de

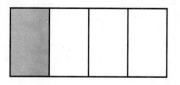

A **fourth of** the shape is green.

fourths cuartos

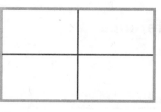

This shape has 4 equal parts. These equal parts are called **fourths**.

half of mitad de

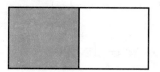

A **half of** the shape is green.

halves mitades

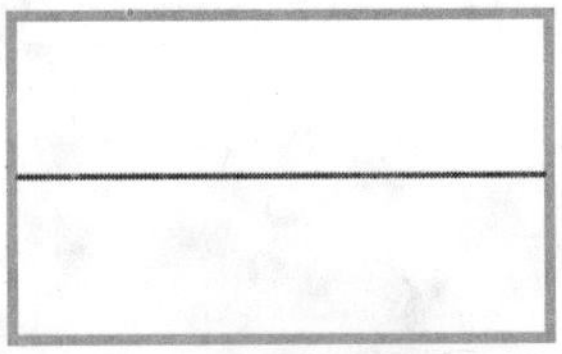

This shape has 2 equal parts.
These equal parts are called
halves.

hexagon hexágono

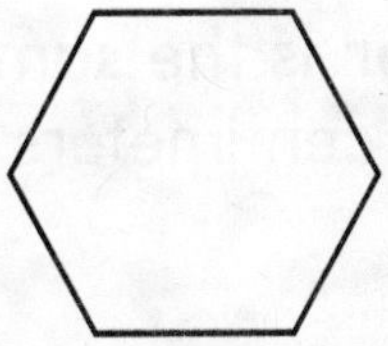

A two-dimensional shape with
6 sides is a **hexagon**.

hour hora

There are 60 minutes in
1 **hour**.

hundred centena

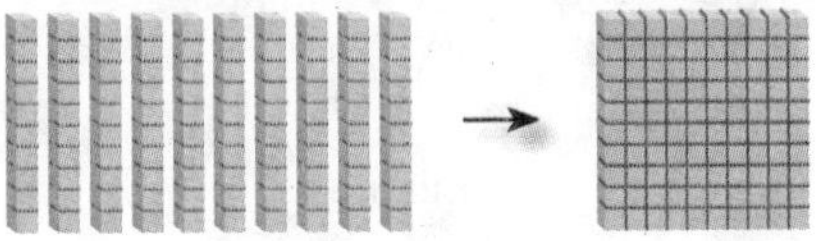

There are 10 tens in
1 **hundred**.

inch pulgada

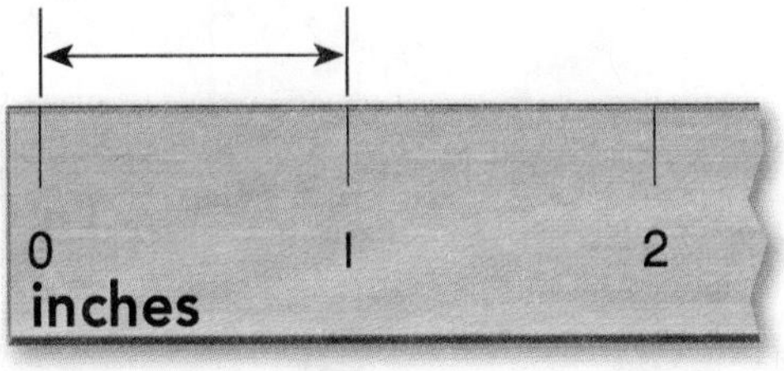

is equal to (=) es igual a

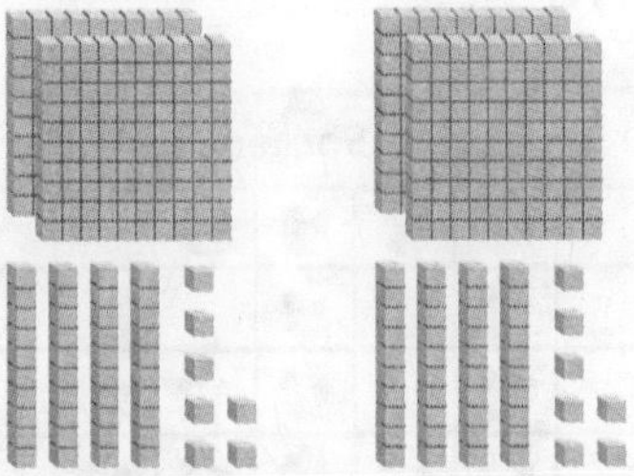

247 **is equal to** 247.
247 = 247

is greater than (>) es mayor que

241 **is greater than** 234.
241 > 234

is less than (<) es menor que

123 is less than 128.
123 < 128

key clave

Number of Soccer Games							
March	⚽	⚽	⚽	⚽			
April	⚽	⚽	⚽				
May	⚽	⚽	⚽	⚽	⚽	⚽	
June	⚽	⚽	⚽	⚽	⚽	⚽	⚽

Key: Each ⚽ stands for 1 game.

The **key** tells how many each picture stands for.

line plot diagrama de puntos

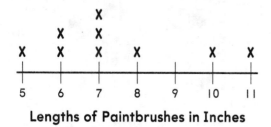

Lengths of Paintbrushes in Inches

measuring tape cinta métrica

meter metro

1 **meter** is the same length as 100 centimeters.

midnight medianoche

Midnight is 12:00 at night.

minute minuto

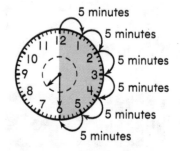

5 minutes
5 minutes
5 minutes
5 minutes
5 minutes
5 minutes

There are 30 **minutes** in a half hour.

nickel moneda de 5¢

A **nickel** has a value of 5 cents.

---

noon mediodía

Noon is 12:00 in the daytime.

---

odd impar

1, 3, 5, 7, 9, 11, . . .

odd numbers

---

ones unidades

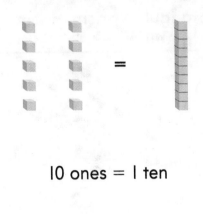

10 ones = 1 ten

penny moneda de 1¢

A **penny** has a value of 1 cent.

---

pentagon pentágono

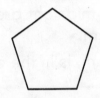

A two-dimensional shape with 5 sides is a **pentagon**.

---

picture graph gráfica con dibujos

Number of Soccer Games						
March	⚽	⚽	⚽	⚽		
April	⚽	⚽	⚽			
May	⚽	⚽	⚽	⚽	⚽	
June	⚽	⚽	⚽	⚽	⚽	⚽

Key: Each  ⚽ stands for 1 game.

plus (+) más

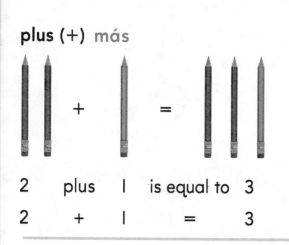

2	plus	1	is equal to	3
2	+	1	=	3

---

p.m. p.m.

Times after noon and before midnight are written with **p.m.**

11:00 p.m. is in the evening.

---

quadrilateral cuadrilátero

A two-dimensional shape with 4 sides is a **quadrilateral**.

---

quarter moneda de 25¢

A **quarter** has a value of 25 cents.

quarter of cuarta parte de

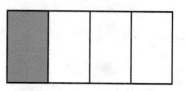

A **quarter of** the shape is green.

---

quarter past y cuarto

8:15

15 minutes after 8
quarter past 8

---

rectangular prism prisma rectangular

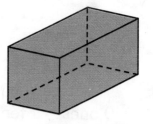

regroup reagrupar

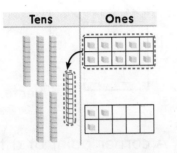

You can trade 10 ones for
1 ten to **regroup**.

side lado

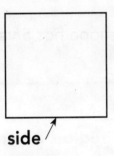

This shape has 4 **sides**.

sphere esfera

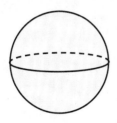

sum suma o total

$$9 + 6 = 15$$

sum

survey encuesta

Favorite Lunch	
Lunch	Tally
pizza	IIII
sandwich	⊞ I
salad	III
pasta	⊞

A **survey** is a collection
of data from answers to
a question.

ten decena

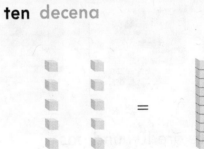

10 ones = 1 ten

third of tercio de

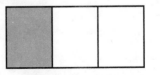

A **third of** the shape
is green.

thirds tercios

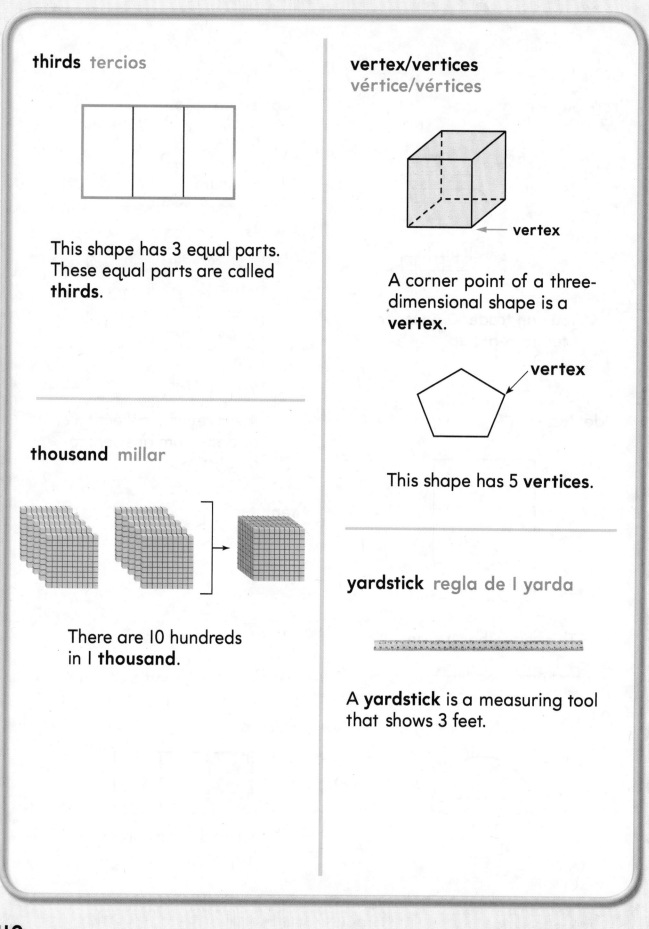

This shape has 3 equal parts. These equal parts are called **thirds**.

thousand millar

There are 10 hundreds in 1 **thousand**.

vertex/vertices
vértice/vértices

vertex

A corner point of a three-dimensional shape is a **vertex**.

vertex

This shape has 5 **vertices**.

yardstick regla de 1 yarda

A **yardstick** is a measuring tool that shows 3 feet.

Correlations

 COMMON CORE STATE STANDARDS

Standards You Will Learn

Mathematical Practices		Some examples are:
MP1	Make sense of problems and persevere in solving them.	Lessons 1.3, 1.5, 2.2, 3.2, 3.3, 4.7, 4.9, 4.11, 5.9, 5.10, 5.11, 6.7, 7.7, 8.5, 9.4, 10.1, 10.2, 10.3, 10.4, 10.6, 11.5
MP2	Reason abstractly and quantitatively.	Lessons 1.2, 2.6, 2.11, 2.12, 3.5, 3.9, 4.9, 4.10, 5.5, 5.9, 5.10, 5.11, 6.1, 8.1, 8.4, 8.5, 8.6, 9.4, 9.7, 10.2, 10.4
MP3	Construct viable arguments and critique the reasoning of others.	Lessons 1.1, 2.5, 2.8, 2.11, 4.6, 5.6, 5.10, 6.8, 8.8, 9.3, 10.5, 10.6
MP4	Model with mathematics.	Lessons 1.4, 1.7, 2.3, 2.11, 3.8, 3.9, 3.11, 4.1, 4.2, 4.5, 4.9, 4.11, 5.4, 5.9, 5.10, 5.11, 6.6, 7.3, 7.4, 7.5, 7.6, 7.7, 8.5, 8.9, 9.4, 10.1, 10.3, 10.5, 10.6, 11.3, 11.4, 11.5, 11.6, 11.10, 11.11
MP5	Use appropriate tools strategically.	Lessons 3.7, 3.10, 4.4, 5.1, 5.2, 5.3, 5.8, 6.1, 8.1, 8.2, 8.4, 8.6, 8.8, 8.9, 9.1, 9.3, 9.5, 11.2, 11.7, 11.9
MP6	Attend to precision.	Lessons 1.3, 1.5, 1.6, 2.1, 2.5, 2.7, 2.12, 3.5, 3.11, 4.1, 4.2, 4.3, 4.6, 4.8, 4.10, 4.12, 5.5, 5.7, 6.1, 6.2, 6.3, 6.4, 6.5, 6.7, 6.9, 6.10, 7.2, 7.3, 7.8, 7.9, 7.10, 7.11, 8.1, 8.2, 8.3, 8.4, 8.6, 8.7, 8.9, 9.1, 9.2, 9.3, 9.6, 9.7, 10.1, 10.2, 10.3, 10.4, 10.5, 11.1, 11.2, 11.6, 11.8, 11.9, 11.10, 11.11
MP7	Look for and make use of structure.	Lessons 1.1, 1.2, 1.6, 1.7, 1.8, 1.9, 2.1, 2.2, 2.3, 2.4, 2.5, 2.6, 2.7, 2.8, 2.9, 2.10, 3.1, 3.2, 3.3, 3.7, 3.10, 4.4, 4.7, 4.8, 5.3, 5.6, 5.7, 7.1, 7.5, 7.6, 7.11, 8.3, 8.7, 9.2, 9.5, 9.6, 11.4, 11.5

Standards You Will Learn

Mathematical Practices		Some examples are:
MP8	Look for and express regularity in repeated reasoning.	Lessons 1.2, 1.6, 2.1, 2.2, 2.4, 2.12, 3.2, 3.3, 3.4, 3.5, 3.7, 4.3, 4.11, 4.12, 5.5, 5.8, 6.2, 6.3, 6.4, 6.5, 6.7, 6.8, 6.9, 6.10, 7.2, 7.3, 7.4, 7.8, 7.9, 7.10, 8.1, 8.8, 9.1, 11.7, 11.8

Domain: Operations and Algebraic Thinking		Student Edition Lessons
Represent and solve problems involving addition and subtraction.		
2.OA.A.1	Use addition and subtraction within 100 to solve one- and two-step word problems involving situations of adding to, taking from, putting together, taking apart, and comparing, with unknowns in all positions, e.g., by using drawings and equations with a symbol for the unknown number to represent the problem.	Lessons 3.8, 3.9, 4.9, 4.10, 5.9, 5.10, 5.11
Add and subtract within 20.		
2.OA.B.2	Fluently add and subtract within 20 using mental strategies. By end of Grade 2, know from memory all sums of two one-digit numbers.	Lessons 3.1, 3.2, 3.3, 3.4, 3.5, 3.6, 3.7
Work with equal groups of objects to gain foundations for multiplication.		
2.OA.C.3	Determine whether a group of objects (up to 20) has an odd or even number of members, e.g., by pairing objects or counting them by 2s; write an equation to express an even number as a sum of two equal addends.	Lessons 1.1, 1.2
2.OA.C.4	Use addition to find the total number of objects arranged in rectangular arrays with up to 5 rows and up to 5 columns; write an equation to express the total as a sum of equal addends.	Lessons 3.10, 3.11

Standards You Will Learn

Domain: Number and Operations in Base Ten

Understand place value.

2.NBT.A.1	Understand that the three digits of a three-digit number represent amounts of hundreds, tens, and ones; e.g., 706 equals 7 hundreds, 0 tens, and 6 ones. Understand the following as special cases:	Lessons 2.2, 2.3, 2.4, 2.5
	a. 100 can be thought of as a bundle of ten tens — called a "hundred."	Lesson 2.1
	b. The numbers 100, 200, 300, 400, 500, 600, 700, 800, 900 refer to one, two, three, four, five, six, seven, eight, or nine hundreds (and 0 tens and 0 ones).	Lesson 2.1
2.NBT.A.2	Count within 1000; skip-count by 5s, 10s, and 100s.	Lessons 1.8, 1.9
2.NBT.A.3	Read and write numbers to 1000 using base-ten numerals, number names, and expanded form.	Lessons 1.3, 1.4, 1.5. 1.6, 1.7, 2.4, 2.6, 2.7, 2.8
2.NBT.A.4	Compare two three-digit numbers based on meanings of the hundreds, tens, and ones digits, using >, =, and < symbols to record the results of comparisons.	Lessons 2.11, 2.12

Use place value understanding and properties of operations to add and subtract.

2.NBT.B.5	Fluently add and subtract within 100 using strategies based on place value, properties of operations, and/or the relationship between addition and subtraction.	Lessons 4.1, 4.2, 4.3, 4.4, 4.5, 4.6, 4.7, 4.8, 5.1, 5.2, 5.3, 5.4, 5.5, 5.6, 5.7, 5.8
2.NBT.B.6	Add up to four two-digit numbers using strategies based on place value and properties of operations.	Lessons 4.11, 4.12

Domain: Number and Operations in Base Ten		
Use place value understanding and properties of operations to add and subtract.		
2.NBT.B.7	Add and subtract within 1000, using concrete models or drawings and strategies based on place value, properties of operations, and/or the relationship between addition and subtraction; relate the strategy to a written method. Understand that in adding or subtracting three-digit numbers, one adds or subtracts hundreds and hundreds, tens and tens, ones and ones; and sometimes it is necessary to compose or decompose tens or hundreds.	Lessons 6.1, 6.2, 6.3, 6.4, 6.5, 6.6, 6.7, 6.8, 6.9, 6.10
2.NBT.B.8	Mentally add 10 or 100 to a given number 100–900, and mentally subtract 10 or 100 from a given number 100–900.	Lessons 2.9, 2.10
2.NBT.B.9	Explain why addition and subtraction strategies work, using place value and the properties of operations.	Lessons 4.6, 6.8
Domain: Measurement and Data		
Measure and estimate lengths in standard units.		
2.MD.A.1	Measure the length of an object by selecting and using appropriate tools such as rulers, yardsticks, meter sticks, and measuring tapes.	Lessons 8.1, 8.2, 8.4, 8.8, 9.1, 9.3
2.MD.A.2	Measure the length of an object twice, using length units of different lengths for the two measurements; describe how the two measurements relate to the size of the unit chosen.	Lessons 8.6, 9.5

Standards You Will Learn

Domain: Measurement and Data		
Measure and estimate lengths in standard units.		
2.MD.A.3	Estimate lengths using units of inches, feet, centimeters, and meters.	Lessons 8.3, 8.7, 9.2, 9.6
2.MD.A.4	Measure to determine how much longer one object is than another, expressing the length difference in terms of a standard length unit.	Lesson 9.7
Relate addition and subtraction to length.		
2.MD.B.5	Use addition and subtraction within 100 to solve word problems involving lengths that are given in the same units, e.g., by using drawings (such as drawings of rulers) and equations with a symbol for the unknown number to represent the problem.	Lessons 8.5, 9.4
2.MD.B.6	Represent whole numbers as lengths from 0 on a number line diagram with equally spaced points corresponding to the numbers 0, 1, 2, ..., and represent whole-number sums and differences within 100 on a number line diagram.	Lessons 8.5, 9.4
Work with time and money.		
2.MD.C.7	Tell and write time from analog and digital clocks to the nearest five minutes, using a.m. and p.m.	Lessons 7.8, 7.9, 7.10, 7.11
2.MD.C.8	Solve word problems involving dollar bills, quarters, dimes, nickels, and pennies, using $ and ¢ symbols appropriately. *Example: If you have 2 dimes and 3 pennies, how many cents do you have?*	Lessons 7.1, 7.2, 7.3, 7.4, 7.5, 7.6, 7.7

Domain: Measurement and Data		
Represent and interpret data.		
2.MD.D.9	Generate measurement data by measuring lengths of several objects to the nearest whole unit, or by making repeated measurements of the same object. Show the measurements by making a line plot, where the horizontal scale is marked off in whole-number units.	Lesson 8.9
2.MD.D.10	Draw a picture graph and a bar graph (with single-unit scale) to represent a data set with up to four categories. Solve simple put-together, take-apart, and compare problems using information presented in a bar graph.	Lessons 10.1, 10.2, 10.3, 10.4, 10.5, 10.6
Domain: Geometry		
Reason with shapes and their attributes.		
2.G.A.1	Recognize and draw shapes having specified attributes, such as a given number of angles or a given number of equal faces. Identify triangles, quadrilaterals, pentagons, hexagons, and cubes.	Lessons 11.1, 11.2, 11.3, 11.4, 11.5, 11.6
2.G.A.2	Partition a rectangle into rows and columns of same-size squares and count to find the total number of them.	Lesson 11.7
2.G.A.3	Partition circles and rectangles into two, three, or four equal shares, describe the shares using the words *halves, thirds, half of, a third of*, etc., and describe the whole as two halves, three thirds, four fourths. Recognize that equal shares of identical wholes need not have the same shape.	Lessons 11.8, 11.9, 11.10, 11.11

Index

A

Act It Out strategy, 217–220, 503–506

Activities

Games. See Games

Hands On Activities: 13, 19, 31, 43, 87, 237, 255, 329, 335, 403, 409, 427, 467, 473, 479, 485, 541, 547, 553, 571, 583, 589, 603, 609, 615, 627, 639, 653, 665, 671, 723, 729, 735, 741, 747

Take Home Activity, 16, 22, 28, 34, 39, 46, 52, 58, 64, 78, 84, 90, 96, 102, 108, 113, 120, 126, 132, 138, 144, 166, 172, 178, 184, 190, 195, 202, 208, 214, 220, 226, 240, 246, 252, 258, 264, 270, 275, 282, 288, 294, 300, 306, 320, 326, 332, 338, 344, 349, 356, 362, 368, 374, 380, 394, 400, 406, 412, 417, 424, 430, 436, 442, 448, 470, 476, 482, 488, 493, 500, 506, 512, 518, 524, 530, 544, 550, 556, 562, 567, 574, 592, 606, 612, 618, 630, 636, 642, 656, 662, 667, 674, 680, 686, 708, 714, 720, 726, 732, 738, 743, 750, 756, 762, 768

Addends

adding 3 one-digit, 181–184

adding 3 two-digit, 297–300

adding 4 two-digit, 303–306

breaking apart to add, 176–177, 237–240, 249–252, 397–400

defined, 170

missing, See Addends, unknown

order of, 169–172, 181–184, 297–300, 303–306

unknown, 183, 194, 212–214, 232, 285–287, 292–293, 300, 305, 309, 371–373, 622–623, 648

Addition

adding three 1-digit addends, 181–184

basic facts, 163–166, 169–172, 175–178, 181–184, 187–190, 211–214

basic fact strategies

doubles and near doubles facts, 163–166

make a ten, 175–178, 182–184

use related facts, 187–190

breaking apart addends to add, 176–177, 237–240, 249–252, 397–400

of equal groups, 217–220, 223–226

regrouping in, 255–258, 261–264, 267–270, 273–275, 280–282, 297–300, 303–306, 403–406, 409–412, 415–417

relate to subtraction, 187–190, 359–362

represented with bar models, 187–188, 205–208, 285–288, 377–380

three-digit numbers, 391–394, 397–400, 403–406, 409–412, 415–417

breaking apart to add, 397–400

regrouping, 403–406, 409–412, 415–417

to find differences, 187–189, 359–362

two-digit numbers, 237–240, 243–246, 249–252, 255–258, 261–264, 267–270, 273–275, 279–282, 285–288, 291–294, 297–300, 303–306

breaking apart addends to add, 237–240, 249–252

finding sums of 3 two-digit numbers, 297–300

finding sums of 4 two-digit numbers, 303–306

using compensation, 243–246

using models and quick pictures, 237–238, 243, 255–258, 261–264, 267, 329, 335–338, 341, 391–394, 397, 403, 409, 419, 421, 427

See also Problem Types, for word problems

Problem Solving Strategies
act it out, 217–220, 503–506
draw a diagram, 285–288, 365–368, 565–567, 621–623, 765–768
find a pattern, 49–52
make a model, 135–138, 421–424
make a graph, 683–686

Problem Types, for word problems
Add to
Change unknown, 285, 378
Result unknown, 153, 154, 163, 172, 178, 184, 214, 230, 237, 243, 252, 264, 270, 279, 286–288, 291, 300, 306, 310, 320, 326, 359, 368, 377, 379–380, 391, 623, 674
Start unknown, 213, 293
Compare
Bigger unknown, 343, 642
Difference unknown, 190, 206–208, 214, 231, 232, 326, 338, 356, 366–367, 372, 384–386, 412, 423, 439, 648, 654–656, 659–662, 672, 674, 680
Smaller unknown, 319, 332, 367, 447, 612
Put Together/Take Apart
Addend unknown, 155, 184, 208, 212–213, 232, 252, 286–287, 292, 332, 347, 367, 374, 385–386, 422, 430, 433, 442, 448, 692
Both Addends unknown, 246, 264, 282, 311, 380, 448, 606, 662, 768
Total unknown, 152, 156, 166, 169, 172, 175, 178, 184, 187, 190, 193, 196, 205, 207–208, 212–214, 230, 233, 237, 240, 246, 252, 255, 258, 261, 264, 267, 273–274, 276, 282, 287–288, 292–294, 297, 300, 303, 306, 310–312, 326, 356, 377, 379, 385, 387, 394, 400, 403, 406, 409, 412, 415, 418, 434–436, 452, 566–567, 595, 598, 622, 636, 655–656, 661–662, 671–674, 677, 680, 692

Take from
Change unknown, 187, 213, 320, 326, 371, 373, 427, 430
Result unknown, 159, 187, 190, 199, 205–207, 212, 229, 313, 320, 323, 329, 332, 335, 338, 341, 344, 348, 350, 353, 359, 362, 365, 367–368, 372, 379, 384–386, 394, 421, 423–424, 430, 433, 436, 445–446, 453, 565–567, 621–623, 642
Start unknown, 338, 373, 424

Properties of Addition,
add in any order, 169–172
adding zero, 170–171
grouping addends in different ways, 181–184, 297–300, 303–306

Q

Quadrilaterals, 723–726, 730–732, 735–738, 741–743

Quarters, 473–476, 479–482, 485–488, 492–493, 497–500

Quick Pictures, 27, 32–33, 49, 87–90, 93, 99, 112–113, 117, 123, 135–137, 141, 238, 243, 255–258, 261–264, 267, 309–310, 329, 335–338, 341, 391–394 397, 403, 409, 415, 427, 433.

R

Real World
Listen and Draw, 25, 31, 37, 43, 75, 81, 87, 93, 99, 111, 117, 123, 129, 141, 163, 169, 175, 187, 193, 199, 205, 211, 223, 237, 243, 255, 261, 267, 273, 279, 291, 297, 303, 323, 329, 335, 341, 347, 353, 359, 371, 377, 391, 403, 409, 415, 427, 433, 439, 445, 467, 473, 479, 485, 491, 497, 509, 515, 521, 527, 541, 547, 553, 559, 571, 583, 589, 603, 609, 615, 627, 633, 639, 659, 671, 677, 705, 717

T

Take Home Activity, 16, 22, 28, 34, 39, 46, 52, 58, 64, 78, 84, 90, 96, 102, 108, 113, 120, 126, 132, 138, 144, 166, 172, 178, 184, 190, 195, 202, 208, 214, 220, 226, 240, 246, 252, 258, 264, 270, 275, 282, 288, 294, 300, 306, 320, 326, 332, 338, 344, 349, 356, 362, 368, 374, 380, 394, 400, 406, 412, 417, 424, 430, 436, 442, 328, 470, 476, 482, 488, 493, 500, 506, 512, 518, 524, 530, 544, 550, 556, 562, 574, 580, 586, 592, 606, 612, 618, 630, 636, 642, 656, 662, 667, 674, 680, 686, 708, 714, 720, 726, 732, 738, 743, 750, 756, 762, 768

Tally charts, 653–656, 659, 666–667

Test Prep
Chapter Review/Test, 67–70, 147–150, 229–232, 309–312, 383–386, 451–454, 533–536, 595–598, 645–648, 689–692, 771–774
Mid-Chapter Checkpoint, 40, 114, 196, 276, 350, 418, 494, 568, 624, 668, 744

ThinkSmarter, 16, 21, 22, 27, 28, 33, 34, 39, 40, 45, 46, 51, 52, 57, 58, 63, 64, 77, 78, 83, 84, 90, 95, 96, 102, 107, 108, 113, 120, 125, 126, 131, 132, 138, 144, 165, 166, 171, 172, 177, 178, 184, 190, 195, 201, 202, 207, 213, 214, 219, 220, 226, 239, 240, 245, 246, 251, 257, 258, 263, 264, 269, 270, 275, 276, 281, 282, 287, 288, 293, 294, 299, 300, 305, 306, 319, 320, 325, 326, 332, 338, 343, 344, 349, 350, 355, 356, 361, 362, 367, 368, 373, 374, 380, 393, 394, 399, 400, 405, 406, 412, 417, 423, 424, 429, 430, 436, 441, 442, 327, 328, 469, 470, 475, 476, 482, 487, 488, 493, 499, 500, 505, 506, 511, 512, 518, 524, 529, 530, 544, 550, 555, 556, 562, 567, 574, 580, 586, 592, 606, 612, 618, 623, 630, 636, 641, 642, 656, 661, 662, 667, 673, 674, 679, 680, 685, 686, 707, 708, 713, 714, 719, 720, 726, 731, 732, 737, 738, 743, 744, 749, 750, 756, 762, 767, 768

ThinkSmarter +, 22, 52, 102, 144, 172, 1256, 252, 264, 332, 344, 394, 430, 500, 530, 544, 586, 606, 642, 680, 686, 720, 750

Thirds, 747–750, 753–756, 759–762, 561–768

Thousand, 99–102

Three-digit numbers
addition, 391–394, 397–400, 403–406, 409–412, 415–417
comparing, 135–138, 141–144
composing and decomposing, 117–120
counting patterns with, 61–64, 123–126, 129–132
different forms of, 111–113
expanded form, 93–96, 111–113
place value, 81–84, 87–90, 93–96, 99–102, 111–113, 123–126, 141–144
subtraction, 421–424, 427–430, 433–436, 439–442, 445–448
using quick pictures to represent, 87–90, 93, 99, 117, 123, 391–394, 397, 403, 409, 415, 421–424, 427, 433, 439
word form, 105–108, 111–113

Three-dimensional shapes
attributes of, 711–714
build, 717–720
identify and describe, 705–708

Time
a.m. and p.m., 527–530
clocks
analog, 509–512, 515–518, 521–524, 527–530
digital, 510–512, 516–518, 521–523, 527–529
noon and midnight, 528
telling time, 509–512, 515–518, 521–524, 527–530

Triangles, 723–726, 729–732, 735–738, 551–750, 753

Try Another Problem, 50, 136, 218, 286, 366, 422, 504, 566, 622, 684, 766